D1596078

Television Series
of the 1970s

Television Series of the 1970s

Essential Facts and Quirky Details

VINCENT TERRACE

ROWMAN & LITTLEFIELD
Lanham • Boulder • New York • London

Published by Rowman & Littlefield
A wholly owned subsidiary of The Rowman & Littlefield Publishing Group, Inc.
4501 Forbes Boulevard, Suite 200, Lanham, Maryland 20706
www.rowman.com

Unit A, Whitacre Mews, 26-34 Stannary Street, London SE11 4AB

British Library Cataloguing in Publication Information Available

Library of Congress Cataloging-in-Publication Data

Names: Terrace, Vincent, 1948– author.
Title: Television series of the 1970s : essential facts and quirky details / Vincent Terrace.
Description: Lanham : Rowman & Littlefield, 2017. | Includes bibliographical references and index.
Identifiers: LCCN 2016044272 (print) | LCCN 2017005614 (ebook) | ISBN 9781442278288 (hardback : alk. paper) | ISBN 9781442278295 (electronic)
Subjects: LCSH: Television series—United States—Catalogs. | Television pilot programs—United States—Catalogs.
Classification: LCC PN1992.8.S4 T483 2017 (print) | LCC PN1992.8.S4 (ebook) | DDC 791.45/750973—dc23
LC record available at https://lccn.loc.gov/2016044272

Printed in the United States of America

Contents

Acknowledgments

The author would like to thank James Robert Parish, Steven Eberly, Bob Leszczak, Nicole Galiardo, and Madison Gorman for their assistance on this project.

Introduction

This is a volume in a series of books that detail the trivia aspects of largely American television programs by decade. This book follows *Television Series of the 1950s* and *Television Series of the 1960s*.

This volume, like its prior editions, is *not* a book of opinions or essays about 1970s programs. It is a presentation of trivia facts associated with specific TV series that premiered from January 1, 1970, through December 31, 1979.

Did you know, for example, that on *All in the Family*, the hospital bill for Gloria's birth was $131.50; that the bionic ear replacement used for Jaime Sommers (*The Bionic Woman*) has the catalog number 6314 KMH; or that on *CHiPs* Jon Baker was the only motorcycle officer to carry a policeman's nightstick?

What about the sitcom *Dusty's Trail* being known as "*Gilligan's Island* out West"? How about Mr. Roarke being an immortal on *Fantasy Island* or that J.J.'s favorite drink on *Good Times* is Kool-Aid (or that his mother, Florida, was *not* named after the state her name implies)?

Do you know what Mary Hartman's strange hope for her daughter Heather was on *Mary Hartman, Mary Hartman*? What Carl Kolchak (*Kolchak: The Night Stalker*) feared most? What name-brand bra Carol wore on *Maude* or who played TV's first African American policewoman on *Get Christie Love*?

These are just a thimbleful of the many thousands of intriguing trivia that can be found within the pages that follow. *Television Series of the 1970s* is a totally different perspective on a past era of what has been shown on American television.

Note: Programs that premiered in the 1960s and that continued first-run production into the 1970s are *not* included here. Information on the following programs can be found in the volume *Television Series of the 1960s*:

Adam 12	*Hawaii Five-0*
The Beverly Hillbillies	*Hogan's Heroes*
Bewitched	*I Dream of Jeannie*
The Brady Bunch	*It Takes a Thief*

The Courtship of Eddie's Father
The Doris Day Show
Family Affair
The Flying Nun
Get Smart
The Ghost and Mrs. Muir
Green Acres

Land of the Giants
Mannix
Mod Squad
My Three Sons
My World . . . and Welcome to It
Petticoat Junction
That Girl

Alice
(CBS, 1976–1985)

Cast: Linda Lavin (Alice Hyatt), Vic Tayback (Mel Sharples), Beth Howland (Vera Gorman), Polly Holliday (Florence Jean Castleberry), Diane Ladd (Belle DuPree), Celia Weston (Jolene Hunnicutt), Alfred Lutter, then Philip McKeon (Tommy Hyatt), Marvin Kaplan (Henry Beismeyer).

Basis: Following the death of her husband Donald, a widow (Alice) with a young son (Tommy) embarks on a journey to pursue her dream of becoming a singer. A temporary setback (inoperable car) strands her in Arizona, where she acquires a waitress job at Mel's Diner. Vera, Flo, Belle, and Jolene are her fellow waitresses (each wearing pink uniforms and earning $2.90 an hour).

ALICE HYATT
Mother: Mona Spevak (Doris Roberts).
Place of Birth: Passaic, New Jersey.
Birthday: October 15, 1937.
Education: Passaic High School (voted "The Girl with the Best Knees"; she was also overweight and called "Pudge Spevak").
New Jersey Occupation: Waitress at Vito's Bar and Grill (where she met Donald Hyatt, a big-rig trucker [later killed in a job-related accident]). She also formed the singing group Alice and the Acorns. In Phoenix, Alice earned extra money singing at the Saddle Sore Bar, Vinnie's House of Veal, and Herman's Hitching Post. She can also dance and drive an 18-wheel truck.
Address: The Desert Sun Apartments (Apartment 103), then the Phoenix Arms (Apartment 108).
Replacement: Poor working conditions forced Alice to protest. Mel temporarily replaced her with Blanche, a robot waitress.
Relatives: Mother-in-law, Rose Hyatt (Eileen Heckart).

Childhood Memory: As a Brownie Scout becoming lost in the woods and being led back to camp by a squirrel that mysteriously appeared before her.

Note: The final episode finds Alice moving to Nashville to sing with Travis March.

MELVIN "MEL" SHARPLES
Year of Birth: 1930.
Mother: Carrie Sharples (Martha Raye).
Occupation: Owner of Mel's Diner at 1030 Bush Highway. On Mel's desk is his third-place bowling trophy; in the diner's backyard, there is a heart painted on a wall with "Lynn Loves Bob" in it. Mel also owns the Mother Goose Preschool building and temporarily worked at the R.J. Catering Company.
Famous Dish: Mel's Chili.
Education: Mentioned that he attended pastry school.
Address: 604 Plainview Drive, Apartment 107. His living room wall first displayed the famous Farrah Fawcett swimsuit pose (later a poster of Loni Anderson).
Military Service: The navy during the Korean War.
Car License Plate: NU 087.
Biggest Worry: His nose. Teased as a kid (called "Hose Nose"), by his navy mates as "Banana Nose," by the Japanese (when stationed overseas) as "Hanasan" ["Mr. Nose"]), and by his bowling team as "Super Schnoz." "Smelly Melly" and "Jelly Belly" were names Mel says he was also called in school.
Diner Guard Dogs: Bobbie Jo and Billy Ray.
Bank: The Desert Bank.
Philosophy: Believes the only way he can be nice to his waitresses is to yell at them.
Marital Status: Single. Mel never married "because I'm married to this diner."
Competition: Mary's Munch-A-Rama and Benny's Beanery.
Dress: Mel wears polyester suits (which he buys at Syd's Stylist Shop) but is most often seen in a white T-shirt at the diner.
Anniversary: Mel celebrated the 25th anniversary of Mel's Diner at Vinnie's House of Veal (where he appeared as "B-Boppin' Mel Sharples").
Relatives: Grandma Sharples (Merie Earle).

Note: Mel sells the diner (after 27 years in business) to the Ferguson Brothers (who plan to tear it down) in the final episode.

VERA LOUISE GORMAN
Birthday: May 28, 1941.
Place of Birth: Los Angeles.

Education: Berkeley University in Los Angeles.

Occupation: Waitress. She also worked the night shift at Big Herb's 24-Hour Gas Station and lived in Boston for a time with her Aunt Agatha (Mildred Natwick).

Nickname: Called "Dinghy" by Mel.

Trait: Shy, sensitive, and a bit clumsy. Although pretty, she feels she has no sex appeal.

Address: The Sun Rise Apartments.

Marital Status: Single.

Pets: Mel (a cat), Mitzi and Harold (hamsters), and Sidney (guppy). She also has a piggy bank she calls "Irving."

Ability: Count money simply by hearing it. She plays the cello and takes lessons at Miss Dana's Academy of Tippy Tappy Toe Dancing.

Hero: Actor-dancer Donald O'Connor is her hero.

Favorite Cartoon: Daffy Duck.

Favorite Candy: Yum Nutties.

Favorite Movie: The African Queen (although she has a poster from the film *Watch on the Rhine* on her living room wall).

Favorite TV Show: One Day after Another (a soap opera).

Quirks: She will not serve Mel's Boston Clam Chowder ("because the clams came from Seattle") and believes everything on TV is real (for example, when Theo Kojak, the bald detective on *Kojak*, caught a cold, she sent him a toupee; when Mary Richards lost her job on the final episode of *The Mary Tyler Moore Show*, she cried).

Fear: Heights. If she finds herself in a situation where she is in a high place, she tells her brain she is on the ground floor "so I don't get scared."

Relatives: Cousin, Art Carney (himself).

Note: Vera marries her boyfriend, police officer Elliott Novak (Charles Levin), in the final episode.

FLORENCE JEAN "FLO" CASTLEBERRY

Birthday: July 2, 1937.

Place of Birth: Cowtown, Texas.

Address: The Desert Trailer Park.

Catchphrase: "Kiss my grits."

Favorite Bar: Shake Chug-a-Lug.

Most Treasured Items: A black velvet painting of singer Johnny Cash; an imitation leopard bedspread and a plush rabbit she won at the Corpus Christi State Fair.

Character: Wisecracking, sassy, and sexy (always attired in tight pants when not working) and known to wear "peekaboo" nightgowns at bedtime.

Make-Out Spot: Lookout Mountain.

Ability: To put up with Mel and all his complaining, especially his objections to her making personal phone calls.

Note: In 1980, Flo leaves Mel's Diner for a hostess job at the Thundering Herd Restaurant in Houston, Texas. After a return visit to her hometown (Cowtown), she decides to stay and open her own bar, Flo's Golden Rose (the basis of the spin-off series *Flo*).

BELLE DUPREE

Age: 41 (born in November 1935).

Place of Birth: Mississippi.

Address: 112 Ashton Drive in Phoenix.

Quirks: Wears bells in her earrings "because my name is Belle"; claims she hears a voice in her head that calls her "Isabelle"; likes a touch of honey in her coffee.

Character: A bit sassy and wisecracking. Belle originally worked for Mel but quit to pursue a singing career. When she failed to impress singers Tammy Wynette and Waylon Jennings, Mel rehired her to replace Flo.

Note: Prior to Belle returning, Mel hired his on-and-off girlfriend Marie (Victoria Carroll) to replace Flo. Mel calls Marie "Cuddle Cups" and "Snooky Tookie"; she calls him "Cookie Nose," "Barrel Bottom," and "Puppy Toes." Marie quits when she acquires a better-paying job (at $400 a week) at the Shake Chug-a-Lug Bar.

The Departure: Belle, vacationing in Nashville, calls Mel to inform him that she has joined a band (formed by her cousin Larry) as a singer.

JOLENE HUNNICUTT

Father: "Big" Jake Hunnicutt (Gregory Walcott).

Brothers: Jesse (Trevor Henley), Jasper (Kent Parkins), Jimmy (Robin Eurich), Jake Jr. (Steve McGriff), and Jonas Hunnicutt (Gurich Koock).

Birthday: December 14, 1951.

Place of Birth: South Carolina.

Address: The Pine Valley Apartments in Phoenix.

Occupation: Waitress (hired by Mel after learning of Belle's departure). Jolene previously worked in a "Stuffing Factory" ("Stuff, staple, stuff, staple," she says), as a stewardess for Desert Airlines (quit when she discovered she was afraid of flying), and as a truck driver.

Nickname: Called "Blondie" by Mel; when he yells at her, it's "Bag it Blondie."

Dream: To open her own beauty parlor (which occurs in the final episode, when she inherits money from her grandmother "Granny" Gumms [Natalie Masters]).

TV Show Appearance: Jolene (along with Alice and Vera) competed on the song-guessing game *Go for It.*

Dislikes: Wearing hairnets ("It makes your hair look like sofa stuffing").

Favorite Magazines: True Romance and *Modern Crime.*

Belief: "A coffee break is like a teensy weensy vacation with pay."

Quirk: At the Laundromat, Jolene uses washing machines 6 and 9 ("because number 8 wobbles") and dryers 16 and 35. She sleeps on Snoopy-decorated sheets.

OTHER CHARACTERS

Tommy Hyatt, Alice's son, is a member of the Coyotes basketball team (high school not named) and later attends Arizona State College (he is a sophomore when the series ends). He had his first crush on actress Brooke Shields, worked as a short-order cook at Mel's Diner, and sang and played guitar at the Dry Gulch Saloon.

Henry Beismeyer, Mel's most faithful customer, always complains about the bad food; he frequents Benny's Beanery for an enjoyable meal. He is a telephone company repairman and married the demanding Chloe (Ruth Buzzi). He dreams of becoming the first intergalactic repairman so that he can hear Chloe say, "Phone home H.B." (in a takeoff of "E.T. Phone Home" from the film *E.T.*). At bedtime, Henry wears Punky Brewster pajamas (from the series *Punky Brewster*), and Chloe has to sing him a lullaby ("Rockabye Henry in the treetop . . .") before he falls asleep. Henry and Chloe become the parents of twins in last-season episodes.

All in the Family
(CBS, 1971–1979)

Cast: Carroll O'Connor (Archie Bunker), Jean Stapleton (Edith Bunker), Sally Struthers (Gloria Bunker), Rob Reiner (Mike Stivic), Danielle Brisebois (Stephanie Mills), Denise Miller (Billie Bunker).

Basis: Life with a bigoted blue-collar worker (Archie Bunker) and his family: his wife, Edith; his daughter, Gloria; and Gloria's husband, Mike. Also included is information from the spin-off *Archie Bunker's Place* (CBS, 1979–1983) and its characters Stephanie Mills and Billie Bunker.

ARCHIBALD "ARCHIE" BUNKER

Address: 704 Hauser Street, in Astoria, Queens, New York.

House Cost: $14,000 (purchased by Archie in 1951).

Occupation: Dock foreman (for the Prendergast Tool and Dye Company). In 1979, after being laid off, Archie purchases Kelsey's Bar (also called Kelsey's

Tavern) from Tommy Kelsey (Bob Hastings) and renames it Archie Bunker's Place (open from 9 a.m. to 4 a.m. daily). He also drove a cab owned by his friend Burt Munson (Billy Halop).

Competition: McFinney's Bar.

Year of Birth: Mentioned as the 1920s. He is three years older than Edith.

Place of Birth: Queens, New York.

Childhood: Wrongly taught by his parents to believe in the superiority of his own race and to distrust foreign-born people of all kinds.

Religion: Christian.

Education: Archie first mentions he is a "public school graduate," then a high school dropout (to help support his family). In 1973, Archie returns to high school to acquire his diploma for a job promotion. In 1979, Archie is seen hosting a reunion of his 1940 Bryant High School graduating class.

Childhood Nickname: "Shoe Bootie" (wearing one shoe and one bootie when his parents were unable to buy him a new pair of shoes).

Trait: Bigoted, loudmouthed, and uncouth. He possesses normal intelligence but speaks very poor English. He is stubborn, set in his ways, and reluctant to accept new ideas, as he feels threatened by anything he was never taught to fear.

Military Service: "The Big One" (as Archie calls World War II; he also calls it "Double-u, Double-u Two"). He was first stationed at Fort Riley in Kansas, then shipped to Italy, where he served 22 months with the Air Corps (as second in command of the motor pool). His hitch earned him a Purple Heart, a good-conduct medal, "and a butt full of shrapnel—which is why I ain't danced with my wife in 30 years." Prior to the injury, Archie and Edith danced at the Stardust Ballroom on Fordham Road (in the Bronx). When attending his annual army reunions, Archie stays at the New Howard Johnson's Hotel in Manhattan.

Blood Pressure: Varies between 178/90 and 168/95.

Vice: Smoking cigars.

Greatest Moment of His Life: Meeting actor-singer Sammy Davis Jr.

Political Affiliation: Strict conservative.

Favorite Chair: The big easy chair in the living room.

Catchphrases: "Whoop-dee-doo" and "Aw, jeez."

Favorite Beer: Schlitz. He has hard liquor he calls the Saturday Night Special.

Favorite Pudding: Rice "with a pinch of milk on top."

Favorite Snack: Twinkies.

Favorite Baseball Team: New York Mets.

Favorite Basketball Team: New York Knicks.

Favorite Newspaper: New York *Daily News.*

Favorite Magazine: The *National Enquirer* ("if it appears in the *Enquirer,* it's true," he says).

Favorite Actor: John Wayne (whom he calls "The Duke" [Wayne's real nickname]).

Favorite President: Richard Nixon.

Hobby: Bowling (member of the Cannonballers).

Heroic Act: Saving the life of female impersonator Beverly LaSalle (Lori Shannon).

Club: The Royal Brotherhood of the Kings of Queens Lodge (555-4378 is its phone number).

Term of Endearment for Edith: "Dingbat." (He also tells her to "stifle it" for talking too much.) Because of Archie's New York accent, Edith's name is heard as "Ee-dit." Archie also has special terms for other people: "Coloreds" (African Americans), "Polacks" (Polish people), and "I-talians" (Italian people).

Temptation: Nearly had an extramarital affair with Denise (Janis Paige) while away on a business trip.

"Pet": A field mouse that invaded his home and that Archie named Marvin.

House Protection: A tape recording of barking dogs.

Wardrobe Accessory: An American flag pin on his coat lapel. He wears his wedding ring on his middle finger and places his eyeglasses in his shirt pocket alongside two pens.

Relatives: Brother, Fred Bunker (Richard McKenzie). Mentioned were Archie's cousin, Rudy (who lives in California); Linda, Archie's niece; and Oscar, Archie's cousin, "who died up in the attic."

EDITH BUNKER

Maiden Name: Edith Baines.

Year of Birth: 1922.

Place of Birth: Queens, New York (where she grew up in a loving family).

Education: Fillmore High School (Class of 1940). Bayside High School is later mentioned by Archie.

Occupation: Housewife. Edith worked as a secretary for the Hercules Plumbing Company (in 1946), then, during the 1970s, as Sunshine Lady at the Sunshine Home for the Elderly (at $2.65 an hour). She also worked as a recreation assistant (at $5 an hour) at the Rego Park Center (for the elderly). She auditioned for a Sunny Suds laundry detergent TV commercial but lost the job when she chose "Brand X" as the better product.

First Meeting: The Puritan Maid Ice Cream Parlor in 1941 (they married shortly thereafter and honeymooned in Atlantic City [stayed in room 822 of the Hotel Atlantic City]). Twenty-five years later, Archie and Edith spent a second honeymoon at the same location.

Television: In the late 1940s, Archie and Edith would watch *The Milton Berle Show* from the window of Tupperman's Department Store. Two years later, they purchased their first set—a console with a six-inch screen.

Disappointment: For her own safety, Edith was advised not have any more children due to a complication that occurred after Gloria's birth.

Religion: Episcopalian.

Award: Citizen of the Week (for saving the life of an elderly man).

Trait: Tries to see the good in people. She cannot lie and finds that knowing when to make a comment or say nothing is her best defense against Archie in an argument.

Disgrace: At the age of six, Edith stole a five-cent Oh Henry! candy bar from Woolworths. She later told the store manager but had to pay 10 cents, as the price had increased.

Favorite TV Show: As the World Turns.

Favorite Magazines: Cosmopolitan and *Reader's Digest.*

Favorite Department Store: Bloomingdale's.

Bank Account: The First Friendly Bank of Queens (where their checking, Magic Potato Cutter, and Christmas Club accounts all total $78).

Favorite Butcher Shop: Kelmer's.

TV First: Edith facing menopause—a situation that caused the doctor to prescribe medication for Archie (who cannot deal with female issues).

Edith's Passing: When Jean Stapleton left the series in 1979, her character was written out when Edith suffered a fatal heart attack in her sleep.

Relatives: Cousins, Maude (Bea Arthur), Amelia (Elizabeth Wilson, then Rae Allen), Roy (Tim O'Connor), Clara (Ruth Manning), and Bertha (Peggy Rae); aunt, Iola (Nedra Volz).

GLORIA BUNKER

Year of Birth: 1944.

Place of Birth: Bayside Hospital in Queens, New York.

Hospital Bill: $131.50.

Childhood: Babied by Edith when she discovered Gloria was anemic.

Trait: Accustomed to being pampered (she fears moving out of the house because she realizes that she will have to grow up, and she is not prepared for that).

Husband: Mike Stivic.

Son: Joey Stivic (Cory and Jason Drager; later, Dick Billingsley and Christopher Johnston). Mike and Gloria wanted to name the baby Stanislaus, but Archie objected—"Kids are mean; they're gonna call him "Louse."

Hair Color: Blonde. She wore a brunette wig in one episode that not only changed her appearance but also caused Mike to become overly romantic (as Gloria claimed, he could have an affair with another woman without cheating on his wife).

Term of Endearment: Called "Little Girl" by Archie.

Education: Queens High School (dropped out at age 16 to take a secretarial course).

Occupation: Housewife. Gloria originally worked as a secretary in Manhattan, cosmetics salesgirl at Kressler's Department Store (earning $80 a week), and artist's model (a career that ended quickly when Archie discovered she was asked to pose nude).

Political Outlook: Conservative (although Mike is trying to make her a liberal).

MICHAEL "MIKE" STIVIC

Father: Casmir Stivic (Michael Conrad).

Place of Birth: Chicago.

Age: While not specifically stated, about the same age as Gloria.

First Meeting: Initially stated that Gloria met Mike, a hippie, when she worked in Manhattan and, later, that Mike and Gloria met through a blind date set up by her girlfriend.

Occupation: College student, then teacher. Mike did not have a job and relied on Archie for support (although Archie balked, he relented because Gloria was his daughter).

Trait: A strict liberal whom Archie believes lives in a vacuum (as he has no job and no responsibilities). Gloria believes Mike is the smartest person she has ever known and is discovering that a lot of what she learned from her conservative parents is wrong.

Terms of Endearment: Called "Meathead" and "You dumb Polack" by Archie.

Mike's Belief: Archie's conservative outlook is harmful to the world, while Edith is ignorant of the ways of the world.

Favorite Soft Drink: RC Cola.

STEPHANIE MILLS

Relationship: The daughter of Edith's "no good" cousin, Floyd Mills (Marty Brill then Ben Slack). Following her mother, Marilyn's, death in a car accident, Stephanie was being raised by Floyd but came to live with Archie and Edith in 1978, when Edith discovered that Floyd was an alcoholic, and Stephanie had to fend for herself.

Date of Birth: May 1967.

Religion: Jewish (attends the Temple Beth Shalom and Hebrew school [called "religious school" by Edith]); she later made her bat mitzvah (a girl's transformation to an adult).

Education: Ditmars Junior High School (member of the chorus and plays right field on its baseball team, the Astoria Hawks [wears a green and white jersey, number 10]). A related story appeared in the *Queens Shopping* newspaper.

Most Difficult Subject: Algebra.

Trait: Shy and insecure.

Favorite Rock Group: The Goo Goos.

Favorite Magazine: Seventeen.

Activities: The Girl Scouts and the Astoria Girls Club. She also attends dance school and enjoys roller and ice skating. She has lunch each day at 12 noon at Archie's bar.

Nicknames: Called "Kid" and "Kiddo" by Archie.

Archie's Fear: Stephanie shedding her tomboyish ways. She is becoming a young woman, and Archie is simply afraid to deal with all the problems associated with adolescence. Any change in Archie's life is a traumatic experience for him.

Restrictions: Stephanie can have a boy "who is a friend but not a boyfriend."

Relatives: Grandmother, Estelle Harris (Celeste Holm); cousin, Sophie (Mitzi Hoag).

BILLIE BUNKER

Full Name: Barbara Lee Bunker.

Date of Birth: July 1963.

Relationship: The daughter of Archie's younger brother Fred (his wife abandoned the family when Billie was seven). Billie left Baltimore to begin a new life in New York and moved in with Archie to help him care for Stephanie (her first cousin).

Fondest Childhood Memory: On Christmas Eve, when she was seven years old, Billie sat on the staircase with a camera hoping to get a picture of Santa Claus. She fell asleep at 3 a.m. and missed her opportunity.

Education: Philosophy courses at Queens College (Tuesday and Thursday evenings).

First Crush: At the age of 12, her orthodontist ("I would go to see him every Saturday to have my braces tightened").

Occupation: Waitress at Archie Bunker's Place.

Trait: A very private person who enjoys quiet evenings at home. During high school, she experimented with drugs.

Favorite Drink: Nestlé Quik chocolate mix for a quick burst of energy.

OTHER CHARACTERS

Bernard "Barney" Hefner (Allan Melvin) is Archie's neighbor, a bridge inspector for the city of New York. He is married to Blanche (Estelle Parsons) and has a dog named Rusty (who likes to do his business on Archie's front lawn). Although Archie disliked Rusty, he accidentally ran him over while driving Munson's taxi cab.

Teresa Betancourt (Liz Torres) is the nurse who rents Gloria's former bedroom (for $100 a month) when Gloria and Mike move next door to Archie. She calls Archie "Mr. Bunkers" (although with her Spanish accent it comes out "Mr. Bonkers").

Murray Klein (Martin Balsam) is Archie's bar partner. In 1981, Archie buys out Murray's share of the bar when he leaves to marry Marie Phillips (Cynthia Harris).

Harry Snowden (Jason Wingreen) is Archie's bartender; Veronica Rooney (Anne Meara) is the bar's cook; Edgar Van Ranseleer (Bill Quinn) is the bar's blind regular.

Stretch Cunningham (James Cromwell) is Archie's friend and dock co-worker; Frank and Irene Lorenzo (Vincent Gardenia and Betty Garrett) are Archie's neighbors; Ellen Canby (Barbara Meek) is the housekeeper whom Archie hires after Edith's passing.

SPIN-OFF
Gloria (CBS, 1982) finds Gloria as a single mother after Mike, who had acquired a teaching job in California, deserts his family. Gloria moves back in with Archie and later acquires a job as a veterinary assistant in Fox County, New York. See also *The Jeffersons* and *Maude*.

Note: Based on the British series *Till Death Us Do Part*. *And Justice for All* (ABC) was the first American pilot with Carroll O'Connor as Archie Justice; Jean Stapleton, Edith; Kelly Jean Peters, Gloria; and Tim McIntire, Richard (Gloria's husband). *Those Were the Days* became the second attempt (ABC) with Carroll and Jean repeating their roles with Candace Azzara as Gloria and Chip Oliver as Richard. Norman Lear produced a third pilot (for CBS) called *All in the Family* with the series regular cast that sold the series.

The Amazing Spider-Man
(CBS, 1977–1979)

Cast: Nicholas Hammond (Peter Parker), Chip Fields (Rita Conway), Robert F. Simon (J. Jonah Johnson), Michael Pataki (Captain Barbera), Ellen Bry (Julie Masters), Fred Waugh (Spider-Man), Irene Tedrow (Aunt May).

Basis: A young man, bitten by a radioactive spider, acquires the proportionate powers of a living spider to battle the forces of evil.

PETER BENJAMIN PARKER
Place of Birth: Queens, New York.

Parents: Richard and Mary Parker (secret agents who were killed during a case assignment). Peter, an infant at the time, was sent to live with his Uncle Ben and Aunt May in Forest Hills, Queens, New York.

Address: 1231 Maple Drive (a home he shares with his Aunt May).

Phone Number: 555-1834.

Height: 5 feet, 10 inches tall.

Weight: 168 pounds.

Medical Condition: Allergies.

Occupation: Freelance reporter/photographer for the *Daily Bugle.*

Education: Midtown High School (honors student); graduate student in physics at Empire State University in New York City. He had excelled in science since his early schooling.

The Change: While working in the school's lab, Peter is bitten by a spider that had been exposed to radiation during an experiment. Later, while on the street, he senses danger (an approaching car) and escapes harm by scaling a wall like a spider.

The Result: With no way to reverse what has happened, Peter vows to use his ability to battle criminals. In the comic book version, Peter is motivated to anonymously battle crime after his Uncle Ben is killed by a burglar.

The Costume: Red (top), blue (bottom), and red mask. His appearance had earned him the name Spider-Man by those who witnessed his actions.

Powers: Spider sense (sense danger), extraordinary strength, amazing agility, and the ability to cling to most surfaces and spin webs (allowing him to use acrobatic-like moves to swiftly move from one place to another).

OTHER CHARACTERS

J. Jonah Jameson, the editor of the *Bugle,* lives on the Upper East Side of Manhattan and drives a Rolls-Royce with the license plate 49NEJJ.

Rita Conway is Jonah's administrative assistant, a woman who is eager to become a crime reporter. She lives at 876 University Place, and 555-6097 is her phone number.

Julie Masters is Peter's rival, a reporter with the *Bugle*'s competition (the *Register*) who is determined to uncover Spider-Man's secret identity. She lives at the Marlowe Apartments and drives a car with the license plate 376 KNP.

Captain Barbera, stationed at One Police Plaza in Manhattan, is the police official who works closely with Peter but is unaware that he is actually Spider-Man. He and Peter work well together, but in the comic book, Barbera was gruff and difficult to work with.

Note: David White played J. Jonah Johnson in the pilot with Jeff Donnell as Aunt May. TV's first attempt at adapting the Stan Lee comic book character to TV was the 1969 ABC animated series *Spider-Man,* wherein Peter Parker (voice of Peter Soles) was a student at Central High School when he was bitten by the spider.

Archie Bunker's Place

See *All in the Family.*

Arnie

(CBS, 1970–1972)

Cast: Herschel Bernardi (Arnie Nuvo), Sue Ane Langdon (Lillian Nuvo), Stephanie Steele (Andrea Nuvo), Del Russell (Richard Nuvo), Roger Bowen (Hamilton Majors Jr.), Charles Nelson Reilly (Randy Robinson).

Basis: A blue-collar dockworker (Arnie Nuvo) attempts to adjust to a new way of life after being promoted to a white-collar management position.

ARNOLD "ARNIE" NUVO

Date of Birth: October 23, 1923.

Height: 5 feet, 6 inches tall.

Wife: Lillian. They honeymooned in Palm Springs.

Sister: Christina Nuvo (Carol Arthur).

Children: Andrea and Richard Nuvo.

Occupation: Dock Foreman for Continental Flange, Inc. After 12 years on the job, Arnie receives a promotion as the head of new product improvement, replacing the former head, "Holly" Hollingsworth (Bob Cummings).

Salary: $20,000 a year.

Weekly Deductions: $81.26 (federal tax), $22.07 (Social Security), $4.21 (state tax), $25 (company pension fund), $10 (secretary's coffee fund), $25 (executive dining table fund). $100 (yearly) for the company charity, Pals of the Poor.

Household Expenses: $200 (various monthly bills), $40 (weekly grocery bill).

Favorite Meal: Stuffed grape leaf.

Least Favorite Meal: TV dinners.

Home Address: 4650 Liberty Lane, Los Angeles, California.

Home Phone Number: 555-6676.

Continental Flange Address: 36 West Pico Boulevard.

Company Membership: The Bowling League and the All-Male Quartet.

LILLIAN NUVO

Maiden Name: Lillian Harrison.

Date of Birth: March 8, 1936 (34 years old when the series begins).

Place of Birth: Paterson, New Jersey.

Education: Paterson High School.

Measurements: 37-23-36 (in real life, Sue Ane had an "hourglass figure"). She has blonde hair and blue eyes and stands 5 feet, 6 inches tall.

Wardrobe: Casual but conservative (first season). The 13-year age difference between Arnie and Lillian became more noticeable during the second season, and Lillian dressed to emphasize her figure and younger age (miniskirts, shorts, and sexy negligee).

Occupation: Model for Perfect Figure Lingerie (before marriage).

Activities: Head of the consumer watch group The Charge of the Wife Brigade (picketing Continental Flange for polluting the environment was their first crusade). Lillian also takes classes in floral arranging, papier-mâché, and art.

Clothing Purchases: Helen's Dress Shop.

Quirk: Insists on giving homemade cookies as Christmas gifts; grocery shops only on a Thursday; buys 10-pound jars of peanut butter for her family.

ANDREA AND RICHARD NUVO

Andrea, a cute blonde, and Richard, a nonconformist, attend Westside High School. Richard, 17 years old, is a junior; Andrea, born on June 9, 1955 (15 years old when the series begins), is a sophomore. Richard strives for good grades and is much like his father in that he will stick up for what he believes in no matter what the consequences. Andrea is musically inclined (plays the guitar) and has not set a future goal. She is not overly fashion conscious or interested in becoming a woman "right now."

OTHER CHARACTERS

Hamilton Majors Jr., called "Ham," is the company president and claims to run Continental Flange "for Dad." He is a member of the Bayshore Polo Club and babies his right hand (his mallet hand) and will shake hands only with his left hand. Hamilton is a bit miserly when it comes to company spending and stresses S-A-V-E to all his employees. He has also instituted a daily exercise routine and drives a vintage Rolls-Royce. He is assisted by Neil Ogilvy (Herb Voland), the plant supervisor.

Randolph "Randy" Robinson is Arnie's neighbor (resides at 4648 Liberty Lane) and star of the television series *The Giddyup Gourmet* (a spoof of the actual TV series at the time, *The Galloping Gourmet*). Randy is single, considers himself a ladies' man, and supposedly traveled the world, where he gathered the most exquisite recipes for his cooking show. While Randy presents an image of being a man of steel, he is rather nervous and unsure of himself (and what he is about to do) at times.

Banacek

(NBC, 1972–1974)

Cast: George Peppard (Thomas Banacek), Christine Belford (Carlie Kirkland), Murray Matheson (Felix Mulholland), Ralph Manza (Jay Drury).

Basis: Freelance insurance investigator Thomas Banacek attempts to solve highly complex cases involving lost, missing, or stolen items.

THOMAS BANACEK

Heritage: Polish.

Place of Birth: Sully Square in Boston, Massachusetts.

Business: T. Banacek—Restorations.

Home Address: 85 Mount Vernon Street in the Beacon Hill section of Boston.

Occasional Clients: National Fidelity Insurance; the Boston Insurance Company (which he prefers, as it was built on the site of his former childhood home).

Character: A suave and sophisticated ladies' man and self-made millionaire.

Military Service: A marine during the Korean War and trained in combat judo.

Background: His father, Leo, a research scientist, was born in Warsaw, Poland, in 1924 and immigrated to America (at the age of 16). He worked as a mathematician for an insurance company, but after 20 years on the job, he was replaced by a computer. Because of this, Thomas will not work in an office or in a nine-to-five job—"I don't work for anybody. I work for myself."

Fees: $100 a day expenses plus 10 percent of the value of the object that is missing.

Lifestyle: Extravagant. He smokes pencil-thin panatela cigars and has exquisite tastes in wine, women, and food.

Favorite Breakfast: "Eggs Banacek" (his variation on Eggs Benedict).

Favorite Strategy Game: Chess.

Quirk: Never hands out a business card. As he says, "I'm in the Boston phone book."

Cars: 1941 Packard convertible, 1969 American Motors AMX, 1973 Cadillac Fleetwood Limousine, and a 1941 Packard 180.

Mobile Phone Number: KL 1-7811.

Specialty: Intrigued by how a crime was committed and why it was impossible for authorities to solve.

Research: "The Assurance Reports." The "Recovery and Rewards" section lists unsolved insurances cases; if they are more than 60 days old, they become public domain and allow anyone to solve them for the reward.

Success Rate: 66 percent. Insurance companies find it cheaper to hire Banacek than assign their own agents to a case. Not solving a case does not seem to anger Banacek; he says simply, "I get a little bit older."

Proverbs: Banacek has an old country saying that begins with "There's an old Polish proverb that goes . . ." (Examples are "Only a truly wise man chooses not to play leap frog with a unicorn," "Only a centipede can hear all the footsteps of his uncle," and "No matter how hot the face of the sun, the mother cat has her kittens under the porch.")

Competition: Caroline Kirkland, called "Carlie," works first for the National Meridian Insurance Company, then the Boston Insurance Company in the Property and Recovery Division. She drives a 1973 Corvette and claims that "Banacek can smell a case just like a rat in a Provolone factory." Carlie would like to leave her job and become an independent like Banacek—"I can be Dr. Watson to your Sherlock Holmes."

Information Man: Felix Mulholland, the owner of Mulholland Rare Books and Prints. He considers himself very intelligent—"I am a walking compendium of man's knowledge."

Chauffeur: Jay Drury, the owner of Jay's Executive Limo Service, drives Banacek's various cars. He believes he is capable of solving crimes and hopes to one day prove that.

Baretta

(ABC, 1975–1978)

Cast: Robert Blake (Tony Baretta), Tom Ewell (Billy Trueman).

Basis: Tony Baretta, an undercover police detective (in an unnamed city that is presumed to be in New Jersey), uses various disguises to apprehend criminals.

ANTHONY "TONY" BARETTA

Heritage: Italian.

Middle Name: Vincenzo.

Address: Apartment 2C of the King Edward Hotel.
Police Precinct: The 53rd (presumably the robbery and homicide division).
Badge Number: 609.
Car: A 1966 blue four-door Chevy Impala that he calls the Blue Ghost.
License Plate: 532 BEN.
Pet Bird: Fred, a smart cockatoo that loves liquor and "thinks he's a chicken."
Trait: Off duty, Tony wears a T-shirt, jeans, and a cap pulled over his forehead. He also holds an unlit cigarette or has one placed behind his ear. He refers to girls close to him as "my cousins."
Catchphrase: "And that's the name of the game" (said after collaring a suspect).
Favorite Hangout: Ross's Billiard Academy.

OTHER CHARACTERS
William "Billy" Truman is the elderly house detective at the King Edward Hotel (a former cop who worked with Tony's father, also a cop); Inspectors Schiller (Dana Elcar) and Hal Brubaker (Ed Grover) are Tony's superiors.

Fats (Chico "Fats" Williams) is the detective who often accompanies Tony on stakeouts, while Detective Foley (John Ward) is the annoying, by-the-book cop that irritates Tony. Rooster (Michael D. Roberts), a pimp, and Little Moe (Angelo Rossitto), a little person who works as a shoeshine "boy," are Tony's informants.

Barnaby Jones
(CBS, 1973–1980)

Cast: Buddy Ebsen (Barnaby Jones), Lee Meriwether (Betty Jones), Mark Shera (J.R. Jones).
Basis: An elderly but shrewd private detective solves crimes through the wisdom and knowledge he has gained through decades of investigating.

BARNABY JONES
Business: Barnaby Jones Investigations (established in 1929). In 1969, Barnaby retired (to raise horses on his ranch) and turned over the agency to his son, Hal. In 1973, Hal's murder during an investigation brings Barnaby out of retirement and back to his former occupation after he solves the case.
Business Address: 3782 Clinton Avenue, Los Angeles, California.
Telephone Number: 467-7935 (then 555-7650).
Office Number: 615.
Home Address: The Jones Ranch in Sun Valley, California.

Barnaby Jones. *CBS/Photofest.* ©*CBS*

Steady Client: The Meridian Insurance Company.

Character: A skilled investigator who analyzes the clues he finds (he has a mini-lab in his office). He claims to be "a long looker and a slow thinker" and is well versed in clinical psychology and the forensic sciences. He feels he is as vibrant as the day he first started and has the needed wisdom to continue in his capacity as a private detective.

Favorite Drink: Milk (he even orders it in bars).

Favorite Sport: Fishing.

Trait: Relaxed manner, positive attitude, and folksy charm.

OTHER CHARACTERS

Elizabeth "Betty" Jones is Barnaby's daughter-in-law (Hal's wife). She works as his secretary and office assistant and assists him in the field when needed.

Jedediah Romano Jones, called "J.R.," is the son of Barnaby's cousin Munroe from Chicago. He is a law school graduate studying for the bar exams in California and working with Barnaby to gain knowledge of criminal behavior. J.R. rushes into a case looking for a clue (what Barnaby often calls "a needle in a haystack") and eager to find it; Barnaby believes "it is best to find the haystack first."

Barney Miller
(ABC, 1975–1982)

Cast: Hal Linden (Barney Miller), Max Gail (Stan Wojechowicz), Abe Vigoda (Phil Fish), Ron Harris (Ron Glass), Steve Landesberg (Arthur P. Dietrich).

Basis: The situations that befall the officers of a New York City police precinct.

BERNARD "BARNEY" MILLER

Position: Captain of the 12th Precinct in Greenwich Village.

Wife: Elizabeth (Barbara Barrie).

Children: Rachel (Anne Wyndham), age 21, and David (Michael Tessier), age 12.

Address: 617 Chestnut Street in Manhattan.

Elizabeth's Job: Agent for the New York City Department of Social Services.

Barney's Character: Patient man who tries to adhere to department policies but often finds that he must bend the rules. At one point, when Barney's work put a strain on his marriage, he separated from Elizabeth and moved into an apartment (45) at the Hotel Greenwich (which had been raided 25 times for prostitution).

Jail Time: Barney witnessed a cocaine bust and was not only cited for contempt of court but also given jail time for being "an uncooperative witness" by a judge.

STANLEY TADEUSZ WOJECHOWICZ

Nickname: "Wojo" and "Stan."

Position: Sergeant (took him eight years to achieve).

Military Service: A marine during the Vietnam War.

Address: Apartment 12 of a building at the corner of Perry Street.

Pet Parrot: Crackers (for which he paid $225).

Medical Issue: Unable to have children (sterile).

Father Figure: Phil Fish ("The closest thing I have to a father since I became a cop").

ARTHUR P. DIETRICH

Position: Detective. He joined the New York Police Department on November 12, 1973.

Original Goal: Actor (in college he played Nick the Bartender in *The Time of Your Life* by William Saroyan; when no one showed up for the play, he changed his mind).

Date of Birth: October 12, 1947 (in another episode, he mentions his birth year as 1943).

Hometown: Allentown, Pennsylvania.

Place of Birth: St. Mary's Hospital.

Current Address: An apartment on West 12th Street.

Favorite Comedy Team: The Three Stooges.
Board Member: The Trilateral Commission of the police department.

RONALD "RON" HARRIS
Position: Detective.
Address: Apartment 34 at West 43rd Street in Manhattan.
Ambition: To become a writer.
Book: Blood on the Badge (originally called *Precinct Diary* and published by
    Wainwright Publishing House; Ron refers to it as "B.O.B").
Screenplay: To set a trap to capture a porno film producer, Ron wrote *4 Women.*
Ancestors: Ezekiel, Ron's great grandfather, owned a liquor store in Cleveland,
    Ohio. His four-times great grandfather commanded the Scottish Dragoons
    in fifteenth-century Scotland.
Family Crest: A bagpipe in a field of tweed. The geological survey cost $35.
Most Proud: His elegant dress as a plainclothes detective.

PHILIP "PHIL" FISH
Position: Sergeant (he has been with the New York Police Department for 38
    years).
Wife: Bernice (Doris Belack, then Florence Stanley); married for 40 years.
Daughter: Beverly Fish (Emily Levine), a schoolteacher.
Address: Apartment 5 at 316 Chambers Street in Brooklyn, New York.
Awards: Three commendations, a Medal of Valor, and citations for bravery.
Character: Cranky, set in his ways, not fond of children, and eager to just get
    through the day with as few hassles as possible.

OTHER CHARACTERS
Nick Yemana (Jack Soo), born in Omaha, Nebraska, in April (year not given),
is the Asian member of the team. While he investigates cases and writes out
reports, he has the unofficial job of making the coffee (a task he first enjoyed
until everyone started complaining about its awful taste). He is also addicted to
gambling (playing the horses at Aqueduct Racetrack) and claims that money
turns him on. While he is seen reading the Racing Form, he also reads the *New
York Times.*

Carl Levitt (Ron Carey), the officer seeking a position as a plainclothes
detective, was born in 1942 in New Brunswick, New Jersey, but raised in Rutherford, New Jersey.

Janice Wentworth (Linda Lavin) is the only female detective in the squad
room during the series' first season; she is later replaced by Officer Maria Bat-
tista (June Gable).

Arnold Ripner (Alex Henteloff) is the rather disreputable lawyer; Frank
Luger (James Gregory) is the police inspector.

The series pilot film, *The Life and Times of Captain Barney Miller*, aired on ABC on August 8, 1974. Abby Dalton played Barney's wife, Elizabeth.

SPIN-OFF

Fish (ABC, 1977). Phil, age 62, retires from the force to join Bernice as host parents of five delinquent children in a group home social services program. Charlie Harrison (Barry Gordon), a 27-year-old studying for a doctorate in child psychology at New York University, assists them. The children are Jilly Papalardo (Denise Miller), Diane Palanski (Sarah Natoli), Mike Feroni (Lenny Bari), Victor (John Cassisi), and Loomis (Todd Bridges). Jilly, whose mother is a prostitute, had a short career as a model for the Yarnell Modeling Agency; nothing is stated about the other children. Phil's home was said to be decorated with discarded furniture from Ellis Island. Prior to returning to the 12th Precinct (when the retirement age became 70), Phil held jobs as a vacuum cleaner salesman and night watchman.

Benson
(ABC, 1979–1986)

Cast: Robert Guillaume (Benson DuBois), James Noble (Gene Gatling), Missy Gold (Katie Gatling), Caroline McWilliams (Marcy Hill), Inga Swenson (Gretchen Krause), Didi Conn (Denise Stevens), Rene Auberjonois (Clayton Endicott), Ethan Phillips (Peter Downey).

Basis: An African American butler (Benson DuBois) and his experiences as he becomes a vital part of a governor's (Gene Gatling) staff.

OVERALL SERIES INFORMATION

Benson was first seen as the butler to Jessica Tate (Katherine Helmond) of Dunns River, Connecticut, on the series *Soap*. When Gene, Jessica's cousin, is elected governor, she loans him Benson to organize his household. Benson soon becomes indispensable and remains with Gene. At this time, Benson was given a full name (Benson DuBois). Previously, he was called only "Benson" (or "Mr. Benson"), which was his last name.

Capitol City, in an unidentified state, is the setting. "If it's not broken, don't fix it" is the state motto, and several towns (named after TV series) are mentioned as making it up: Springfield (*Father Knows Best*), Pine Valley (*All My Children*), Walnut Grove (*Little House on the Prairie*), Somerset (*Somerset* [NBC soap opera]), and Eastland (*The Facts of Life*). Hamilton County is said to be the site of a U.S. Air Force base.

In episodes that show Gene making a political speech, there is a symbol on the podium that reads, "Seal of the Great State of . . ." It is just impossible to read the name that follows "of." In dialogue, it is called "The State" or "Our State."

BENSON DUBOIS
Year of Birth: 1927.

Place of Birth: Baltimore, Ohio.

Mother: Lois DuBois (Beah Richards); his father is deceased.

Siblings: Brothers, Russell DuBois, an orthodontist (Tim Reid), and Earl DuBois (Kene Holliday), and sister, Elaine DuBois (Vernee Watson).

Occupation: Director of household affairs, then state budget director and lieutenant governor.

Residence: The governor's Mansion, then an apartment in a historic building designed by J. Robert Emerson and owned by Clayton Endicott (Benson is president of the tenant's association), a condo with the street number 639, and Apartment 2H at 7209 Dorsett Avenue.

Military Service: Private, then sergeant, with the army during the Korean War (first stationed at Fort Dix in New Jersey, then Hawaii). He mentions sharing a foxhole with actor George Kennedy in Korea, and, unknown to Benson and his squad, they were used as guinea pigs when germ warfare was tested on them without their knowledge.

Dog Tag Number: 52136045.

Favorite Breakfast: Eggs over easy.

Favorite Song: "As Time Goes By" (from the film *Casablanca*).

Christmas Memory: The smell of caramel swirl coffee cake baked by his mother.

Childhood Recollections: Had a dog named Jack and was called "Puddin' Head" by his family (as he would hog the dinnertime desserts).

Favorite Sport: Hockey.

Honor: Named "Bachelor of the Month" by *City View* magazine; presented with an honorary doctorate degree from Reynolds University in Florida.

Dream: To become a jazz pianist in a smoky nightclub.

Undercover Assignment: Posing as convict Danny Ballard to expose conditions in the Kingsley State Prison.

Favorite Eatery: Sing's Chinese Restaurant.

Inheritance: The *Playbird* men's magazine and its club, the Playbird Nest (from its late owner, Hugh Howard, who remembered a kind deed Benson did for him in 1953).

Relatives: Nephew, Benson Hawkins; prefers to be called "Clete" (Keenan Ivory Wayans); aunt, Lil (Helen Martin); uncle, Buster (Julius Harris); cousin, Saundra (Alva Petway).

GENE XAVIER GATLING
Father: Gibson Gatling (David Huddleston); mother not mentioned.

Siblings: Sister, Libby (Dorothy Green), and brother, Jack Gatling (Sandy McPeak).

Daughter: Katherine, called "Katie" (who is left handed).

Marital Status: Widower. Gene was married to Olivia Bennett, a woman he mentions by name only once (he refers to her as "His wife" or "Katie's mother"). Gene married Olivia when he was 37 years old; Katie was born when Gene was 40. Her demise was quite tragic: at a country club costume party, Olivia dressed as a sugarplum fairy (with real sugar cubes attached to her dress). As Gene says, "She was attacked and eaten by horses." Gene mentions that Gloria Costello was his first girlfriend.

Birth Sign: Sagittarius.

Height: 6 feet, 3 inches tall.

Place of Birth: Unclear. Gene mentions being born in "The State," which is "a nice place to raise kids." However, when Jessica Tate visits Gene, it is learned that she and Gene grew up together in Connecticut. Gene teased Jessica all the time (she called him "Mean Gene"); because Jessica was untidy, Gene called her "Messy Jessie." Jessica traveled by plane, indicating that "The State" is some distance from Connecticut.

Education: Breckenridge Prep School; Crandall High School. (A member of the swim team until he learned he was allergic to chlorine. He was president of the student counsel and voted, due to his chemistry class "expertise," "Most Likely to Dissolve"; his sister, Libby, was his prom date.) In his unnamed college, he was voted "Spinach King."

Occupation: Governor of the State (replaced the former governor; said to be Governor Mulligan, then Governor Mountford). Gene's political party is never revealed (simply called "The Party").

Prior Occupation: Unclear. Gene's family owns the Gatling Lumber Mill, and Gene mentions only "working down at the lumber mill" (situated in the Devil's Peak region). He is also said to be the owner of a paper mill, a lumberjack, and a logger. The mystery continues: In high school, Gene entered a dance marathon and endured 39 hours of nonstop dancing, leading him to believe he should become a professional dancer. He next took flying lessons and contemplated becoming an airline pilot. It was at this time that he thought that becoming governor was his life's goal: to give the people an honest government. He later says that he was approached to run for governor while working at the paper mill.

Residence: The Governor's Mansion in Lawrence County. It is said to be haunted by the ghost of Governor Hardwick, who was poisoned by an ambitious aide over 100 years ago.

Pets: As a kid, Gene had two dogs named Max and Max (only he could tell them apart).

Hobby: History and logrolling (he entered his first logrolling contest at age 14).

Favorite Breakfast: Poached eggs.

Favorite Sport: Fishing.

Favorite TV Shows: The Big Valley, The Six Million Dollar Man, and *The Fall Guy* (all starring his favorite actor, Lee Majors).

Military Service: The navy during World War II (where he received a Purple Heart for stubbing his toe and breaking it during a battle).

Ability: Cooking (famous for his "Bunkhouse Biscuits," which he made when he worked at the lumber mill).

Yearly Christmas Gift for Benson: A wallet.

Trait: Singing in his sleep and telling long stories about his past.

Coffee: Black (but not too strong).

Flaw: Although he needs to travel by car, he often gets carsick.

KATHERINE "KATIE" GATLING

Age: 9 (when the series begins).

Middle Name: Olivia (after her mother).

Place of Birth: Unknown until the 1981 episode "Lumber Mill," when Katie recalls the lumber mill as a child, indicating that she too was born in "The State."

Education: Capitol City Grammar School (played the cello in the school orchestra), then Capitol City High School (called C.C.H., where she is a cheerleader).

Club: The Capitol City Girls' Softball League (wears jersey 5).

Pet Cat: Napoleon.

Favorite Part of Christmas: Picking out a tree with Benson.

Favorite Music Group: Kiss.

Nickname: Called "Sugar" by Benson. Benson also gives Katie 50 cents a day for her school milk money and acts like a substitute for Katie's mother (e.g., taking her to the Mother-Daughter Church Picnic). Gretchen calls her "Lipschkin," and Clayton calls her both "Munchkin" and "Princess."

Favorite Breakfast: Oatmeal.

Favorite Sixth-Grade Activity: Going to the library on Saturday afternoons.

Business Venture: Katie's Cookies (based on a recipe from Benson's mother).

Character: Very sweet and charming girl who almost always does what she is told. She takes her schoolwork seriously and strives for perfect grades.

Relatives: Cousin, Laura (Tracy Gold).

GRETCHEN KRAUS

Place of Birth: Germany.

Mother: Fritzi Kraus (Sudie Bond); father not mentioned.

Position: Head of household affairs; later seen as Benson's assistant. Billie Bird as Mrs. Cassidy becomes the new housekeeper. Gretchen was previously an actress, then housekeeper, for former State Governors Pat Mulligan and Harold Mountford. She also designs costumes for the local State Community Theater.

Middle Name: Willomina.

Age: 47.

Residence: The Governor's Mansion.

Favorite Sport: Bowling.

Favorite Actor: John Wayne.

Favorite Cuisine: French food.

Favorite Dance: The waltz.

Favorite Movie: The Sound of Music.

Childhood: While Gretchen rarely talks about her past, she mentioned that her parents sought a better life and came to America when she was a young girl. On occasion, she sings songs from "the Old Country," and as a child she and two girlfriends formed a band and played songs for the people of her village.

Marital Status: Single (as Benson insinuates, there is no man in his right mind who would marry her). However, through dialogue, it is implied that Gretchen was once married.

Character: A stern woman who is set in her ways. She is very demanding (wants things done her way) and simply dislikes Benson (both quarrel and insult each other). It appears that Gretchen (virtually always called "Krause" by Benson) is the only one who is able to control the two large guard dogs that patrol the grounds. She refers to them as "Doggies" (but did call one "Sheba").

Dream: To travel across America by train.

MARSHA "MARCY" HILL

Mother: Louise Hill (Allyn Ann McLerie); father not mentioned.

Position: Gene's executive secretary.

Year of Birth: 1945.

Place of Birth: St. Paul, Minnesota.

Trait: Very efficient and dedicated to her job.

Fear: Losing her job to someone who is better at organization.

Boyfriend: Dan Slater (Ted Danson), the producer of Gene's "Fireside Chat" TV program (wherein he addressed the public). Dan and Marcy married on February 20, 1981. Gretchen was Marcy's maid of honor, and Katie was bridesmaid; Benson gave the bride away. A year later, Marcy and Dan move to Buffalo, New York, to open an advertising agency.

Relatives: Uncle, Henry (Robert Rockwell).

DENISE STEVENS

Position: Marcy's replacement (but as Benson's secretary). She worked previously in a Wall Street accounting firm, then in the legislative secretarial pool on Capitol Hill.

Middle Name: Florence.

Place of Birth: Brooklyn, New York.

Birthday: July 13, 1951.

Education: The New York School of Business.

Ability: To read papers that are upside down (which she calls her hobby) and, saying that numbers are her second language, to solve complex mathematical problems in her head.

Dream: To become a rock musician (playing drums).

Favorite Breakfast: Scrambled eggs.

Boyfriend: Peter Downey (born in Florida and works as Gene's press secretary). He and Denise married in a forest in 1983 and a year later became the parents of a baby boy (delivered by Benson when he, Denise, and Gene were trapped in a hospital elevator).

Peter is an outdoorsman (attended forestry school) and addicted to fast food (Fatso's is his favorite eatery; he works out at Morry's Gym). He mentioned that his ex-wife was named Jeannine and that he attended Reynolds University. He previously worked as a restaurant reviewer for an auto club magazine and was called "Bunny Wabbitt Face" by Denise. In 1984, Denise and Peter leave when Denise accepts a job with NASA.

CLAYTON ENDICOTT III

Position: Chief of staff (also called chief political aide), then budget director (when Benson is elected lieutenant governor).

Place of Birth: Manhattan.

Parents: Whitney (Stephen Elliott) and Harriet (Billie Bird) Endicott.

Childhood Nickname: Called "Skippy" by his mother.

Marital Status: Single.

Military Service: The Marines. He also served with the adjutant general's office in Washington, D.C., and spent a summer as an intern with the Foreign Service.

Background: A nonpracticing attorney who is descended from royalty (first said to be the sixteenth-century Maurice Claude of Normandy, then from Pilgrims on the *Mayflower*). He is now heir to Endicott Industries and is a member of an unnamed polo team.

Education: Princeton University.

Second Language: Chinese (able to speak both dialects).

Trait: Prim and proper and very demanding. He fears that Gene's "backwoods" upbringing is not a powerful tool to be state governor.

Dream: To become a poet.

Relatives: Aunt, Carney (Ernestine Mercer).

LIFE WITHOUT BENSON

In the 1984 Christmas episode, Benson is injured in a car accident and envisions what life would be like in 1991 if he were not a part of Gene's life. Clayton had become governor (Benson was not there to keep Clayton in check). He is unscrupulous and, feeling sorry for Gene, has made him his butler. Katie is a Madonna-like, sexy girl who dropped out of college to marry a football player named Lunkhead. Gretchen is a bag lady known as "Nuts and Fruit Cake" ("She got off at the wrong exit on the interstate of life and sells nuts, fruitcakes, and Christmas candy door-to-door").

Note: The last two episodes find Benson running for governor against Gene. As Gene and Benson watched the election results, the program ended with an announcer saying, "And the Winner Is . . ." (the title of the final episode). Benson was a candidate for an unnamed political party, and his romantic interest, Senator Diane Hartford (Donna LaBrie), became his campaign manager.

Three possible endings, none of which aired, were considered: Benson winning, Gene being reelected, or a wild-card candidate becoming governor. It is rumored that a trailer for an eighth season was made showing that Gene was elected and that Benson became a state senator. Gene had previously mentioned that he plans "to move back to the lumber mill with Katie" after his term is up.

The Bionic Woman
(ABC, 1976–1977; NBC, 1977–1978)

Cast: Lindsay Wagner (Jaime Sommers), Richard Anderson (Oscar Goldman), Jennifer Darling (Peggy Callahan), Martin E. Brooks (Dr. Rudy Wells).

Basis: Jaime Sommers, seriously injured during a skydiving accident, is saved when Oscar Goldman, head of the O.S.I. (Office of Scientific Intelligence), authorizes a cost-classified bionic operation to save her life. Now, endowed with superhuman powers, Jaime performs dangerous and sensitive missions for the O.S.I. The program is a spin-off of *The Six Million Dollar Man* (see entry).

JAIME SOMMERS

Parents: James and Ann Sommers (both of whom were college professors, now deceased; Ann worked secretly as an undercover agent for the U.S. government).

Birthday: June 27, 1949.

Place of Birth: Ojai, California.

Measurements: 34-27-34. She stands 5 feet, 7 inches tall and weighs 132 pounds.

Education: Ojai High School.

Occupation: Former tennis pro turned schoolteacher (grades 7 to 9) at the Ventura Air Force Base in California.

Residence: A small apartment over a garage on Decatur Road in Ojai.

Romantic Interest: Colonel Steve Austin, the American astronaut who received the world's first bionic operation (making him "The Six Million Dollar Man").

First Meeting: In high school, where Jaime was a freshman and Steve a senior. Another episode mentions that Steve and Jaime met in third grade. (When Jaime dared Steve "to eat all that food." He did and became ill.)

First Kiss: At a New Year's Eve party (Steve was teased for "robbing the cradle").

Nickname: "Babe" (as called by Steve).

Favorite Hangout: The Capri (a pizza parlor). When they became troubled, the downed tree near the shore of a lake provided a refuge for working things out. While it looked like they would eventually marry, their career goals separated them.

The Accident: After a four-year separation, Steve reunites with Jaime when he returns to Ojai. Shortly before Jaime is to leave for a tennis match in Spain, she and Steve decide to skydive. Everything is normal until Jaime's parachute malfunctions and she plunges to the ground. The ensuing fall produces injuries so serious that she cannot be saved under normal circumstances. Seeing that Jaime's only hope for survival rests with a bionic operation, Steve convinces a reluctant Oscar Goldman to authorize the operation.

The Outcome: Jaime's life is saved when her legs, right arm, and right ear are replaced with atomic-powered artificial limbs.

The Payback: Feeling that she owes the government a debt, Jaime relinquishes her tennis career to become an agent for the O.S.I. (her cover is that of a schoolteacher).

Characteristic: The world's first female cyborg (cybernetic organism).

Abilities: Incredible speed (can run the mile in 58 seconds), enhanced hearing, and extraordinary strength.

Telephone Number: 311-555-2376 (given verbally); 311-555-7306 (seen on camera).

Car License Plate: 826 OPP (then TVU 566).

Favorite Flower: Yellow roses.

Childhood Dog: Puzzles.

Best Friend: Peggy Callahan (also called "Janet Callahan"), Oscar's secretary at O.S.I. headquarters in Washington, D.C. She resides as 232 Landcroft Street, was born on April 7, has blonde hair and blue eyes, and measures 36-24-35. Her Type 3 driver's license (number S5 64607) expires on January 20, 1979.

Evil Double: Lisa Galloway (Lindsay Wagner), a surgically altered woman made to look like Jaime to learn the secret of her strength. Through a taffylike substance called Hydrazene (developed by Jaime's bionic surgeon Dr. Rudy Wells), Lisa was able to literally become another Jaime, but the substance was unstable and caused illness.

NBC Change: Jaime is teamed with Maximillion, a bionic German shepherd she calls "Max" (injured in a fire and saved when a million-dollar bionic operation [hence the dog's name] replaced his jaw and legs).

JAIME'S BIONICS

Ear: Bionic Audio Micro Sensor. Catalog number 6314 KMH.
Right Arm: Bionic Neuro Link Forearm. Catalog number 2821/WLY.
Right Hand: Bionic Neuro Link Hand. Catalog number 2022/PJI.
Legs: Bionic Neuro-Link Bipedal Assembly. Catalog number 914 PAH.
Power Supply: Atomic Type AED-4, 1,500-Watt Continuous Duty, and Atomic Type AED-9A, 4,920-Watt Continuous Duty.

REBOOT

Bionic Woman (NBC, 2007) wherein "The" was dropped from the title and Jaime's history completely altered. *Cast:* Michelle Ryan (Jaime Sommers), Lucy Kate Hale (Becca Sommers).

JAIME SOMMERS

Birthday: February 23, 1983.
Place of Birth: Van Horne, Iowa.
Parents: Ethan and Madeline Jo Sommers.
Sister: Becca Sommers (born on May 5, 1991).
Education: Meskwaki High School.
Life-Changing Event: In 2004, after Madeline Jo's passing from breast cancer, Jaime moves to San Francisco to begin a new life (Becca later comes to live with her). While working as a bartender, Jaime enrolls in a college psychology program and befriends her bio/environmental ethics professor, Dr. Will Anthros (Chris Bowers), the head surgeon at the Berkut Group (aka the Wolf Creek Bio Tech Research Center), a secretive organization founded by Will's father, Anthony (Mark Sheppard), and its chief executive officer, Jonas Bledsoe (Miguel Ferrer). The center was established to treat wounded soldiers and then rebuild them as fierce fighters.
The Operation: Jaime and Will are riding in a car when they are struck by a truck. Will receives few injuries, but Jaime is seriously hurt with little hope for survival. Jaime is rushed to Berkut, where, through a $50 million bionic operation (performed by Will), Jaime's right arm, ear, eye, and both legs are replaced with nuclear-powered, synthetic limbs. Jaime, now endowed with incredible abilities, agrees to help the agency in its secret operations.
The First Bionic Woman: Sarah Corvis (Katee Sackhoff), a renegade with deteriorating bionics who is seeking to encompass Jaime's advanced bionics to

save her life. Jaime's bionics are supported by a bloodlike substance called Anthrocytes. Over time, these "become fatigued" and the bionics shut down, causing death. It is estimated that Jaime has five years to live—but Jason promises, "We'll find a way to save you."

B.J. and the Bear
(NBC, 1979–1981)

First-Season Cast: Greg Evigan (B.J. McKay), Claude Akins (Elroy P. Lobo), Mills Watson (Deputy Perkins), Brian Kerwin (Birdie Hawkins), Sam (Bear).

Second-Season Cast: Greg Evigan (B.J. McKay), Murray Hamilton (Rutherford T. Grant), Judy Landers (Jeannie Campbell), Candi Brough (Teri Garrison), Randi Brough (Geri Garrison), Barbra Horan (Samantha Smith), Linda McCullough (Callie Everett), Sherilyn Wolter (Cindy Grant), Sheila DeWindt (Angie Cartwright), Jock Mahoney (Jason T. Willard), Eric Server (Jim Steiger), Sam (Bear).

First-Season Basis: An honest, independent truck driver (B.J. McKay) tries to maintain an honest operation despite the dishonest people out to get him.

Second-Season Basis: B.J. establishes his own trucking business and now, with a crew of seven beautiful assistants, again faces difficult times—from both a rival trucking company and a corrupt law enforcer.

BILLIE JOE "B.J." MCKAY (1979–1980)
Birthday: October 14, 1953.
Place of Birth: Milwaukee, Wisconsin.
Sister: Shauna McKay (Debra Ryan).
Occupation: Independent trucker.
Assistant: Bear, his pet chimpanzee.
Fees: $1.50 a mile plus expenses.
Cargo: Haul anything that is legal anywhere.
Truck: A red-with-white-trim Kenworth 18-wheeler.
Milwaukee License Plate: As seen: 806-356, UT 3665, 635-608, 4T-3665.
CB Handle: "The Milwaukee Kid."
Favorite Watering Hole: The Country Comfort Truckers Stop in Bowlin County.
Military Service: Chopper pilot during the Vietnam War.
Band: Sang with a group called Ghettoway City.
Bear: Named by B.J. after Paul "Bear" Bryant, the University of Alabama football coach. During a mission in Vietnam, B.J.'s helicopter was shot down, and he became a prisoner of war. A friendly chimpanzee befriended B.J. and brought him food to help him survive. When B.J. was rescued, he took Bear with him.

Nicknames: B.J. calls Bear "Kid" or "The Kid."

Character: A clean-cut young man simply attempting to do his job. He is easy-going, comes to the aid of people in trouble, and can take care of himself in a fight.

Competition: J.P. Pierson (M.P. Murphy), owner of the shady Hi Ballers Trucking Company (who is against independents for stealing business).

Enemy: Elroy P. Lobo, the corrupt sheriff of Orly County, Georgia (seeks to jail B.J. for breaking up his white slavery ring); his dim-witted assistant, Deputy Perkins; and his levelheaded, honest deputy, Birdwell "Birdie" Hawkins.

B.J. MCKAY (1980–1981)

Business: Bear Enterprises. Trucks are fixed at Deke's Truck Repair Shop.

Business/Living Quarters Address: 800 Palmer Street, Hollywood, California, above Phil's Disco, a bar/restaurant.

Business "Partner": Bear, his simian companion.

OTHER CHARACTERS

Jeannie Campbell, nicknamed "Stacks," measures 37C-24-36. She is sweet and feminine and somewhat of a dumb blonde. Her ability for distraction often helps B.J. solve a case. She does show ample cleavage, and perilous situations do not seem to bother her until she thinks about what is happening to her. She loves to have cheesecake pictures taken (especially if she is wearing a bikini or low-cut blouse). Stacks, as she is always called, drives a truck with the plate 4JJ 0167 and dreams of getting married but falls for men who are most often despicable.

Callie Everett is the toughest and most physically violent of the girls. She can handle herself in a fight and, as B.J. says, "has a smart mouth." Callie secretly loves B.J. but believes that "B.J. sees me only as a girl who can drive a rig and fix a flat tire." While very pretty, she is not as feminine as the other girls (dresses in nonflattering clothes) and drives a truck with the plate IXT 403. Edward Andrews played her Uncle Barney.

Geri and Teri Garrison are identical twins who also work as waitresses at Phil's Disco. Geri is impatient and likes to take matters in her own hands. Teri prefers to take things slow and easy; they drive a truck with the license plate UJJ 4004.

Angela "Angie" Cartwright, the only African American member of the team, is also the least active of the girls, as she moonlights as a radio disc jockey called "The Nightingale." Her truck license plate reads 040-3777.

Samantha "Sam" Smith is sweet and feminine and not prone to violent confrontations. She accompanies B.J. on assignments but most often looks after Bear while B.J. investigates. She shares a truck (license plate XTR 7162) with Cindy.

Cynthia "Cindy" Grant is easily upset and a bit irrational. She has knowledge of criminal law and often warns B.J. that what he is about to do to crack a case could be construed as breaking the law. Cindy always sides with B.J. against her corrupt father (Captain Grant), as she knows he is wrong in what he is doing.

Enemy: Rutherford T. Grant, the corrupt head of S.C.A.T. (Special Crimes Action Team), Southern Division of the Los Angeles Police Department. Grant has made it his top priority to put B.J. behind bars, as he feels that B.J. is a threat to his illegal activities (catering to the mob). He is assisted by Lieutenant Jim Steiger, a man who is not as dishonest as Grant, but follows his orders.

Competition: Jason T. Willard, the head of the corrupt Trans-Cal Trucking Company.

SPIN-OFF

The Misadventures of Sheriff Lobo (NBC, 1979) deals with the unorthodox dealings of Elroy P. Lobo, the corrupt sheriff of Orly County, Georgia, and his deputies: the corrupt (but dim-witted) Perkins and the honest Birdwell "Birdie" Hawkins.

Elroy's corruption continues in *Lobo* (NBC 1980), wherein Lobo (now the chief of detectives) and his deputies (Perkins and Birdie) are hired by the mayor of Atlanta (who believes Lobo is honest) to curb the city's crime rate.

The Bob Newhart Show
(CBS, 1972–1978)

Cast: Bob Newhart (Bob Hartley), Suzanne Pleshette (Emily Hartley), Bill Daily (Howard Borden), Peter Bonerz (Jerry Robinson), Marcia Wallace (Carol Kester).

Basis: A psychologist (Bob Hartley) attempts to deal with problems at home with friends and family as well as patients at the office.

DR. ROBERT "BOB" HARTLEY

Parents: Herb (Barnard Hughes) and Martha Hartley (Martha Scott). Martha was originally called "Eleanor" (she calls Bob "Sonny"); her maiden name is Smith.

Occupation: Psychologist. Bob also held a temporary job as an agent for the Loggers' Casualty Life Insurance Company (slogan: "We Gotta Insure These Guys").

Place of Birth: Illinois in 1929.

Sister: Ellen Hartley (Pat Finley).

Wife: Emily.

Address: Apartment 523 (a building owned by the Skyline Management Corporation in Chicago).

Office Number: Varies between 751 and 715 at the Rampo Arts Building.

Office Telephone Number: 726-7098.

Social Security Number: 352-22-7439.

Birth Sign: Virgo.

Shoe Size: 8½B.

IQ: 129.

Military Service: The army's 193rd Combat Support Orchestra during the Korean War (played drums and was called "best wrists south of the 38th Parallel"). After his discharge, Bob traveled to New York and auditioned for the Buddy Rich Band. Buddy's response, "You stink, man," set Bob on the course to become a psychologist. Bob also played drums in his high school band.

The Bob Newhart Show. *CBS/Photofest. ©CBS*

College Friend: Clifford "Cliff" Murdock (Tom Poston), nicknamed "The Peeper" (Bob had the nickname "The Mooner"). Cliff, born in Montpelier, Vermont, later married Connie (Jean Palmerton); "Moonlight in Vermont" was their song.

TV Appearance: "Psychology in Motion" (the announcer called him "Dr. Robert Hartman").

Regular Patients: Elliot Carlin (Jack Riley), Lillian Bakerman (Florida Friebus), Michele Nardo (Renee Lippin), and Victor Gianelli (Noam Pitlik). In the episode "Death of a Fruitman," tragedy strikes when Bob ejects Victor from his group, and he is, in turn, killed when a truckload of zucchini falls on him.

Overall Series Catchphrase: "Hi Bob" (apparently said 256 times).

Final Episode: Bob and Emily move to Oregon when Bob accepts a college teaching job.

Relatives: Uncle Harry and Aunt May (not seen).

EMILY HARTLEY

Maiden Name: Emily Harrison.

Parents: Cornelius "Junior" Harrison (John Randolph) and Agatha "Aggie" Harrison (Ann Rutherford). Emily is also said to have a younger sister (not named or seen).

Place of Birth: Seattle, Washington.

Education: Seattle High School; college not named.

Birthday: January 3, 1937 (she is eight years younger than Bob).

Measurements: 37-26-38. She has brunette hair and stands 5 feet, 4 inches tall.

Dress Size: 8.

Occupation: Teacher (taught third grade at Gorman Elementary School), then vice principal of Tyler Grammar School.

IQ: 151.

Nickname: "Cupcake" (as called by Bob's father).

Wedding Date: April 15, 1970.

First-Anniversary Gifts: A cat from Emily's parents; a radio from Bob's parents.

HOWARD MARK BORDEN

Siblings: Sister, Debbie Borden (Heather Menzies); brothers, Gordon Borden, the game warden (William Redfield); and Norman Borden, the Mormon doorman (not seen).

Relationship: Bob and Emily's neighbor.

Occupation: A 747 airline navigator. After nine years, he was replaced by a computer and became a navigator for an airline called EDS (European Delivery Service).

Date of Birth: September 15.

Marital Status: Divorced.

Son: Howard Borden Jr. (Moosie Drier), who was conceived "during the great airplane strike of 1963."

OTHER CHARACTERS

Jerome Merle Robinson, called "Jerry," is Bob's friend, a children's orthodontist (they share the same office floor). He was adopted (later found his mother, but his father, an American plumber working in World War II England, was killed during an air raid alert). Jerry washes his hands on average 46 times a day and often becomes involved in Bob's personal and business affairs.

Carol Kester works as both Bob and Jerry's receptionist-secretary. She was born in Collinsville, Iowa, and lives at 2601 Grace Avenue, Apartment 2J. She has a tape of a barking dog (Lobo) that is activated for protection when the doorbell rings. She married Larry Bondurant (Will MacKenzie), a travel agent, and first mentioned she was overweight growing up, then "tall, thin, and red-haired." Larry calls her "Big Red."

Bridget Loves Bernie
(CBS, 1972–1973)

Cast: Meredith Baxter (Bridget Fitzgerald), David Birney (Bernie Steinberg).

Basis: An Irish Catholic girl (Bridget) and a Jewish man (Bernie) marry and attempt to live a normal life despite the fact that their parents object to a mixed religious marriage.

BRIDGET FITZGERALD

Parents: Walter (David Doyle) and Amy Fitzgerald (Audra Lindley). Walter, the owner of Global Investments, is a rich, staunch Republican, while Amy, accustomed to society life, is timid and very reserved. She is a member of the Daughters of Isabella Charity League.

Full Name: Bridget Theresa Mary Colleen Fitzgerald Steinberg.

Brother: Father Michael Fitzgerald (Robert Sampson), a priest at Immaculate Heart Church.

Place of Birth: Manhattan.

Date of Birth: June 1947 (25 when the series begins; same as in real life).

Education: Immaculate Heart Academy; New York University.

Bra Size: 38C. She has blonde hair and blue eyes and stands 5 feet, 8 inches tall.

Dress Size: 4.

Occupation: Fourth-grade schoolteacher at Immaculate Heart Academy.

Address: 1041 Central Park West (before marriage); an apartment over Steinberg's Delicatessen (after marriage).

Trait: Very sweet and caring young woman who tries to avoid confrontations and settle disputes, especially between her and Bernie's parents, amicably.

Childhood Memories: Bridget broke her wrist after falling off her roller skates; *Mrs. Snuggle Bunny and the Tree Toads* was her favorite TV show.

BERNARD "BERNIE" STEINBERG

Parents: Sam (Harold J. Stone) and Sophie Steinberg (Bibi Osterwald). They are the owners of Steinberg's Delicatessen and typical parents (although they continually have disagreements, especially over their son's marriage).

Place of Birth: Manhattan's Lower East Side.

Age: Mid-20s (David Birney was born in 1939, making him 33 when the series begins).

Education: P.S. 52 grammar school; Roosevelt High School.

Occupation: Yellow Cab driver (cab number 12; identification number JC-56; rates are 60 cents for the first mile; 10 cents each one-fifth of a mile). It was in this cab that a passenger (Bridget) met Bernie, and the two fell instantly in love.

The Marriage: Originally wed in a civil ceremony, but to please their parents, Bridget and Bernie remarried in a ceremony presided over by a priest and a rabbi.

Ambition: Become an actor and Broadway playwright.

Address: Steinberg's Delicatessen on Third Avenue and 17th Street (next to Goldstein's Bakery). Bridget and Bernie chose to live over the deli (which closes at 8:00 p.m.) after they refused Walter's wedding gifts (a portfolio of blue-chip stocks, a trip around the world, and a year's free rent at the Manchester Arms) to make it on their own.

Relatives: Sophie's brother, Moe Plotnic (Ned Glass), runs the catering end of the deli.

Buck Rogers in the 25th Century
(NBC, 1979–1981)

Cast: Gil Gerard (Buck Rogers), Erin Gray (Wilma Deering), Tim O'Connor (Dr. Elias Huer), Pamela Hensley (Ardala), Jay Garner (Ephraim Asimov).

Basis: A 20th-century astronaut (Buck Rogers), suspended in time during the flight of an exploration ship, awakens to and must deal with the world of the 25th century.

WILLIAM "BUCK" ROGERS

Birth Month: January.

Occupation: Astronaut (holds the rank of captain).

Mission: Pilot the *Ranger III*, the last of NASA's deep-space probes.

The Year: 1987.

The Place: The John F. Kennedy Space Center, from which the *Ranger III* is launched.

Code: "Flight 711 to Houston Central."

The Accident: The *Ranger III* is propelled into a mysterious orbit where a perfect combination of the gases oxygen, ozone, and ethylene seep into the ship and instantly freeze and preserve Buck.

The Time: Earth in the year 2491 (when the planet is still recovering from a 21st-century holocaust and the Earth is now dependent on trade with other planets for survival).

Capital of the United States: New Chicago. Other cities mentioned are Boston Complex, New Manhattan, New Tulsa, New Phoenix, and New Detroit.

Travel: Star Gates (also called "warp travel," similar to wormholes in space) are man-made portals that allow travel between planets (they are seen as a diamond quartet of bright lights that shimmer when ships pass through them).

Housing: People reside in cone-protected cities (like the City on the Sea, formerly New Orleans), as the atmosphere still has traces of radiation.

Retirement Age: 85.

Government: The Federation of the New Alliance (laws are dictated by the Inner City Council; Dr. Theopolis, a computer [voice of Eric Server] is its leader).

Headquarters: The Capitol Building.

Military: The Earth Directorate (also called the Earth Federation).

Agency Head: Dr. Elias Huer.

Military Commander: Colonel Wilma Deering of the Earth Defense Force, Delta Sector Division.

Military Ships: Terran Star Fighters.

The Awakening: After drifting in space for 504 years, the *Ranger III* is found, and Buck is awakened and told of his fate.

First-Season Assignment: Member of the Third Force of the Earth Directorate (Wilma is his superior). Buck has no official ranking and is considered an honorary captain due to his U.S. Air Force service in the 20th century.

Earth Enemy: King Draco the Conqueror (Joseph Wiseman), ruler of the planet Draconia and three-quarters of the universe; he is represented by his daughter Ardala.

Second-Season Assignment: Buck and Wilma are members of *The Searcher*, a spaceship seeking the lost tribes of Earth.

Searcher Motto: "Per Ardua Ad Astra" (seen on the bottom of the ship; it is Latin for "Through Adversity to the Stars").

Superior: Admiral Ephraim Asimov (also called "Isaac Asimov"). He is assisted by Dr. Goodfellow (Wilfred Hyde-White), a leading scientist, and Hawk (Thom Christopher), an alien man-bird.

Searcher Robot: Chrichton (voice of Jeff Davis), a robot that refuses to believe it was man-made.

Buck's Assistant: Twiki, a silver AmbuQuad (voice of Mel Blanc; played by Felix Silla, Bob Elyea, and Patty Maloney). Twiki originally spoke with a "Biddi-Biddi" sound.

Twiki Stats: A model 2223-T, built by the AmbuQuad Facility in New Chicago. The only other AmbuQuad seen is the gold-colored Tina (acts like a "love interest" for Twiki).

Buck's Nickname for Dr. Theopolis: "Theo."

WILMA DEERING

History: Born into a military family and continued in that tradition by joining the Defense Force; her daring and resourcefulness eventually earned her the rank of colonel.

Measurements: 36-24-35. She has light brown hair and blue eyes.

Nickname as a Kid: "Dizzy Dee."

PRINCESS ARDALA

Father: King Draco; mother not mentioned.

Family Position: The eldest of 29 daughters.

Spaceship: Commands the two-mile-wide *Draconia* battleship.

Measurements: 34-24-34 (by Buck's estimation).

Assistant: Commander Kane (also known as Killer Kane; played by Henry Silva, then Michael Ansara), a former student of Dr. Huer's who defected and joined the Draconian race (to become Ardala's adviser and protector).

Ambition: Defy her father and live her own life "by beginning a magnificent new dynasty with Buck" (a goal never accomplished when Ardala was dropped in a format change).

Charlie's Angels
(ABC, 1976–1981)

Cast: Kate Jackson (Sabrina Duncan), Farrah Fawcett (Jill Munroe), Jaclyn Smith (Kelly Garrett), Cheryl Ladd (Kris Munroe), Shelley Hack (Tiffany Welles), Tanya Roberts (Julie Rogers), John Forsythe (voice of Charlie), David Doyle (John Bosley).

Basis: Sabrina, Jill, and Kelly, detectives called Angels, solve crimes for Charlie Townsend, the never-seen head of the Townsend Detective Agency. Kris replaces Jill in second-season episodes, Tiffany joins with Kelly and Kris in the fourth season when Sabrina leaves, and Tiffany's departure teams Kelly and Kris with Julie in the final season.

OVERALL SERIES INFORMATION

The agency, with the building number 193, is located in Los Angeles; it is also called the Townsend Agency, Townsend Investigations, and Townsend and Associates. The Hawaiian branch is located at 4376 Kalahai Avenue. Fees are mentioned only as "you're paying a great deal of money for our services" or "a substantial fee." The agency receives 10 percent of the value of stolen items they recover.

Charlie, also the owner of the all-girl Venus Trucking Company, is rich and apparently a man of leisure (often seen in luxurious settings with a beautiful girl by his side). He has a tropical fish aquarium (Mildred is his favorite fish) and assists the Angels through his numerous contacts. It is revealed only that Charlie served in the military (the OSS [Office of Strategic Services]) during World War II.

The girls are not really angels. They lie, steal, and cheat to accomplish their goals. The Angels have one wish—to see Charlie. Jill suspects that Charlie remains anonymous because he has sent many people to prison and those people will one day get out and seek revenge. Not revealing himself is his way of protecting them in the long run. Kelly is the only Angel who believes she has seen Charlie. In the episode "Let Our Angel Live," Kelly, recovering from an operation after being shot, is in a dazed state but believes that the man disguised in hospital greens and standing by her side is Charlie.

Charlie's Angels is credited as initiating "jiggle TV" (the Angels' not wearing bras and "plots that caused the Angels to trot"). While this is especially obvious in the episodes "Angels in Chains" and "Angel in a Box," it appears that only Farrah Fawcett did not wear a bra. Hawaiian-based episodes display Kelly and Kris's shapely figures.

Charlie contacts the Angels via a Bell System 4A Speaker Phone (555-9626 is his direct contact number; 213-555-0267 is the business phone number). John Bosley, called "Boz," is Charlie's lawyer (the only one who has seen Charlie). He hates paperwork but always gets stuck with it. He mentioned appearing with the Gilbert and Sullivan Acting Troupe while in college and that Jill and Kris have a peculiar sense of humor.

The Mother Goose Toy Company produced action figures of Sabrina, Kelly, and Kris (as seen in the episode "Mother Goose Is Running for His Life"). Sabrina favors standing behind the bar in the office; Kelly and Kris sit on the sofa next to the bar.

SABRINA DUNCAN

Occupation: Private detective. Divorced from Bill Duncan (Michael Bell) and previously an officer with Division 28 of the Los Angeles Police Department (where she handed out parking tickets).

Nickname: "Bree."

Expertise: Fingerprint dusting, deductive reasoning, and the ability to plan and execute an undercover operation.

Attributes: Loyal, caring of others, and always stylishly dressed. She believes in doing things by the book ("although I follow a different book") and claims, "I've got a Guardian Angel [Charlie] who keeps an eye on me."

Belief: The only Angel who admits they have a fault—"We're the biggest chauvinists of them all. Who says the murderer can't be a woman?"

Oddity: The only Angel to never appear in a bikini, bathing suit, or skimpy outfit.

Departure: Sabrina left after three seasons (two working with Jill and Kelly) to marry for a second time. According to Charlie, she was happy and expecting her first child.

JILL MUNROE

Occupation: Private detective (previously an officer with Division 28 of the LAPD, where she was relegated to typing files).

Place of Birth: San Francisco in 1952. She is 24 years old and says, "In my tomboyish youth I was a real *Roy Rogers* [TV series] freak."

Nickname: Calls herself, Bree, and Kelly "a team like the Supremes."

Measurements: 33½B-23-34 (also given as 35-24-35).

Education: Union Bay High School; San Francisco State University.

Inspiration: TV crime shows like *Dragnet* made her want to become a police officer.

Attributes: Blonde and gorgeous with the ability to distract others. Jill, the most aggressive Angel, is always willing to help others at the risk of her own safety. She carries a pocket watch in her purse that was given to her by her father.

Favorite Activities: Skateboarding and meditating for relaxation.

Hobby: Motorcar racing. She is also an expert poker player and loves tennis.

Car: A white Cobra (license plate 861-BM6).

Residence: A small home on the beach (address not given).

Departure: Jill left after one season to pursue her racing career (hopes to become the first woman to win at Le Mans).

Oddity: The only Angel to create a sensation when, in the episode "Angels in Chains," her mostly unbuttoned blouse opened to reveal part of her right breast and nipple.

KELLY GARRETT

Occupation: Private detective (previously an officer with Division 28 of the LAPD, where she worked as a school crossing guard).

Place and Year of Birth: San Diego in August 1955.

Background: Sketchy. Kelly, an infant, and her mother were involved in a 23-car accident on a Texas highway. Kelly's mother was killed, and Kelly, taken to a hospital, "was misplaced." When Kelly remained unclaimed, she was sent to the St. Agnes Home for the Orphaned in Dallas (given her last name by the nun who raised her; it was not mentioned how she acquired her first name). She was adopted in 1964 and grew up in Texas.

Skills: An expert shot ("I learned to shoot from my father"); ability to sing (lead alto in a glee club) and dance; brilliant at deciphering complex clues; has a knack for picking locks; an expert motorcyclist.

Attributes: Faithful and caring. She is the only Angel not to depart for another career. She worked with Sabrina, Jill, Kris, Tiffany, and Julie.

Bra Size: 34B.

Favorite Drink: Tequila straight up with a lime chaser.

Favorite Eatery: Guido's Italian Restaurant.

Residence: A private home with the street number 10426.

Car License Plate: 129 UBO.

KRIS MUNROE

Relationship: Jill's younger sister.

Occupation: Private detective (previously an officer with the San Francisco Police Department, where she worked as a telephone switchboard operator).

Place of Birth: San Francisco.

Education: Union Bay High School (the first one in her class to learn Pig Latin). Jill had been paying for Kris's college education at State University, where she believed she was studying to become a teacher, not a law enforcer. Before she left, Jill recommended Kris to Charlie as her replacement.

Skills: Expert at distraction and picking locks.

Attributes: Cares for others. (Charlie says a bit too much, as this is also her biggest fault. Her enthusiasm could get her killed.) Kris worked with Sabrina, Kelly, Tiffany, and Julie.

Habit: Taking her childhood Raggedy Ann doll and a book, *Hansel and Gretel*, given to her by her mother, with her when she travels (she considers them good-luck charms).

Measurements: 35-23-34.

Car: A white Cobra (license plate 590-VGG).

Favorite Drink: Scotch on the rocks.

Relatives: Aunt, Lydia Danvers (Jeanette Nolan); uncle, Paul Danvers (John McIntire), the sheriff of Paylon, Arizona.

TIFFANY WELLES

Occupation: Private detective. Although she appears to have just stepped out of the pages of a fashion magazine, she was an officer with the Boston Police Department (where she filed reports). She became an Angel through a connection (her father, a detective lieutenant, and Charlie are good friends); her mother is a schoolteacher.

Place of Birth: Boston.

Education: Whitney College (lived in Tracy Hall and was a member of the Kappa Omega sorority house). As a senior in high school (unnamed), she worked as a nurse's aide.

Attributes: Caring but vulnerable if she lets her guard down. She has the ability to communicate with spirits (she is considered a "sensitive" and worked with Hans Kemper, a famous ghost hunter).

Expertise: The ability to fool people. Her stunning good looks and air of sophistication provide the perfect cover for her job.

Nickname: "Tiff."

Musical Ability: Plays the violin.

Bra Size: 34C.

Departure: Tiffany left after one season to pursue a modeling career in New York. She worked with Kelly and Kris.

JULIE ROGERS

Occupation: Private detective. Previously a fashion model who appeared on the cover of *Elite* magazine representing a reducing drink called Joggerade.

Place of Birth: New York City.

Measurements: 37-24-35.

Background: Julie's father deserted the family when she was very young; her mother died of acute alcoholism in a charity hospital. Julie, practically raised on the streets of Manhattan, drifted to Los Angeles, where she was arrested for shoplifting a dress (which she needed for a job interview). After serving time, she found work with the Woodman Modeling Agency (where she helped Kelly and Kris capture a killer). Charlie was impressed by her work and hired her when Tiffany left.

Attributes: Street knowledge and able to think and act quickly in adverse situations.

Fault: Too impulsive; acts without thinking; feels her beauty can accomplish a goal.

REBOOT

Charlie's Angels (ABC, 2011) features the new Angels: Rachael Taylor (as Abby Sampson), Anne Ilonzeh (Kate Prince), and Minka Kelly (Eve French). Ramon Rodriquez is John Bosley, and Victor Garber is the voice of Charlie.

Townsend Investigations is now based in Miami Beach, Florida, and Charlie's operatives are called Angels "because they show up when you least expect it and when you need them the most."

ABBY SAMPSON

Background: Daughter of the wealthy Sampson family of New York City. At age 13, her life changed when her father (Victor), a Wall Street power broker, was exposed as a swindler, convicted, and sent to prison. Abby turned to a life of crime and became an expert thief and scam artist. She was saved by Charlie when one of her cons to rip him off failed but gained her a position as one of his operatives.

Expertise: A skillful con artist with a knack for getting into any building at any time.

KATE PRINCE

Background: Born in New Orleans and moved to Miami after her father's death. She attended Miami Southern University on a basketball scholarship and joined the Miami Police Department after graduation. She became a detective, then an agent, with the Organized Crime Unit. Corruption within the unit corrupted Kate: she took kickbacks and developed a serious drug problem. She was caught in a sting operation but saved by Charlie when he helped her get her life back together and hired her as an Angel.

Expertise: Knowledge of the city's criminal population and its network of informers.

EVE FRENCH
Background: Eve was five years old when her parents, aid workers in El Salvador, were killed in a civil war. She was sent to St. Theresa's Orphanage and ran away 12 years later. She crossed the border and went to Miami, where she became part of a car theft ring (the Carol City Crew). One such theft caused a collision that resulted in a death, and Eve, convicted of manslaughter, was sent to the Tallahassee State Prison. When Charlie learned of her fate, he stepped in and secured her a job as an Angel.
Expertise: Thievery and an ability to adapt to any situation.

JOHN BOSLEY
Background: Born in New York City and at an early age showed signs of extraordinary intelligence, especially with computers. At age 14, he hacked his way into the Division of Motor Vehicles and issued himself a driver's license. By the age of 24, he used his skills to amass a $57 million fortune. An Internal Revenue Service investigation exposed him—but Charlie's intervention saved him from a long prison sentence, and he became Charlie's right-hand man.
Expertise: Using his computer knowledge to help the Angels on cases.

CHiPs
(NBC, 1977–1983)

Cast: Erik Estrada (Francis Poncherello), Larry Wilcox (Jonathan Baker), Robert Pine (Joseph Getraer), Randi Oakes (Bonnie Clark), Tom Reilly (Robert Nelson), Brianne Leary (Sindy Cahill), Tina Gayle (Kathy Linahan), Bruce Penhall (Bruce Nelson).
Basis: The work of California Highway Patrol officers (called CHiPs) is depicted through the assignments of Francis Poncherello and Jonathan Baker.

OVERALL SERIES INFORMATION
Kawasaki motorcycles are ridden by the patrol officers (equipped with Motorola radios). The truck seen in the opening theme is Golden Home Repair; the address of CHP is 777 West Washington Boulevard, Los Angeles, California 90015; 555-7374 is its telephone number, and car accident victims are taken to Valley General Hospital.

MERV (Maximum Efficiency Robotization Victor Series 1; built by Space Tech Industries) was the department's attempt to introduce efficiency in CHP via robotics; the Children's Liver Foundation is the unit's favorite charity.

CHiPs. *NBC/Photofest. ©NBC*

The CHP officers depicted are with the A Watch Unit of the Central Division of the California Highway Patrol (also called the Motorcycle Enforcement Division and referred to as highway patrol motor officers). They are also members of the department's basketball team, Central CHP, and are referred to as "Chippies" by civilians. The series title encompasses a lowercase "i" and "s" for pronunciation purposes.

The Freeway Angels, an unauthorized (by CHP) civilian organization led by Emily Daniels (Melody Anderson), helps the unit by calling in crimes they witness. Emily started the patrol after her seven-year-old brother was killed by a hit-and-run driver.

FRANCIS PONCHERELLO
Mother: Name not mentioned; lives in Chicago (Anna Navarro).
Siblings: Sister, Patricia Poncherello (Maria O'Brien), a nurse; brothers, Martin and Robert (not seen).
Nicknames: Called both "Frank" and "Ponch." Llewellyn is his middle name.
Education: South Polly Technical High School (called "Polly High"), where Ponch was a troublemaker and holds the record for the most visits to the principal's office.

Occupation: Highway patrol officer. Ponch was technical adviser on the TV series *Angel Patrol* (about Midge [Candi Brough] and Marge [Randi Brough], blonde, motorcycle-riding twins who solve crimes); a model (The Barcelona Man) for Barcelona Men's Jeans. He also appeared on the game show *Name Your Price* (a *Price Is Right* parody where Ponch failed to correctly guess the price of a motorcycle).

Residence: An unidentified mobile home (where he is not the tidiest housekeeper), then Apartment 127 (later 402) at 240 Bayshore Drive in a complex with a pool (and gorgeous bikini-clad girls); the rent is $500 a month.

Badge Number: 2140 (also given as B-600).

Kawasaki License Plate: 16A95.

Mobile Code: LA-15-Mary 4 (later LA-15-Mary 6).

Heritage: Latino. Ponch first mentions he was born in Van Nuys, California (where he was called "The Latino Flash"), then in the Barrio on March 16, 1949. He also mentions being born on a bus.

Record: Issuing the most citations (278) in one month.

Favorite Eatery: Marinino's.

Favorite Meal: Baked veal stuffed (as made by his mother).

Favorite Ice Cream Flavor: Tutti-frutti.

Favorite TV Soap Opera: The Troubled World (mythical). As a kid, he watched the series *Highway Patrol* with Broderick Crawford (who made a guest appearance in the 1977 episode "Hustle"); he watches the then–Saturday morning kids series *H.R. Pufnstuf.*

Favorite Sport: Basketball. Ponch mentions he was raised on basketball and was called "High Points Ponch." He also believes he is an expert (but isn't) on bowling and has a black belt in karate. Prior to joining CHP, Ponch was involved in illegal street car racing.

Cars: A bronze Firebird that he purchased for $83; a gold Pontiac Trans Am (both with the plate 033 PCE), then a blue truck, plate LE4 9937.

Vice: Junk food, especially snack cakes.

Expertise: Square Dancing.

Church: Attended St. Angela's Church while growing up.

Bank: The Southwest Savings Bank.

Coffee: Black with sugar.

Shoe Size: 9½C.

Replacement: Officer Steve McLeish (Bruce Jenner) temporarily replaced Ponch when Erik Estrada left over a contract dispute. LA-15-Mary 19 is his mobile bike code.

JONATHAN "JON" BAKER

Place of Birth: Rawlings, Wyoming.

Birthday: August 18, 1948 (a Leo).

Marital Status: Single. He mentions having a brother and sister.

Residence: The Raintree Condominiums and Town Homes (Apartment 302).

Occupation: Highway patrol officer.

Badge Number: 8712.

Mobile Code: LA-15-Mary 3.

Kawasaki License Plate: 16A60.

Favorite Eateries: The fast-food stand Gooey and Brigit's Café.

Distinguishing Feature: Carries a nightstick (it is a natural wood color, not the typical black club associated with patrol officers).

Partnership: It is first mentioned that Ponch, a somewhat reckless cop, was assigned to Jon as a means of reforming him; later, after Ponch's prior partner Gary is killed in an accident while pursuing a speeding car, he was teamed with Jon; and, finally, Ponch mentions that he was a rookie when assigned to Jon for training in the field. Jon first saw Ponch when he rode a patrol car and caught Ponch, who worked in a gas station, illegally riding a dirt bike. Jon felt Ponch had what it takes to become a member of CHP and gave him an application.

Favorite Ice Cream Flavor: Strawberry.

Favorite Music: Country and western.

Yellow British Car License Plate: JAB 5.

Blue Pickup Truck License Plate: 1E49937 (also seen as E99499).

Military Service: Soldier during the Vietnam War. It is mistakenly believed that Jon was the first TV character to be called a Vietnam vet. In actuality, Linc Case from the TV series *Route 66* in 1963 was the first such character.

Coffee: Black with sugar.

Shoe Size: 10D.

Character: Certified flight instructor and enjoys all types of sports (tennis, handball, and skiing are his favorites). He teaches children how to bowl (worked as a bowling instructor while in high school), likes the outdoors, and has a clean police record. As a kid, Jon raised parakeets.

Favorite Riding Horse: Old Grey.

Nervous Habit: Adjusts his guns and pulls on his gloves.

Replacement: In 1982, when Larry Wilcox left the series (Jon returned home to work on the family farm), Officer Robert "Bobby" Truval Nelson became Ponch's new rookie partner (a descendant of the Vikings). His mobile code was LA-15-Mary 7 and he was called "Hot Dog" by Ponch. He prefers his coffee without sugar or milk and has a younger brother (Bruce), who is a CHP rookie.

Relatives: Nephew Wes Miller (Christopher Knight).

OTHER CHARACTERS

Sergeant Joseph "Joe" Getraer, born in 1945, has the badge number 572 and is the superior officer. He is married to Betty (Gwynne Gilford) and the father of Timmy (Lindsay Kennedy) and Ellen (Lynn Holly Johnson). Joe's motorcycle license plate reads 68C24, and he considers himself "a closet expert on gemstones." LA-15-S5 is his mobile code, 555-7871 is his home phone number, and 1E49908 is his car license plate. He mentioned serving with the navy as a petty officer third-class. It was Joe who made the decision to form the CHiPs patrol teams as a better way to protect highways. He claims to be allergic to dogs in one episode, while he is around them in other episodes. Delta Delta Tau was his unnamed college fraternity.

Sindy Cahill is the first regularly seen CHP female officer (introduced in the 1978 episode "Family Crisis." The prior week's episode, "The Volunteers," featured Rana Ford [Jane Turner], a CHP patrol officer who assisted Ponch and Jon but whose character was not continued). Sindy has the mobile code LA-15-Mary 11; 4372 is her badge number, and 999056 (also seen as 462 085) is her patrol car license plate. Sindy, who breaks a serious CHP rule (rarely fastens her seat belt), has the mind of a detective and tries to solve crimes through deductive reasoning.

Bonnie Clark (Sindy's replacement) is a cruiser officer with the mobile code LA-15-7 Charles; her Plymouth Fury cruiser license plate reads 999001 (also seen as 62085 and 999 957). She earns $15,000 a year, took sign communications at Cal State, and is now a part of the CHP Deaf Liaison Program. Ponch calls her "Bon Bon," and her 1980 Futura car license plate reads 085 YIN. Randi Oakes originally played Kim Belford, a car thief in the 1979 episode "Down Time."

In 1982, Bonnie was replaced by Kathleen "Kathy" Linahan, a former CHP computer operator (in the Report Room) turned motorcycle patrol officer. She often rides with patrol officer Arthur Grossman (Paul Linke) and has the mobile code LA-15-Mary 10 (Grossman, nicknamed "Grossie," has the mobile code LA-15-Mary 5, then Mary 9). Kathy lives in a beach house at 153½ Malibu Beach Road ("the guesthouse in the back") and has an orchid named after her ("The Kathalina") as a gesture of kindness from an orchid grower (Phil Silvers) whom Kathy stopped for speeding. Robbie Rist played Arthur's cousin, Russell.

Officer Barry Baricza (Brodie Greer) has the mobile bike code LA-15-Mary 23. His parents, Pete (Sandy McPeak) and Vera (Diana Douglas), own a business called Baricza Crop Dusting (where Barry worked before deciding to become a police officer). His cruiser mobile code is S-4-7-Adam.

Harlan Arliss (Lou Wagner) is the CHP mechanic (he lives at 9246 Beech Drive in Los Angeles and has a dog named Dave); Officer Bruce Nelson, Bobby's younger brother, is a world speedway champion learning to become a CHP motorcycle cop. His mobile code is LA-15-Mary 8, and 6A7175 is his motorcycle license plate.

Note: In the TNT TV movie *CHiPs 99*, Ponch and Jon are reunited in a story wherein they investigate a series of car thefts. Joe Getraer was now the CHP commissioner.

Columbo

(NBC, 1971–1978; ABC, 1989–1991)

Cast: Peter Falk (Lieutenant Columbo).

Basis: A brilliant but disheveled police detective (Lieutenant Columbo) solves crimes of the most deadly nature—murder.

LIEUTENANT COLUMBO

Place of Birth: New York City.

Heritage: Italian. In some episodes, Columbo mentions he can speak fluent Italian; in others, he says he cannot.

Siblings: Five brothers and one sister (never seen or named).

First Name: He admits to having one but says, "My wife is about the only one who uses it." In the episode "Dead Weight," when Columbo shows his badge, the name "Frank Columbo" can be seen and is presumably his actual first name.

Wife's Name: Kate (not mentioned until the spin-off series *Mrs. Columbo* aired; see below. He also has a daughter named Jenny). In the series, Columbo refers to her as "The Wife," "The Missus," or "Mrs. Columbo." They have been married for 23 years in 1989.

Pet: A basset hound he calls "Dog" ("He's a dog, so we call him dog"). He sometimes refers to the dog as "Fang" and mentioned he tried the name "Beethoven" but felt the dog didn't like it. Dog's favorite food is ice cream.

Occupation: Homicide detective with the Los Angeles Police Department (although he is also said to be with the Hollenbeck Division and Central Division). He was originally with the New York Police Department before moving to Los Angeles in 1958.

Childhood Influence: The gangster movies of the 1930s and 1940s that instilled in him a desire to uphold the law.

Military Service: The army during the Korean War.

Car: A weather-beaten Peugeot Model 403 (although Columbo says it is a 1950 car, it is actually a 1959 model).

License Plate: 044 APD, then 448 DBZ.

Quirks: Rarely uses a gun, often neglects his yearly firing range tests, and rarely stays in his office, as he needs to do field investigating. He often helps himself to food at murder scenes and takes a hard-boiled egg to a crime scene if he is awakened in the middle of the night to assist on a case. His biggest problem is how to dispose of the eggshells. When not able to have dinner at home, Columbo eats chili and crackers at local diners, and when on a case, he will often whistle the song "This Old Man."

Columbo. *ABC/Photofest.* ©*ABC*

Badge Number: 436 (also seen as 416).

Favorite Sandwich: Peanut butter and raisins (he feels it is far superior to peanut butter and jelly sandwiches).

Noticeable Wardrobe Feature: A rumpled raincoat.

Character: A master of deductive reasoning but claims to have a bad memory. He tends to slouch, is always early for appointments, and studies people's faces for their reactions to his questions. He is always fascinated by the evidence he finds, as small, insignificant details bother him, and he will not rest until he can tie up every loose end.

Personality: Very persistent. He often believes there is something wrong with him because "I seem to bother people and make them nervous."

Catchphrase: When questioning a suspect, his "Oh, just one more thing" line is an indication that Columbo has found a prime suspect.

Home Life: Columbo enjoys comedy and variety programs on TV. He has given up listening to the radio—"Perry Como [singer] and Louis Armstrong [singer and orchestra leader] I understand, but those rock groups give me a headache." He enjoys western movies and Italian opera and would like Saturday nights off, "but I can't take it off if duty calls." He considers himself an excellent cook and likes to play pool.

Dislikes: Flying and boating, as they tend to make him sick.

Habit: Smoking cigars (he carries three cigars in his jacket pocket). "I know it's a filthy habit and that I should have given it up years ago. Even my wife complains and sends me out to the back porch." The Mrs. would like him to smoke a pipe, "but that's too much for me to carry around."

Drinks: A hot cup of tea and hot, strong, black coffee ("No decaf for me").

As a Teacher: Taught a criminology course at Fremont College in Los Angeles.

Note: Bert Freed first played Columbo on the "Enough Rope" episode of *The Chevy Mystery Show* on NBC in 1960; Peter Falk first played Columbo in the 1968 TV movie *Prescription: Murder.* This was followed by a second TV movie, *Ransom for a Dead Man,* in 1971.

SPIN-OFF

Mrs. Columbo (NBC, 1979). Here, Katherine "Kate" Columbo (Kate Mulgrew), the wife of the lieutenant, and their daughter, Jenny (Lili Haydn), live at 728 Valley Lane in San Fernando, California (555-9861, then 555-9867, is their phone number). The lieutenant is never seen (always away on business), and Kate works as a writer for the *Weekly Advertiser,* then the *Weekly Advocate.* Her boss is Josh Alden (Henry Jones), and while assigned to human interest stories, Kate often manages to find murder. Their dog, called both "Dog" and "Fang," is also present, as is the lieutenant's Peugeot.

The series was revised as *Kate Loves a Mystery*, wherein Kate and the lieutenant were divorced. Kate, using her maiden name (Callahan), was now more actively involved in criminal cases and worked closely with Mike Varrick (Don Stroud) of the Valley Municipal Police Department. Jenny, who attends Valley Elementary School, resides with Kate, while the lieutenant received only the Peugeot in the divorce settlement.

Kate Facts: Wears Maidenform bras; writes her grocery list with a brown eyeliner pencil, drives a sedan with the license plate 859 KTL. *Madame Butterfly* is her favorite opera, and she spoils movies for hubby by always guessing the wrong person as the killer.

Dallas

(CBS, 1979–1991)

Cast: Larry Hagman (J.R. Ewing), Patrick Duffy (Bobby Ewing), Linda Gray (Sue Ellen Ewing), Victoria Principal (Pamela Barnes-Ewing), Charlene Tilton (Lucy Ewing), Barbara Bel Geddes, then Donna Reed (Eleanor Ewing), Jim Davis (Jock Ewing), David Wayne, then Keenan Wynn (Digger Barnes), Ken Kercheval (Cliff Barnes), Steve Kanaly (Ray Krebs), Joan Van Ark (Valene Ewing), David Ackroyd, then Ted Shackelford (Gary Ewing).

Basis: A look at the dealings of J.R. Ewing, the greedy, self-serving head of the Ewing Oil Company in Dallas, Texas.

OVERALL SERIES INFORMATION

It is the 1930s, when oil wildcatters John "Jock" Ewing and Willard "Digger" Barnes strike oil in Pride, Texas. The men form a partnership, but greed on the part of Jock leads Digger to believe he is being cheated out of his fair share of the company. Bitterness consumes Digger, and he has sworn to reclaim what he believes is rightfully his. Adding fuel to the fire is Eleanor Southworth, the daughter of Aaron Southworth, the owner of the Southfork Ranch (in Braddock, Texas), when she chooses to marry Jock over Digger (in 1936).

The ranch was founded by Enoch Southworth in 1858; his son, Aaron, inherited it in 1901, and Eleanor, called both "Miss Ellie" and "Ellie," became its owner in 1959. Eleanor and Jock became the parents of John Ross Ewing Jr. (called "J.R."); Garrison, called "Gary" (born in 1943); and Bobby.

A helicopter crash in South America claimed the life of Jock in 1982, and Ewing Oil was split evenly between J.R. and Bobby. It is also revealed that Jock had a prior wife, Amanda Lewis Ewing (Lesley Woods, then Susan French), who had been institutionalized.

JOHN ROSS "J.R." EWING
Place of Birth: The Southfork Ranch.
Year of Birth: 1939.
Education: Braddock High School; the University of Texas.
Military Service: The army (initially sent to Vietnam, but he manipulated officials and spent the remainder of his service in Japan).
Favorite Drink: Bourbon.
Occupation: Vice president of Ewing Oil (then president when Jock retired in 1977).
Childhood: Learned the ins and outs of the oil business by accompanying Jock to the office. He later chose to become a businessman, not the ranch owner Jock had hoped.
Wife: Sue Ellen Shepherd (see "Sue Ellen Ewing" below).
Son: John Ross Ewing Jr. (Tyler Banks, then Omri Katz).
Character: Ruthless and uncaring, seeking only to further his position, acquire money, and make Ewing Oil the most profitable oil company in the world. J.R. is "the man everybody loves to hate" and is not only a brilliant schemer but a conniver as well. He claims that the name of the game is huge profits—no matter what it takes to attain them. In his tenure at Ewing Oil, his dealings cost the company $2 billion in bad deals.
J.R.'s Nickname for Sue Ellen: "Sugar" and "Darlin'."
The Marriage: J.R. and Sue Ellen, married in 1971, were both unfaithful to each other and divorced in 1981. They remarried in 1982 and divorced again in 1988.

ROBERT "BOBBY" EWING
Year of Birth: February 16, 1950 (in dialogue, he is also said to have been born in 1949 and 1952). A camera shot of Bobby's driver's license shows his birthday as November 1, 1956.
Education: Braddock High School; the University of Texas.
Occupation: Roadman for Ewing Oil, then company executive (1978) and chief executive officer (1980). He also headed Ewing Construction, became a Texas state senator (1981), and, after a falling out with J.R., became the chief executive officer of the rival oil company Petro Group Dallas (PGD). In 1991, Bobby became the owner of the Southfork Ranch.
Wife: Pamela Barnes (see "Pamela Barnes" below), the daughter of Willard Barnes. They married in 1978, divorced in 1983, and remarried in 1986.
Children: Lucas (with Pamela) and Christopher (adopted).
Bobby's Original Love Interest: Jenna Wade (Morgan Fairchild, then Francine Tacker), his childhood sweetheart (they broke up when Jenna moved to Europe).

Political Party: First hinted at Republican, then Democrat.

First Claim to Fame: All–Southwest Conference football player.

SUE ELLEN EWING

Maiden Name: Sue Ellen Shepherd.

Place of Birth: Dallas, Texas.

Year of Birth: 1947.

Parents: Patricia Shepherd (Martha Scott) and an unnamed alcoholic father who deserted the family and later died.

Husband: J.R. Ewing.

Sister: Kristen Shepherd (Mary Crosby), the woman responsible for shooting J.R. in the 1980 episode "A House Divided" (also referred to as "Who Shot J.R.?")

Education: The University of Texas at Austin (where she became the reigning beauty on campus). She entered the 1967 Miss Texas Pageant and won not only the title but also the heart of one of the judges—J.R., then vice president of Ewing Oil.

Character: A member of the Daughters of the Alamo (with Miss Ellie), founder of the Home for Wayward Boys, and head of a fund-raising committee for the unfortunate. She loved to cook, was graceful at social functions, and attempted her own business (Valentine Lingerie) in 1986. She was also an alcoholic.

Refuge: After divorcing J.R., Sue Ellen moved in with Stephen "Dusty" Farlow (Jared Martin), the owner of the Southern Cross Ranch in San Angelo, Texas (and married to Linda Farlow [Melody Anderson]).

PAMELA "PAM" BARNES

Place of Birth: Corpus Christi, Texas.

Year of Birth: 1953.

Parents: Thought to be Willard and Rebecca Blake Barnes (until it is revealed that Rebecca had an extramarital affair with Hutchinson "Hutch" McKinney and Pamela was the child born of that affair). Rebecca deserted the family in 1954 when Pamela was an infant. Willard's sister, Maggie Monahan (Sarah Cunningham), raised Pamela and her brother Cliff. Rebecca was presumed dead until she resurfaced in 1981 as the wife of Herbert Wentworth (a businessman) and the owner of the Wade Luce Oil Company (which became Barnes-Wentworth Oil in 1983). In 1983, Rebecca was injured in a plane crash and later died at Dallas Memorial Hospital.

Pam's Half-Sister: Katherine Wentworth (Morgan Brittany). Katherine, a broadcast journalist, longed for Bobby Ewing and was responsible for shooting him (1984) and accidentally running him down with her car (1985) when Pamela was the target.

Education: Pamela was a good student and a member of the cheerleading squad (at the age of 15, she performed at the Sun Bowl football game in El Paso, Texas).

Occupation: Wife. Pamela originally worked at a clothing boutique called the Store. After a miscarriage (due to a fall in the barn), she studied to become a lawyer.

Husband: Bobby Ewing. She and Bobby first met when Ray Krebs, foreman of the Southfork Ranch (born in 1945 and later revealed to be half Ewing [a child from Jock's extramarital affair]), invited her to a barbecue, and she and Bobby immediately fell in love. Because of the Ewing–Barnes family feud, they became known as "The Romeo and Juliet of Braddock" and eloped (they were married in New Orleans in a 10-minute service performed by a Southern Baptist minister).

The Aftermath: Pamela was disliked by J.R. and Sue Ellen, as they felt she was a spy for their rivals and married Bobby only to get a part of Ewing Oil for her father (Willard).

LUCILLE "LUCY" EWING

Place of Birth: Braddock, Texas.

Year of Birth: 1961.

Parents: Gary and Valene Ewing. J.R. considered Gary a weak link in the Ewing empire, especially since he worked as a rodeo rider and married a diner waitress (Valene). J.R. forced Gary and Valene to flee (to California), leaving their daughter, Lucy, to be raised by Jock and Ellie. The spin-off series *Knots Landing* (1979–1993) emerged with Gary and Valene taking up residence in the community of Knots Landing (where Gary worked as a salesman for Sid Fairgate, the owner of Knots Landing Motors, and Valene became famous when she wrote the book *Capricorn Crude*, an exposé of the Ewing family).

Education: Braddock High School; Southern Methodist University.

Occupation: Varies: Young Miss Dallas fashion model for Ward Publications; freelance model for the Blair Sullivan Agency; waitress at the Hot Biscuit in Fort Worth, Texas; half partner in a construction business; patron of the arts.

Husband: Mitchell "Mitch" Cooper (Leigh McCloskey), a medical student, then doctor, she later divorced.

Character: Appears to be sweet and innocent but is actually very promiscuous. She dates "losers," was kidnapped, was raped, had an addiction to drugs, and had an abortion. Lucy felt that no matter what happens, she could bounce back, as it could never happen again.

CBS TV MOVIE UPDATES

Dallas: The Early Years (1986) recounts the early wildcatting days of Jock (Dale Midkiff) and Digger (David Marshall Grant). Molly Hagan is Miss Ellie.

Dallas: J.R. Returns (1996) finds J.R. out to reclaim Ewing Oil after Cliff Barnes takes control of the company. Bobby now runs the Southfork Ranch with his son Christopher (Christopher Demetral).

Dallas: The War of the Ewings (1998). Sue Ellen and Bobby are in control of Ewing Oil, with J.R., now managing an oil company conglomerate, seeking to regain the family oil empire. The series regulars repeat their roles.

Dallas: Return to Southfork (2004). A reunion of the original cast members as they recall highlights from the series.

TNT SERIES UPDATE

Dallas (2012–2014). A look at the Ewing empire through the eyes of its current owners, cousins John Ross Ewing (Josh Henderson) and Christopher Ewing (Jesse Metcalf). Bobby Ewing (Patrick Duffy) is now the owner of the Southfork Ranch; Larry Hagman and Linda Gray repeated their roles as J.R. Ewing and Sue Ellen Ewing.

Diana
(NBC, 1973–1974)

Cast: Diana Rigg (Diana Smythe), David Sheiner (Norman Brodnik), Barbara Barrie (Norma Brodnik), Richard B. Schull (Howard Tolbrook), Robert Moore (Marshall Tyler), Carl Androsky (Holly Green), Richard Mulligan (Jeff Harmon).

Basis: Diana Smythe, an elegant and sophisticated fashion illustrator living in England, relocates to New York City to begin a new career in Manhattan's fashion district.

DIANA SMYTHE

Place of Birth: Yorkshire, England.

Date of Birth: October 26, 1943 (in real life, Diana Rigg was born on July 30, 1938).

Parents: James (a barrister) and Millicent (housewife) Smythe.

Address: 254 Bristol Place.

Education: The Doncaster School; the British Fashion Institute.

Marital Status: Divorced.

Occupation: Fashion illustrator at Lindley's Fashion Boutique in London.

Measurements: 34-25-34. She has auburn hair and stands 5 feet, 8½ inches tall.

Manhattan Address: Apartment 11-B at 4 Sutton Place (owned by her brother, Roger; Diana resides there while Roger, an anthropologist, is on assignment in Ecuador).

Phone Number: 555-7755.

Roger's Dog: Gulliver (a Great Dane).

Problem: Retrieving the numerous apartment house keys Roger gave to friends and drinking companions to use when he was out of town or needed a place to stay.

Diana's Neighbors: Holly Green, a television commercial hand and foot model, and Jeff Harmon, a mystery novelist.

Manhattan Employment: Fashion coordinator at Butley's Department Store.

Business Address: 37 West 34th Street.

Employer: Norman Brodnik, the store president. His wife, Norma, is the merchandising head (and possessed by money, which she claims is her hobby).

Fellow Employees: Howard Tolbrook, the gambling-addicted copywriter, and Marshall Tyler, the flamboyant window dresser.

Note: The episode "You Can't Go Back" reunites Diana Rigg with her former *Avengers* costar Patrick Macnee (as Bryan Harris, a former suitor seeking to win Diana back). The program was originally produced as *The Diana Rigg Show*, where Diana Smythe was the assistant to Mr. Vincent (Philip Proctor), the head dress designer at Sue Ellen Frocks. David Sheiner was the store owner (Rodney Brodnik), and Nanette Fabray was his wife Norma.

Diff'rent Strokes
(NBC, 1978–1985; ABC, 1985–1986)

Cast: Conrad Bain (Phillip Drummond), Dana Plato (Kimberly Drummond), Gary Coleman (Arnold Jackson), Todd Bridges (Willis Jackson), Dixie Carter (NBC) and Mary Ann Mobley (ABC) (Maggie McKinney), Danny Cooksey (Sam McKinney).

Basis: Arnold and Willis Jackson, the adopted African American children of a Caucasian millionaire and widower (Phillip Drummond) with a young daughter (Kimberly) tackle life in a world that they have never experienced before.

OVERALL SERIES INFORMATION

Arnold and Willis, the sons of Lucy Jackson (a widow working for Phillip as his housekeeper), live in Harlem at 259 East 135th Street (Apartment 12); their late father was named Henry. When Lucy passes, Phillip keeps a promise he made:

Diff'rent Strokes. *NBC/Photofest.* ©*NBC*

to care for her sons if anything should happen to her. Arnold and Willis became part of a new family and are later adopted by Phillip.

PHILLIP DRUMMOND
Mother: Not named (Irene Tedrow).
Sister: Sophia (Dody Goodman).

Year of Birth: 1923.

Address: 679 Park Avenue in Manhattan. The thirtieth-floor apartment is seen as both Penthouse A and Penthouse B.

Telephone Number: 555-9470.

Business: Owner of Drummond Industries (also said to be Trans-Allied, Inc.).

Education: The Digby Prep School.

Health Club: The Riverside Athletic Club (where he is called "L&M"—Lean and Mean).

Second Wife (1984): Margaret "Maggie" McKinney, a divorcee with a young son named Sam. Maggie owns an unnamed mid-Manhattan health club and is the host of a daily TV series called *Exercise with Maggie.* She mentioned that her first paycheck amounted to $37 (Phillip's first paycheck was for $1.8 million). Before acquiring the role of Maggie, Mary Ann Mobley played Arnold's teacher, Miss Osborne, in 1979. Sam has a goldfish named Montgomery and is a member of Scout Troop 14. He is also on the Hawks baseball team, and peanut butter and tuna fish is his favorite sandwich.

Relatives: Anna, Philip's Dutch cousin (Conrad Bain); Wes McKinney, Maggie's ex-husband (Hoyt Axton).

KIMBERLY DRUMMOND

Birthday: November 7, 1964.

Hair: Blonde.

Eyes: Blue.

Education: The Eastlake Academy for Girls in Peekskill, New York, then Garfield High School in Manhattan. Kimberly was seen at Eastlake, and her character provided the basis for the spin-off series (for information, see *The Facts of Life*).

Allowance: $10 a week.

Nickname: "Pumpkin" (as called by Phillip).

Occupation: Student. She worked after school as a waitress at the Hula Hut, a fast-food store in Manhattan, and as a teenage fashion model at Baun's Department Store. When Kimberly turned 18, she moved to Italy to become the nanny for the son of a young couple (Anna and Rudy Valente). She later attended school in Paris.

Ability: Prima ballerina (starred in the Eastlake Academy production of *Swan Lake*).

Career Ambition: Professional ice skater (she received lessons from Olympic ice-skating champion Dorothy Hamill [playing herself] but faked a pulled hamstring when she was unable to handle the rigorous training).

Shampoo: Mother Brady's All Natural Shampoo.
Relatives: Hans, Kimberly's Dutch cousin (Dana Plato).

ARNOLD JACKSON

Education: P.S. 89; P.S. 406; Roosevelt Junior High; Edison Junior High; Garfield High School. At P.S. 89, Arnold was a reporter for the school newspaper, *The Weekly Woodpecker*, and editor of the Edison Junior High paper, *The Beacon.* At Garfield High, he played Abraham Lincoln in the school play "Abe Lincoln in Illinois."
School Bully: "The Gooch" (never seen).
Hobby: Model railroading (he has both H-O and O-Scale electric trains).
Catchphrase: "What you talkin' about . . ."
Arcade Champ: Scored 1 million points on the video game "Space Sucker."
Pets: Abraham (goldfish) and Lucky (cricket).
Rag Doll: Homer. As a kid, he had a plush cow called "Fuzzy Wuzzy Moo Moo."
After-School Hangout: Hamburger Heaven (later called the Hamburger Hanger).
Club: The Super Dudes Gang.
Band: The Frozen Heads.
Stock: Owns 10 shares in Phillip's company.
Ability: Considers himself to be a magician and calls himself "Arnoldo."
Occupation: Student. He earned money by handing out circulars for Guido's Pizza Palace on 63rd Street and selling Slam Roach Spray door-to-door.

WILLIS JACKSON

Relationship: Arnold's older brother.
Education: Roosevelt Junior High School; Garfield High School; an unnamed college.
Catch Phrase: "Say what?"
Trait: A bit conceded and thinks he is a ladies' man. He enjoys looking in a mirror and tries to act like "Superfly with the girls, but I come off like Big Bird."
Rock Band: The Afro Desiacs. Willis and his girlfriend, Charlene DuPres (Janet Jackson), were the lead singers.
Gang: The Tarantulas.
Occupation: Student. He earns money as an assistant at Kruger's Garage.
Stock: Ten shares in Phillip's company.
Doll as a Kid: Wendy Wetems.
Relatives: Cousin, Muriel Waters (LaWanda Page).
Phillip's Housekeepers: Edna Garrett (Charlotte Rae); Adelaide Brubaker (Nedra Volz); Pearl Gallagher (Mary Jo Catlett).

The Dukes of Hazzard
(CBS, 1979–1985)

Cast: John Schneider (Bo Duke), Tom Wopat (Luke Duke), Catherine Bach (Daisy Duke), Denver Pyle (Jesse Duke), Sorrell Booke (J.D. Hogg), James Best (Rosco P. Coltrane).

Basis: Cousins Bo and Luke Duke risk their lives to protect their hometown, Hazzard County, Georgia, from a corrupt politician (J.D. Hogg) who seeks only to increase his wealth and community standing.

BEAUREGARD "BO" DUKE
Place of Birth: Hazzard County, Georgia.

Birthday: April 8, 1954.

Education: Hazzard High School (where he was a linebacker on the football team).

Military Career: U.S. Marines.

Occupation: Stock car racer.

Favorite Sport: Fishing.

Boast: Claims he can sweet-talk any girl into accepting a date with him.

Car: The General Lee, a 1960 orange Dodge Charger. The car, found by Bo and Luke in a junkyard, was purchased so they could repair it for a race. It was originally black, but when it was brought in for repairs, garage owner Cooter Davenport had only orange paint in stock; Uncle Jesse suggested the name.

Car License Plate: CNH 320.

Distinguishing Marks: A Confederate flag on the roof, doors welded shut (like a racing car), the number "01" on the doors (however, some scenes involving the car are flipped, and the number is seen backwards as "10").

Car Horn: Plays a 12-note musical selection from the song "Dixie."

LUCAS "LUKE" DUKE
Place of Birth and Education: Same as Bo.

Birthday: November 6, 1951.

Military Service: Marine Force recon sergeant (he also participated in camp boxing matches).

Expertise: "The Hood Jump" (sliding across the car roof from one side to the other). Luke occasionally drove the *General Lee* but preferred to ride shotgun while Bo drove it.

Competition: Luke and Bo enter the *General Lee* in the Cherokee County Dirt Road Classic, the Hazzard County Derby, and the Smokey Hollow Race.

Weapons: Like Bo, Luke uses a bow with dynamite-tipped arrows; they never use guns. They had been arrested for running moonshine and are now on probation (carrying firearms is a violation and will send them to jail); Boss Hogg is their probation officer.

Catchphrase: "Yeeee haaaa" (which he said when driving the *General Lee*).

DAISY DUKE

Place of Birth and Education: Same as Bo and Luke.

Home: The Duke family farm on Mill Pond Road (18 miles outside of town, where Bo, Luke, and Uncle Jesse also live).

High School Reputation: Known as "The Wildest Girl."

Occupation: Waitress at the Boar's Nest, the local bar (off Highway 30), where her wardrobe consists primarily of tight-fitting short shorts; she also held a part-time job as a reporter for the Hazzard County *Gazette*.

Pageant Winner: Crowned "Best All-Around Gal in Three Counties" at the Miss Tri-Counties Beauty Pageant (for her "beauty, mechanical abilities, and driving skills").

Car: A yellow Plymouth Road Runner with a black stripe (destroyed when Bo and Luke lost control and the car went off a cliff).

Jeep: A white 1980 Jeep Eagle CJ-5 she calls Dixie.

Favorite Store: The Capitol City Department Store.

Activity: Den mother to the Junior Patrol, a Girl Scout troop.

Wardrobe: Known for her short shorts (called Daisy Dukes) and bikinis (especially the red one seen in the opening theme).

Favorite Sport: Archery. In song, the balladeer claims that Daisy "drives like Richard Petty, shoots like Annie Oakley, and knows the words to all of Dolly Parton's songs."

UNCLE JESSE DUKE

Position: The family patriarch. It is believed (never really made clear) that Bo, Luke, and Daisy's parents were killed in a car accident and that Jesse, a widower with no children of his own, accepted the responsibility of raising them. It is also suggested that Bo and Duke were born on Jesse's ranch (with Jesse acting as a midwife).

Family History: Making moonshine (alcohol by the light of the moon). It has been a family tradition for over 200 years (before it became against the law).

Occupation: Ranch owner. Jesse originally ran moonshine in the Range Runner Association (in a car he first called Sweet Tillie, then Black Tillie). He was caught by the FBI and gave his word that he would never make moonshine again (he makes mouthwash instead, as "making" is in his blood). Jesse now stands for law and order: "The law is the law, and us Dukes gotta obey it no matter what."

Pet Goat: Bonnie.

CB (Citizen's Band) Codes: To keep in touch with each other, Jesse is "Shepherd"; Bo and Luke are "Lost Sheep"; and Daisy is "Bo Peep" (later called "Country Cousin"). They broadcast on frequency channel 9.

Ability: Wizard at card tricks.

Truck: A 1950s Ford stepside pickup.

Relatives: Cousins Holly Comfort (Miriam Byrd Nethery), Jeb Stuart Duke (Christopher Hensel), and Gaylord Duke (Simon MacCorkindale). Lori Lethin played Holly's daughter, Laurie, and Edward Edwards played Holly's son, John Henry.

JEFFERSON DAVIS HOGG

Place of Birth: Hazzard County, Georgia.

Nicknames: "J.D." and "Boss Hogg."

Official Title: County commissioner (responsible for allocating funds for various projects. He is, however, corrupt and diverts such government monies to fund his illegal operations). J.D. is also president of the Hazzard County Bank and justice of the peace. It is mentioned that the county seat is in Hazzard; however, Coryville is mentioned as being the county seat in another episode. He previously ran moonshine with Jesse Duke.

Businesses: Owns most of Hazzard County, including the Boar's Nest Bar (where Daisy is allowed to keep 25 percent of her tips; the bar also has a one-dollar cover charge "to keep out the riffraff"), the Hazzard County Garage (which sells Hoggo Mulllers, Hoggoco Motor Oil, the Hogg Car Charger Kit, and J.D. Shocks), the Coffin Works, Hogg's Happy Burgers (fast food—"The only burgers that make you straighten up and fly right"), Hogg Alarm Systems, and the local radio station, WHOGG. He may also own (not clearly stated) the Dawn to Dusk Bowling Alley and the Hazzard Movie Theater.

Belief: That the *General Lee* is half human and that Bo and Luke were born with silver gas pedals in their mouths (as they often use the car to foil his plans).

Boss's Office: One will see a plaque that reads, "Do Unto Others Before They Do Unto You" and the "J.D. Hogg War Memorial: Dedicated to J.D. Hogg and Less Important War Heroes."

Car: The Gray Ghost (a white Cadillac convertible).

Fear: His identical twin brother, Abraham Lincoln Hogg (Sorrell Book), "the white sheep of the family." Abraham, who wore black, is as honest as J.D. (who wore white) is dishonest, and he believes Abraham will stop him from becoming a rich man.

Enemies: The Duke family, who are trying "to clean up Hazzard County." Boss wants the Duke farm so he can foreclose and sell the land to the Crystal Mountain Brewery. Boss often resorts to framing the Dukes for a crime as a way of achieving his goal.

Relatives: Wife, Lulu Hogg (Peggy Rea); father, Big Daddy Hogg (Les Tremayne); nephews, Hughie Hogg (Jeff Altman) and Jamie Lee Hogg (Jonathan Frakes).

Hazzard County Traditions: April 1 is Saddy Hogg Day (women take over government jobs); the Lulu Hogg Stakes Horse Race (a highlight of the annual Hazzard County Fair); and hunting (Boss has declared that hunting is "three weeks for deer, two weeks for quail, and open season on Dukes and moonshiners)."

OTHER CHARACTERS

Rosco P. (Purvis) Coltrane is the corrupt sheriff who obeys J.D.'s every command, especially enforcing the "Hogg Celebrity Speed Trap" (where victims are often country-and-western singers and forced to perform at the Boar's Nest). Rosco rides with his lazy basset hound (also called a bloodhound) Flash (a female dog that Rosco calls a "he"; Bo calls her "Girl"). He occupies office 101 in the Hazzard County Police Department, and his squad car license plate reads 835 32 (he also has a plate on his office wall that reads 442 629). He yells, "Hot pursuit" when he begins chase of Bo and Luke. As Boss says, "What Rosco lacks in brains he makes up in stupidity." Rosco was an honest cop for more than 20 years until the city budget was changed and he lost his retirement fund. Lucille Benson appeared as Rosco's mother, Mama Coltrane, and Mary Treen appeared as Rosco's aunt, Clara Coltrane.

Enos Strate (Sonny Shroyer) is the honest but naive deputy who assists Rosco. An attempt was made to spin the character off in the failed 1980 series *Enos* (wherein Enos becomes a police officer with the Los Angeles Police Department). He was also Daisy's romantic interest.

Cletus Hogg (Rick Hurst) is Boss's second cousin twice removed and the reserve deputy. Cooter Davenport (Ben Jones) owns Cooter's Garage and has a farm on Jessup Road; his truck license plate reads SU 0265. Mickey Jones appeared as his cousin, B.B. Davenport; Ernie Lively was his cousin, L.B. Davenport.

Note: John Schneider and Tom Wopat left the series in 1982 in a dispute over merchandising. Vance Duke (Christopher Mayer) and Coy Duke (Byron Cherry) replaced them with the explanation being that they returned to Hazzard County to help Jesse run the farm while Bo and Luke left to pursue the NASCAR circuit. Coy and Vance were dropped six months later (leaving to care for their Aunt Bessie and Uncle Albert) when Bo and Luke returned (settling the dispute) after a successful racing tour.

In 1983–1985, CBS aired the animated series *The Dukes*, wherein the Dukes compete against Boss and Rosco in an around-the-world car race for a cash prize that the Dukes need to save their farm. Series regulars supplied their own voices.

TV MOVIE UPDATES

The Dukes of Hazzard Reunion (1997) reunites the cast (except for Sorrell Booke, who had passed away) in a story that finds Rosco scheming to acquire the Duke farm to build a theme park. Here it is mentioned that Daisy had married (after the series ended) but later divorced. She returned to Hazzard County to pursue a graduate degree.

The Dukes of Hazzard: Hazzard in Hollywood (2000) finds Bo, Luke, and Daisy teaming with Rosco, Cletus, and Cooter and traveling to Hollywood to sell songs and raise money for a hospital in Hazzard.

The Dukes of Hazzard: The Beginning (2007) details the life of the Duke Cousins before the events of the series. It is set in modern times, not the 1960s (when the series Dukes would have been teenagers). It is revealed that as teenagers, Bo and Luke (James Bennett and Randy Waynes) were caught by authorities for reckless driving and running fireworks and sent to their Uncle Jesse (Willie Nelson) by their parents for rehabilitation. Daisy (April Scott), said to be an orphan, was being cared for by Uncle Jesse on his farm in Hazzard County. She is first seen as a conservative high school girl (in dress and personality). It is when Daisy first acquires a job at the Boar's Nest and seeks to acquire the attention of Hughie Hogg (Boss's nephew) that she experiments with several wardrobe changes before choosing her sexy attire.

Here it was said that the *General Lee* was found by Bo and Luke in muddy water in Hogg's Ravine (not a junkyard). Christopher McDonald played Boss Hogg.

Dusty's Trail

(Syndicated, 1973–1974)

Cast: Forrest Tucker (Mr. Callahan), Bob Denver (Dusty), Jeannine Riley (Lulu McQueen), Lori Saunders (Betsy McGuire), Ivor Francis (Carter Brookhaven), Lynn Wood (Daphne Brookhaven), Bill Cort (Andy Boone).

Basis: A wagon and a fancy coach, part of a wagon train heading west from St. Louis, Missouri, are separated from the main body and lost. It is the 1850s (by mention of the recent gold rush), and the adventures encountered by its wagon master (Callahan) and scout (Dusty) are depicted as they lead their passengers (Lulu, Betsy, Carter, Daphne, and Andy) to California. The program is known as "*Gilligan's Island* out West."

MR. CALLAHAN

Full Name: Thomas Callahan (although he is always called either "Callahan" or "Mr. Callahan"). He compares to the Skipper on *Gilligan's Island*.

Occupation: Scout and wagon master (organizing pioneers for trips from St. Louis to "the promised land" of California).

Military Service: Sergeant in the U.S. Cavalry (called "Yellow Leg" for the yellow stripe that ran down the side of his blue uniform pants).

Military Title: "United States Boxing Champion of the U.S. Cavalry" (called "Kid Callahan") from 1835 to 1840. He won 43 victories, 38 of which were knockouts.

Weight: 220 pounds.

Dream: To buy a horse ranch.

Horse: Blarney.

Ability: To read and make Indian smoke signals; understands Indian drum language.

DUSTY

Relationship: Callahan's lifelong friend. His full name is never revealed.

Occupation: Trail scout.

Duties: Gather firewood, cook, tend the horses, and share guard duty with Mr. Callahan.

Horse: Freckles.

Pet Bear: Hercules (he removed a thorn from a bear's paw and had "a best friend").

Trait: Bumbling and trouble prone (his misguided scouting caused the wagons to separate and become lost). He compares to Gilligan on *Gilligan's Island*. He is also thin but says, "I always look starved even after I've eaten."

Shooting Ability: He can hold a gun, but that's about it (he is a very poor shot).

Distinguishing Mark: A scar, shaped like a half-moon on his back (caused by an ax). Chief Full Moon of the Amowona Indian tribe believes he is his long-lost son Half Moon.

LULU MCQUEEN

Occupation: Dance hall girl. She compares to Ginger on *Gilligan's Island*.

Dream: To open Lulu's, an elegant dance hall in San Francisco.

Distinguishing Feature: A small birthmark on the left side of her face (upper cheek). This could be just makeup, as in some episodes she has no birthmark at all.

Hair Color: Blonde.

Wardrobe: Very sexy, cleavage-revealing dresses (typical of what a Wild West saloon girl would wear); as Lulu says, "Tight, form-fitting dresses."

Trait: Beautiful and "fearless" (pretends to be brave. As she says when Indians pose a threat, "I'll match my war paint [makeup] against their war paint at any time").

Ability: Can sing, dance, and "seduce any man. If I can't, I'll turn in my beauty mark."

Weapon: She considers her beauty her weapon but does carry a gun in her garter belt on her right leg ("Men say I'm a woman. This little baby [the gun] keeps the odds even").

Name for Mr. Callahan: Calls him "Cal" at times.

About Dusty: "I always thought I understood men, but you shake my confidence."

ELIZABETH "BETSY" MCGUIRE

Place of Birth: Pennsylvania.

Occupation: Schoolteacher.

Dream: To establish a school, as she believes that "the children out West need an education."

Ability: Medical knowledge (it is assumed that Betsy was a nurse at one time).

Character: Pretty, shy, and demure. Although she is just as beautiful as Lulu, she hides her sexuality behind long dresses and often buttoned-up-to-the-neck blouses.

Hair Color: Brunette.

Trait: Always a lady but almost always frightened by the situations she faces. She is, in essence, Mary Ann from *Gilligan's Island*.

CARTER AND DAPHNE BROOKHAVEN

Position: A very wealthy married couple (the Thurston and Lovey Howell of *Gilligan's Island*) who are heading to California to become even wealthier. Here they have a fabulous wardrobe and their own elegant traveling coach (driven by Dusty).

Dream: To open a bank and cash in on the gold rush.

Carter's Brokerage House: The New York firm of Jones, Bean, Bean and Stringfellow.

Trait: Carter is very pompous and knows only one thing: how to make money. He cries when he hears that someone else is making money and feels the delay in reaching California is costing him thousands of dollars a day. Daphne is totally devoted to Carter and appears to come from a socially prominent family; she is amazed "that everything out West is so western." Carter explains that Daphne is a little naive "as she sees the good in everyone." Carter says he is a member of "The Wealthy Club," and the family motto is "A Brookhaven never turns his back on danger." Lulu calls Daphne "Mrs. B."

The Journey: It appears by episode dialogue that Carter and Daphne, living in St. Louis, organized the journey and hired Mr. Callahan as their leader. It is not explained what happened to the other wagons in the train or who is leading them.

ANDY BOONE

Position: A resourceful pioneer (possibly a former school science teacher).

Trait: Compares to the Professor on *Gilligan's Island.* He is resourceful and helps with knowledge in just about everything.

Ability: Can take nothing and make something; able to speak several Indian languages.

Dream: To change the landscape of California: "Dam up rivers for irrigation; clear the land for cities; build a railroad from coast to coast."

Note: Four episodes have been edited together to form the feature film *The Wackiest Wagon Train in the West.*

Eight Is Enough
(ABC, 1977–1981)

Cast: Dick Van Patten (Tom Bradford), Diana Hyland (Joan Bradford), Betty Buckley (Abby Bradford), Lani O'Grady (Mary Bradford), Laurie Walters (Joanie Bradford), Dianne Kay (Nancy Bradford), Connie Needham (Elizabeth Bradford), Susan Richardson (Susan Bradford), Grant Goodeve (David Bradford), Willie Aames (Tommy Bradford), Adam Rich (Nicholas Bradford), Joan Prather (Janet McCarther), Brian Patrick Clarke (Merle Stockwell).

Basis: A widowed father (Tom Bradford) and his eight children (David, Mary, Joanie, Nancy, Susan, Elizabeth, Tommy, and Nicholas) navigate life in Sacramento, California.

THOMAS "TOM" BRADFORD

Father: Matt Bradford (David Wayne).

Sister: Vivian Bradford, called "Auntie V" (Janis Paige). She calls him "Tommy Bellybutton."

Address: 1436 Oak Street.

Telephone Number: 555-0263 (later 555-6023).

Station Wagon License Plate: 460 EKA.

Sedan License Plate: 842 CU1.

Occupation: Newspaper columnist for the Sacramento *Register*.

First Wife: Joan (maiden name Joan Wells). They married in 1950 (when Tom was editor of a small, unnamed magazine); 27 years later, Joan succumbs to cancer (in 1977, reflecting the real-life passing of Diana Hyland). Joan was a freelance photographer and called "Joanie" by Tom. She enjoyed reading, especially poetry, and bought Christmas gifts for the family months in advance. Joanie filing her fingernails most annoyed Tom.

Suit: 39 regular.

Key to Remembering His Children's Names: Using the first letter of each child's name: "Never Try Eating Nectarines Since Juice May Dispense." In a later episode, Tommy tells Abby that the key is, "Dumb Martians Just Sit Nearby Eating Tender Noodles."

Cooking Specialty: Chili con Bradford.

Joanie's Parents: Gertie (Joan Tompkins) and Paul Wells (Robert F. Simon).

Second Wife: Sandra Sue "Abby" Mitchell. She and Tom married in 1979.

Abby's Parents: Harry (Dennis Patrick, then Robert Rockwell) and Katherine Mitchell (Louise Latham).

Abby's Occupation: Guidance counselor at Memorial High School. She wrote her college thesis on "Modern Sex Roles."

Prior Address: 1412 Compton Place.

Late Husband: Frank Mitchell (died as a prisoner of war in Vietnam).

Horse as a Child: Blaze.

Car License Plate: YNH 872 (a British M6 that Abby calls Gwendolyn).

Relatives: Abby's nephew, Jeremy Andretti (Ralph Macchio); Abby's Aunt Felicity (Sylvia Sidney).

DAVID BRADFORD

Relationship: The oldest male child.

Education: Sacramento Central High School.

Occupation: Private contractor (license number 789 3383). He worked for the Mann Construction Company, then formed the Bradford Construction Company with his father.

Tradition: On the first Sunday in November, he and Tom go duck hunting.

Home: Apartment 207 (address not given).

Van License Plate: HIR 312.

Wife: Janet (maiden name Janet McCarther), a lawyer with the firm of Goodman, Saxon and Tweedy. She later worked for the firm of Ted O'Hara and Associates.

Janet's Address: 2475 DeVanna Place. Marital difficulties led to their separating and then divorcing in 1981.

Janet's Parents: George (Richard Herd) and Sylvia McCarther (Fay de Wit, then Emmaline Henry).

Note: Mark Hamill played David in the pilot episode.

MARY BRADFORD

Relationship: The eldest of the female children (second-born).

Trait: The most studious of the children; hoping to become a doctor.

Education: Sacramento Central High School, then Berkeley College (where she was a radical and stood up for what she believed in). Her medical school is not named.

Internship: St. Mary's Hospital.

Inspiration: Dr. Craig Maxwell (Michael Thoma), a family friend she calls "Dr. Max" (he is associated with St. Mary's Hospital and Sacramento Memorial Hospital).

Politics: When the pressures of medical school made Mary unsure of her career, she ran for political office (a seat on the Eighth District School Board) but lost.

Favorite Breakfast: Cold pizza.

Revelation: Mary's mother told her that she and three other children (not named) were accidents ("Not that you're not loved, just not planned for").

JOAN "JOANIE" BRADFORD

Relationship: The second-born girl (third-born child). While all the Bradford children found it difficult to adjust to Abby, it was Joanie who felt the most out of place; she had her mother's name and looked just like her and believed that Abby resented her.

Hair: Frizzy (something her mother didn't have); she uses Frizz Free shampoo.

Occupation: Researcher, then news reporter, for KTNS-TV, Channel 8, in Sacramento. She also entertains (as a clown) at the Charles Street Children's Home and dressed as an ice cream cone advertisement (at $3.25 an hour) for the Sweet Tooth Dessert Shoppe. She also attempted acting by appearing without clothes in a play called *Shakespeare in the Nude* (as she said, "I've never seen a look like that on Dad's face").

SUSAN BRADFORD

Relationship: The third-born sister (fourth child).

Trait: The most sensitive of the children.

Education: Sacramento Central High School.

Occupation: An unnamed children's day care center. She originally attempted to become a police officer (but failed the physical endurance test).

Husband: Merle Stockwell.

Merle's Occupation: Minor league pitcher for the Cyclones baseball team (called "Merle the Pearl"). He later became a pitcher for the New York Mets, but in 1981 an arm injury ended his career. He then became a coach at Central High School.

Relatives: Merle's sister, Linda Mae Stockwell (Sondra West).

NANCY BRADFORD

Relationship: The fourth-born girl (fifth child).

Trait: The prettiest of the sisters.

Education: Sacramento High School (where she was a cheerleader); State College (dropped out when she felt she could not handle the workload).

Occupation: Model (appeared on the cover of *Epitome* magazine); the Sunshine Soda Girl in TV commercials; secretary at the Bates, Callahan and Chester Brokerage House. She originally worked for Hot Wires (delivering singing telegrams over the telephone) and gave up possible stardom when she refused to expose her breasts in an ad campaign for Vernon Isley Jeans (Nancy felt she could break into modeling with "my outgoing personality and nice features").

Hobbies: Playing tennis and riding horses.

Shampoo: Extra Body.

Note: Kimberly Beck played Nancy in the pilot episode.

ELIZABETH BRADFORD

Relationship: The youngest of the sisters (the sixth-born child).

Trait: The most impatient of the children (eager to grow up and become an adult). She follows other people's leads and often gets into mischief.

Education: Sacramento High School, then Sacramento Junior College.

Hope: To become a professional dancer.

Fear: Boys. She feels awkward around them ("I'm like a cross between Marie Osmond [popular singer at the time] and a kewpie doll").

Fourth-Grade Memory: Wore braces and was called "Metal Mouth" by the boys. This caused her to fight the name callers and became a hero to the other girls; she was also elected "Blackboard Monitor."

Pilot Character: Elizabeth is depicted as a troublesome girl (here arrested for drug possession) but not so in the series.

Nickname: When Joanie gets angry at Elizabeth, she calls her "Baby." Elizabeth in turn sulks and locks herself in the bathroom.

THOMAS "TOMMY" BRADFORD

Relationship: The second-born son (the seventh-born child).

Trait: The most troublesome child. He constantly rebels against authority and longs to quit school and become a rock musician.

Education: Sacramento High School.

Band: Tommy and the Actions.

Hangout: Cluck 'n' Chuck (fast-food chicken); Bennie's Burger Bin.

Car License Plate: 553 VFZ.

Note: Chris English played Tommy in the pilot.

NICHOLAS BRADFORD

Relationship: The youngest of the children (the eighth-born child).

Trait: Eager to grow up and find unique ways to make money. He started a neighborhood courier service called N&M Delivery Service. When there is a water crisis in the state and people need to conserve, Tom appoints Nicholas as the family's water monitor (for example, Nancy practices her lines in the shower, and Elizabeth takes two showers a day). He also attempted to sell Guca Dew, a wrinkle remover, door-to-door. He was ring bearer at Tom and Abby's wedding and best man at Susan and Merle's wedding.

Favorite Sport: Basketball (although he was rejected for being too short on the Youth League basketball team).

Education: The Goodwin-Knight Elementary School.

Pet Hamsters: Ron and Marsha.

UPDATES

The 1987 TV movie *Eight Is Enough: A Family Reunion* finds Tom as the editor of the Sacramento *Register*. Abby (now played by Mary Frann) is the owner of her own restaurant, the Delta Supper Club. Mary, now a doctor, is married to Chuck (Jonathan Perpich); Susan and Merle have a daughter named Sandy (Amy Gibson).

Elizabeth is married to Mark (Peter Nelson), the owner of a car restoration business. Tommy is a struggling lounge singer; Joanie is now an actress and married to Jean Pierre (Paul Roselli), a film director. Nicholas is attending college, and Nancy is married to a sheep rancher named Jeb (Christopher McDonald).

A second TV movie, *An Eight Is Enough Wedding* (NBC, 1989), finds that David and Janet have divorced and David is marrying his second wife, Marilyn "Mike" Fulbright (Nancy Everhard). Sandy Faison plays the role of Abby Bradford.

The Facts of Life
(NBC, 1979–1988)

Cast: Charlotte Rae (Edna Garrett), Cloris Leachman (Beverly Ann Stickle). *The Students:* Lisa Whelchel (Blair Warner), Nancy McKeon (Jo Polniaszek), Kim Fields (Tootie Ramsey), Mindy Cohen (Natalie Green).

Basis: The Eastland School in Peekskill, New York, provides the backdrop as a group of young girls tackle life, growing from children to adults.

EDNA GARRETT

Occupation: School dietician. Edna previously worked as the housekeeper to Phillip Drummond (from the series *Diff'rent Strokes,* of which *The Facts of Life* is a spin-off). Phillip's daughter, Kimberly, attended the school, which was then called the Eastlake Academy for Girls. On a visit to see Kimberly, the school dietician quits unexpectedly, and the school's headmaster, Harold Crocker, recruits Edna.

Place of Birth: Appleton, Wisconsin.

Marital Status: Divorced from Robert Garrett (Robert Alda).

Son: Raymond Garrett (Joel Brooks).

Life Changer 1: When Edna discovers that her pension fund has been lost and the school will not give her a raise, she quits and begins her own business, Edna's Edibles, a gourmet food shop at 320 Main Street in Peekskill. It was originally Ara's Deli.

Life Changer 2: A fire destroys Edna's Edibles. Edna uses the insurance money to rebuild the store as Over Our Heads, a 1950s-styled malt shop (that also employs Blair, Jo, Natalie, and Tootie).

Life Changer 3: In 1987, Edna marries Dr. Bruce Gaynes (Robert Mandan) and moves to Africa to help him in his work with the Peace Corps. Beverly Ann Stickle, her divorced sister, now cares for the girls (who live above the Over Our Heads store). Beverly Ann later adopts an orphan named Andy

(MacKenzie Astin), who attends South Junior High School, and becomes the guardian of Pippa McKenna (Sherrie Krenn), a foreign exchange student from Eastland's sister school, Colunga, in Sydney, Australia.

Car License Plate: 845 DUD.

Catchphrase: "G-i-r-r-r-r-l-s" (which she yells to stop their bickering).

Relatives: Frank Stickle, Beverly Ann's ex-husband (Dick Van Patten); Pippa's father, Kevin McKenna (Mike Preston); Andy's Grandma Polly (Billie Bird).

BLAIR WARNER

Parents: Steve (Nicholas Coster) and Monica Warner (Pam Huntington, then Marj Dusay).

Sisters: Meg Warner (Eve Plumb) and Bailey Warner (Ashleigh Sterling).

Place of Birth: Manhattan.

Character: Beautiful, conceited, and a bit of a snob. With her stunning good looks, almost perfect figure (she tends "to gain a little weight"), and fashionable wardrobe, Blair is simply a picture of beauty. When Blair sustained a black eye in an accident, Tootie best summed up the situation: "It's like defacing a national treasure." As Blair grew and began to develop her figure, Lisa Whelchel mentioned in a TV interview "that the facts of life were not allowed on *The Facts of Life.*"

Hair Color: Blonde.

Heritage: Wealthy and heir to the Warner Textile Industry.

Awards: "Eastland Harvest Queen"; the blue ribbon for being "Most Naturally Blonde" and the Small Business Woman's Association award for inventing contour top sheets.

Favorite Horse at Eastland: Chestnut.

College: Langley, where she is studying to become a lawyer.

Final Episode: When Blair learns that Eastland has gone bankrupt and will soon close, she uses the money she had been saving to open her own law offices and buys the school. She becomes the headmaster and changes the policy to allow boys.

Relatives: Cousin, Geri Warner (Geri Jewell).

JO ANN "JO" POLNIASZEK

Parents: Charlie (Alex Rocco) and Rose (Claire Malis) Polniaszek.

Place of Birth: Bronx, New York.

Character: Blair's complete opposite and attending Eastland on a scholarship. She hails from poor parents (her mother is a waitress; her father is in jail) and appears a bit rough around the edges. She wears little makeup, rides a motorcycle, has an attitude problem, and is a constant source of aggravation to Blair (over the years, Jo mellowed, and she and Blair became good friends). Jo's name is also said to be Jo Anna.

Regret: The school library has no books on automotive engineering: "You'd be surprised how many girls don't know how to drain a crank case."

Fashion Sense: Jeans and sweatshirts (called "polyester and pretzels" by Blair).

Attitude: Normally "mean and rotten" (as Blair believes; and when Jo isn't herself, Blair thinks "Jo must be coming down with something").

College: Langley (where she is a disc jockey at its radio station WLG, 90.8 FM).

Occupation: Counselor at the Hudson Valley Community Center. She, Blair, Tootie, and Natalie also began a business called Mama Rosa's Original Bronx Pizza. She later marries her boyfriend, Rick Bonner (Scott Bryce).

Relatives: Grandfather, Joseph Polniaszek (Sheldon Leonard); cousins, Terry Largo (Megan Follows) and Sal Largo (Donnelly Rhodes); aunt, Evelyn (Rhoda Gemignani).

DOROTHY "TOOTIE" RAMSEY

Parents: Jason (Duane LePage, then Robert Hooks) and Diane Ramsey (Chip Fields). Diane was originally called "Pauline Ramsey."

Brother: Marshall Ramsey (Kevin Sullivan).

Place of Birth: Washington, D.C.

Character: The youngest and cutest of the students. She appeared to live on roller skates in her first year at Eastland and is also the most helpful and ambitious of the girls (Blair calls her "my little helper"); when she gets upset, she oils her roller skates. Kim Fields was nine years old at the time, and the skates were used to make her appear taller.

Favorite Pastime: Playing checkers with Natalie.

Idols: Michael Jackson and Jermaine Jackson.

Ambition: To become an actress (she was the first African American to play Juliet in the school's production of *Romeo and Juliet*). She later leaves to pursue her acting career at the Royal Academy of Dramatic Arts in London.

Pets: Romeo and Juliet (rabbits) and Jeffrey (cat).

Relatives: Cousin, Michael (Peter Parros).

NATALIE GREEN

Mother: Evie Green (Mitzi Hoag).

Place of Birth: Manhattan.

Character: The only one able to keep the peace between Jo and Blair. She is sweet and trusting and washes her hair when she gets angry. Tootie believes that Natalie is the most honest person she knows.

Career Ambition: To become a reporter. She wears a "thinking cap" when she writes (a blue baseball cap with orange lightning bolts over each ear).

Occupation: Waitress at a taco stand called El Sombrero; reporter for the *Peekskill Press* (where her first article, "An Eighth Grader Gets Angry," was published). She later moves to New York's Soho district to pursue a writing career.

OTHER CHARACTERS

Molly Parker (Molly Ringwald) is the school's newspaper photographer and has a ham radio with the call letters WGAIO. She chews on pencils when she gets angry.

Nancy Olson (Felice Schachter) is a gorgeous teenager who hopes to become a model. She is continually seen talking about or to (over the phone) her boyfriend Roger.

Sue Ann Weaver (Julie Piekarski) is the school's star track runner (runs the mile in 4:58 and won the silver-plated track trophy two years in a row). She has blonde hair and was called "The Eastland Streak."

Cynthia "Cindy" Webster (Julie Ann Haddock) is the school's pretty tomboy. She loves tennis and baseball and jumps rope when she gets angry (especially when Blair calls her "Thunder Thighs"). She is a member of the track team (runs the mile in 5:03), wears her hair in pigtails, and wears jersey number 14.

The episode "The Reunion" reveals that Cindy (not Nancy) was a model, while Nancy became a successful businesswoman. While it is not explained, Cindy now had the last name of Brady. It was also revealed that Sue Ann was not the success she hoped to be and lied (saying she was the vice president of a large company to conceal her real job as a gofer). Molly did not appear.

The 2001 ABC TV movie *The Facts of Life Reunion* reveals that Jo is a police officer and has a daughter named Jamie; Blair is the owner of the Warner Park Hotel in New York City (and married to a tycoon named Tab Warner, making her Blair Warner-Warner); Natalie was first a newspaper reporter, then a behind-the-scenes news producer for the cable news channel CNN; and Tootie, preferring now to be called "Dorothy," is the host of a TV talk show called *Wake Up, Los Angeles* (she is also married and the mother of a daughter named Tisha). Dorothy later quit the talk show to pursue her acting career in New York (while 10-year-old Tisha attended the Eastland School).

The headmasters are Harold J. Crocker (Jack Riley), Mr. Harris (Ken Mars), Stephen Bradley (John Lawlor), and Charles Parker (Roger Perry).

Fantasy Island
(ABC, 1978–1984)

Cast: Ricardo Montalban (Mr. Roarke), Herve Villechaize (Tattoo).

Basis: Visitors to a strange island overseen by Mr. Roarke find their fantasies becoming reality when they experience what was once believed to be impossible.

MR. ROARKE

Character: Suave, debonair, and charming. Mr. Roarke, whose full name is never revealed, dresses in white and speaks with a Spanish accent.

Occupation: The apparent owner of Fantasy Island, a tropical resort in an unspecified West Coast location.

Catchphrase: From the program's opening: "My dear guests, I am Mr. Roarke, your host, welcome to Fantasy Island."

Fantasy Cost: Mentioned as $50,000 in one episode.

The White Room: Located behind Mr. Roarke's office in his white Victorian cottage. It has the ability to send people into the past (or future) to fulfill their fantasies. It also allows Mr. Roarke to enter that person's fantasy and control (or monitor) its progression.

True Being: An immortal; a messenger of God who has been sent to Earth to help deserving individuals by allowing them to experience or relive a past event.

Age: Over 300 years old.

Enemy: Satan (Roddy McDowall), who is seeking Mr. Roarke's soul. Satan has always been defeated by Mr. Roarke but always remarks, "We'll play again. We have all eternity before us. Sooner or later I vow to win."

The Love: Mr. Roarke once loved a woman named Elizabeth, but they never married.

The Ghost: Elizabeth lived in bitter resentment that she and Mr. Roarke never wed. A year regarding Elizabeth's passing is not mentioned, but her restless spirit is determined to destroy Mr. Roarke. In 1980, it is first learned that Elizabeth has returned when she possesses the body of island guest Marge Corday (Tina Louise) to fulfill her vow.

A Marriage: In 1979, Mr. Roarke falls in love with and marries Helena Marsh (Samantha Eggar), a fashion designer with a young son named Jamie (Paul John Balson). The reunion is short lived as Helena was found to have an inoperable brain tumor.

The Mermaid: Princess Nyah (Michelle Phillips) is the beautiful Mermaid that inhabits the waters surrounding Fantasy Island.

Relatives: Granddaughter, Julie (Wendy Schaal). She also served as his assistant (as did Kimberly Beck as Cindy) in 1983.

TATTOO

Occupation: Assistant to Mr. Roarke (and a friend for many years).

Character: Not known by any other name and stands four feet tall. Like Mr. Roarke, he is always elegantly dressed (most often in white). He is trusting and has an eye for the ladies. He longs for a family but has not found the right woman.

Catchphrase: "Da plane, da plane" (which he says as he rings the tower bell to announce passengers arriving by seaplane).

Nickname for Mr. Roarke: "Boss."

Trait: Hoping to make a fortune by inventing something that everybody needs.

Transportation: Tattoo is first seen driving a Jeep CJ-7, then a customized 1976 Plymouth Volare station wagon.

Funny Face

See *The Sandy Duncan Show.*

Get Christie Love
(ABC, 1974–1975)

Cast: Teresa Graves (Christie Love), Andy Romano (Joe Caruso), Jack Kelly (Arthur P. Ryan).

Basis: Christie Love, a stunning African American police sergeant with the Special Investigations Division, Metro Bureau of the Los Angeles Police Department, solves cases involving murder, robbery, and kidnapping. The first series to feature an African American policewoman as the central character (airing at the same time as Angie Dickinson's *Police Woman*).

CHRISTINE "CHRISTIE" LOVE
Parents: Mel (a police officer) and Rose Love (a homemaker).
Birthday: April 19, 1953.
Place of Birth: Los Angeles.
Measurements: 36-24-34. She stands 5 feet, 10 inches tall.
Address: 3600 La Paloma Drive.
Telephone Number: 462-4699.
Car License Plate: 343 MCI (later 089 LIR).
Badge Number: 7332.
Mobile Car Code: 5-Baker-5.
Expertise: Marksman (practices shooting at a range called Hogan's Alley).
Self-Imposed Rule: Never shoot to kill—"just close enough to stop 'em."
Weapons: "My wit, beauty, and understanding of human nature" (she will also show cleavage and wear short skirts to accomplish a goal). She is not as brave as she pretends to be and will scream for help when situations become dangerous.
Catchphrase: "Sugah" (normally said when she captures a killer—"You're under arrest, Sugah!").
Favorite Restaurant: Papa Caruso's. Christie is a good cook but prefers to eat out.

Partner: Lieutenant Joseph "Joe" Caruso. He claims, "My partner is one mean lady." His father, "Papa" Luigi Romano, owns the restaurant. In the pilot episode, Andy Romano played the role of Sergeant Seymour Greenberg.
Superior: Captain Arthur P. Ryan. He has the car code 10-William-10.

Good Times
(CBS, 1974–1979)

Cast: John Amos (James Evans), Esther Rolle (Florida Evans), Jimmie Walker (J.J. Evans), Bern Nadette Stanis (Thelma Evans), Ralph Carter (Michael Evans), Ja'net DuBois (Willona Woods), Janet Jackson (Penny Gordon), Johnny Brown (Nathan Bookman), Ben Powers (Keith Anderson).
Basis: A poor African American family (the Evanses) struggles to survive the difficult economic times of the 1970s on little money and a hope that better times are just ahead.

OVERALL SERIES INFORMATION
James and Florida Evans are the parents of James Jr. (called "J.J."), Thelma, and Michael. They live at 963 North Gilbert (also given as 763 North Gilbert) in Apartment 17C of the Cabrini Housing Project in Chicago. Their rent is $104.50 a month, and 555-8264 is their telephone number.

JAMES EVANS SR.
Father: Henry Evans (Richard Ward).
Year of Birth: 1932.
Place of Birth: Mississippi (he later says he was born on a farm in Minnesota).
Education: Limited; dropped out of sixth grade to help support his family.
Childhood Nickname: "Patches."
Military Service: Army private during the Korean War.
Occupation: Laborer (takes whatever jobs he can to support his family). He most often mentions being the assistant foreman for a company called Brady's.
Character: Very strict but loving father. After graduating from trade school in 1975, James is killed in a car accident while seeking a job in Mississippi.

FLORIDA EVANS
Place of Birth: Detroit.
Year of Birth: 1932.
Name Origin: Named after her Aunt Florida (who was named after her mother, Florida, who was pregnant and picking oranges in a Florida grove when she

Good Times. *CBS/Photofest. ©CBS*

went into labor. Ten minutes later, she gave birth to a baby girl and named
her Florida; "it was either Florida or Sunkist").

Childhood Memory: Attending the local carnival with her father and buying
Cracker Jack (hoping to find her prize to be a tin whistle).

Education: Limited; dropped out in tenth grade to help support her family.

Character: A frugal, God-fearing woman with a knack to stretch every dollar.

Occupation: Housewife. She previously worked as a maid, then as a school bus
driver for the Roadway Bus Company after James's passing.

Second Husband: Carl Dixon (Moses Gunn). They married in 1977 and moved
to Arizona (due to Carl's health issues). A year later, Florida returns to her
children (but no mention is made of what happened to Carl).

Relatives: Cousins, Edgar Edwards (Percy Rodriques) and Raymond (Calvin Lock-
hart); nephew, Cletus (John Anthony Bailey). Kim Hamilton appeared as
Betty, Raymond's wife. Florida mentions she has four sisters and one brother.

JAMES "J.J." EVANS JR.

Relationship: The eldest child (age 17).

Career Ambition: To become an artist.

First Painting: At the age of 12, J.J. painted a naked lady eating grits on the
elevator door (he claims he didn't know how to paint clothes at the time).

Catchphrase: "Dy-No-Mite!" He first answered the telephone with "Hel-looooooo," then with "Chel-lo."

Favorite Drink: Kool Aid.

Nicknames: Called "Junior" by James and "Beanpole" by Thelma.

Education: Harding High School.

Occupation: Lake Shore movie theater usher; Chicken Shack (later the Beef Shack) fast-food store delivery boy; art director for the Dynamic Greeting Card Company.

Comic Book Creation: "Dyno-Man" (about an African-American super hero).

Money: J.J. hides what cash he has in "that sock in the dresser drawer." He borrows money from Marion "Sweet Daddy" Williams (Teddy Wilson), a loan shark who charges 25 percent interest a week. As J.J. says about Sweet Daddy, "It's hard to think of some people as plain folks like Jack the Ripper, Attila the Hun, and Darth Vader."

Fantasy: Believes he is a ladies' man (calls himself "The Ebony Prince") and has numerous girlfriends with outlandish names (like Samantha "The Human Panther," "Boom Boom" Belinda, and Francine "The Furnace").

Blood Type: U-negative (very rare, and he shares it with Sweet Daddy).

Note: J.J.'s pictures (executed by real-life artist Ernie Barnes) feature elongated features of African Americans in everyday scenes.

THELMA EVANS

Relationship: The middle child (age 16).

Date of Birth: June 15, 1957.

Education: Harding High School; theater classes at the Community Workshop. She received a scholarship to the Allison School for Girls (but felt it was not right for her).

Career Ambition: First a doctor, then an actress, and finally a professional dancer.

Occupation: Thelma has no specific job but earns money by babysitting.

Posters: Thelma's bedroom wall displays posters of Sly Stone and Carlos Santana.

Personality: Despite comical insults from J.J., Thelma is a beautiful girl with a generous heart. She is loyal to her family and finds it difficult to lie, especially to her mother.

Boyfriend: Keith Anderson (whom Thelma met at a civic center while performing a dance routine). Keith was a professional football player (Heisman Trophy winner) who, after suffering a knee injury, became a driver for the Windy City Cab Company. The final episode finds Keith returning to football and the Evans family moving to a home at 743 Baker Street. Keith was also seen as an alcoholic.

MICHAEL EVANS

Relationship: The youngest child (age 11).

Education: Harding Elementary and High School (where he is an "A" student).

Occupation: Student. He worked for Carl Dixon, a fix-it-shop owner.

Ambition: To become a Supreme Court justice and change the image of the black man. He is rather radical (for TV at the time) and is forever involving himself in the black cause. He is, however, opposed to violence as a means of achieving something.

Gang: Joined the Junior War Lords Gang.

Nickname: Called "The Little Militant" by James and "Miguel" by J.J.

Bedroom: Michael and J.J. share a foldaway bed in the living room. Only Thelma and her parents have their own room.

Organizations: Michael receives mail from SNCC (Student Nonviolent Coordinating Committee) and CORE (Congress of Racial Equality).

WILLONA WOODS

Relationship: Friend of the family (has been friends with Florida for 25 years).

Birthday: August 5, 1945.

Marital Status: Divorced from Ray Woods (Carl Lee), whom she first called "Alvin."

Occupation: Salesgirl at George's Fashion Boutique (also called the Boutique). She worked previously as a beautician and department store salesgirl.

Nickname: Because she is a gossip, James calls her "The Rona Barrett of the Projects" (referring to a famous gossip reporter of the time).

Child: Millicent "Penny" Gordon, an abused girl she adopted. Celeste was her doll.

Nickname for Michael: "Gramps."

Relatives: Penny's unnamed natural mother (Chip Fields).

NATHAN MILLHOUSE BOOKMAN

Occupation: Building superintendent.

Trait: Overweight and henpecked.

Wife: Violet Bookman (Marilyn Coleman), a woman he fears.

Club: A member of the Jolly Janitors Club.

Nickname: Called "Buffalo Butt" (also "Booger") by Willona.

Note: The program is a spin-off of *Maude*, where Florida worked as the maid to Maude Findlay. John Amos played Florida's husband as Henry (a firefighter); their children were mentioned but not seen.

Happy Days
(ABC, 1974–1984)

Cast: Ron Howard (Richie Cunningham), Henry Winkler (Fonzie), Tom Bosley (Howard Cunningham), Marion Ross (Marion Cunningham), Anson Williams (Potsie Weber), Erin Moran (Joanie Cunningham), Donny Most (Ralph Malph), Lynda Goodfriend (Lori Beth Allen), Cathy Silvers (Jenny Piccalo), Scott Baio (Chachi), Pat Morita (Arnold Takahashi).

Basis: Life in the 1950s (and early 1960s) as experienced by the Cunningham family: parents Howard and Marion and their children, Richie, Joanie, and Chuck.

RICHARD "RICHIE" CUNNINGHAM

Address: 618 Bridge Street in Milwaukee, Wisconsin.

Nickname: "Freckles" (because of his red hair and freckles, he was said to resemble Howdy Doody, the puppet from the TV series of the same title). In the family yearbook, a full page is devoted to Richie, as a baby, eating his first bowl of oatmeal.

Education: Jefferson High School (member of the French Club, the basketball team [wore jersey 17], the ROTC [Third Squad Leader], and reporter for the *Bugle*); the University of Wisconsin. In grammar school, he won a medal for reading comprehension.

Trademark: The song "Blueberry Hill" (he would often sing the first line, "I found my thrill on Blueberry Hill . . .") by Fats Domino.

Hangout: Arnold's Drive-In (fast-food hamburgers).

Make-Out Spot: Inspiration Point.

Favorite Breakfast: Blueberry pancakes with fresh-squeezed orange juice.

Favorite Dinner: Meat loaf.

Car: A 1952 Ford he called the Love Bandit.

License Plate: F 7193.

Happy Days. *ABC/Photofest.* ©*ABC*

Career Ambition: First a lawyer, then a journalist. He was a radio disc jockey ($25 a week) at station WOW, cub reporter for the Milwaukee *Journal*, cofounder (with his friends Potsie and Ralph) of Cheap Work ("Any Job for Money"), and waiter at Arnold's Drive-In. He appeared on the WZAZ-TV game show *Big Money* and exposed the program as being fixed when he was given answers for his category of baseball.

Wife: Lori Beth Allen. She called him "Sizzle Lips," and they had a son, Richard (Bo Sharon). Lynda Goodfriend previously played Richie's friend, Kim. Ron Howard left the series when Richie joined the army and was transferred to Camp Silverman in Greenland.

ARTHUR HERBERT FONZARELLI

Nicknames: "The Fonz" and "Fonzie." Only Mrs. Cunningham calls him "Arthur."

Reputation: The cool high school dropout. He rode with the Falcons and Demons motorcycle gangs.

Occupation: Mechanic at Otto's Auto Orphanage, Herb's Auto Repairs, and Bronco's Auto Repairs. After acquiring his diploma at Jefferson High, he taught shop class, then became the dean of boys at George S. Patton High School.

Hangout: Arnold's Drive-In (where the "Guy's Room" bathroom and the photo booth are "his offices").

Address: He originally lived in Apartment 154 (address not given), then above the Cunningham's garage for $50 a month rent.

Pet Dog: Spunky.

TV Hero: The Lone Ranger.

Movie Idol: Actor James Dean.

Trademark: His brown leather jacket.

Aftershave Lotion: Mr. Musk.

Background: Questionable. Fonzie first mentions that his father deserted the family when he was three years old (later, it's "my father split when I was two and my mother [Angela] two years later"). He next says his father left him when he was 12 years old (no mention of his mother). He was then raised by his grandmother, who called him "Skippy."

Possessions: His motorcycle, a toolbox with the name "Sweetums" on it ("Hey, it's a gift from a girl"), and an autograph from Annette Funicello (of *The Mickey Mouse Club* Mouseketeers). As he explains, "She gave me hers; I gave her mine."

Family Disgrace: "The Fonzarelli Curse" (when a male family member is asked to be a best man at a wedding, disaster will result).

Dance Creation: "The Fonz" (written by musician Leather Tuscadero).

Uncanny Ability: To command attention simply by snapping his fingers and attracting girls.

Catchphrases: "Aaayh" and "Whooa."

Trademark: Two-thumbs-up gesture.

Girlfriends: Pinky Tuscadero (Roz Kelly), Leather Tuscadero's older sister, a biker who dressed in pink; Ashley Pfister (Linda Purl), a widow with a young daughter named Heather (Heather O'Roarke). They broke up when Ashley returned to her estranged husband in the hope of reconciling. Craig Stevens and Marla Adams were Ashley's parents, George and Millicent Pfister.

Adopted Child: Danny (Danny Ponce), an orphaned boy.

Attempt at Fame: For the TV series *You Wanted to See It*, "Fearless Fonzarelli" attempted to jump over 14 garbage cans at Arnold's Drive-In but crashed into the Arnold's Milwaukee Fried Chicken stand.

Relatives: Grandma Nausbaum (Frances Bay); cousin, Angie (Charles Galioto).

HOWARD CUNNINGHAM

Brother: Richard "Dick" Cunningham (Richard Paul).

Occupation: Owner of the Cunningham Hardware Store on 8th Street and East Boulevard (which he began in 1946). He previously worked as a hardware store stock boy, then a hot dog vendor at Yankee Stadium in the Bronx. His fascination with hardware began as a boy when he was sent to buy a plunger.

Middle Initial: First given as "C," then "T."

Military Service: Army private during World War II (where he was called "Cookie").

Political Party: Republican.

Car: A black DeSoto, license plate F 3680 (later a red 1960 Studebaker Lark).

Club: The Leopard Lodge, Local 462 (entered as Leopard First Class; worked his way up to Grand Puba).

Favorite Color: Blue.

Favorite Breakfast: Omelets.

Quirk: Gets a headache if he doesn't have dinner by 7 p.m.; his back goes out if he has an irritating day.

Saddest Day of His Life: When he could no longer hold Joanie in his arms ("It was the day I knew she was no longer my little girl").

Relatives: Cousin, Nancy Blansky (Nancy Walker); niece, K.C. Cunningham (Crystal Bernard); uncle, Joe Cunningham (Pat O'Brien).

MARION CUNNINGHAM

Maiden Name: Marion Kelp.

Occupation: Housewife (worked previously as a secretary).

Wedding Night Song: "Moonlight in Vermont."

Honeymoon: Suite 325 at the Holiday Shore Lodge in Lake Geneva.

Nicknames: Howard calls her "Baby Cakes"; she calls Howard "Snookems."

Club: Member of the Milwaukee Women's Club and Howard's bowling team, the Ten Pins (she bowls a 119).

Favorite TV Shows: The Secret Storm and *The Edge of Night* (actual soap operas).

Allergies: Allergic to cayenne pepper.

Favorite Drinking Cup: The one with a picture of silent-screen actor Rudolph Valentino.

Relatives: Marion's "Mother Kelp" (Billie Bird); she calls Howard "Fatso"; nephew, Roger Phillips (Ted McGinley), the basketball coach at Jefferson High School. Not seen was her Uncle Ben (the owner of a dude ranch in Colorado).

WARREN WEBER

Relationship: Richie's best friend.

Nickname: "Potsie" (named by his mother for making things out of clay; he is especially proud of an ashtray he made).

Weight: 145 pounds.

Height: 5 feet, 10 inches tall.

Education: Jefferson High School; the University of Wisconsin.

Band: Potsie (lead singer), Richie (sax), and their friend Ralph (keyboard) formed the Velvet Clouds (originally called the Happy Days Band). In one episode, Potsie performed professionally at the Vogue Terrace Club.

College Fraternity: Potsie, Richie, and Ralph were members of the Alpha Tau Omega fraternity (also called Pi Kappa Nu fraternity).

Character: Potsie wears a white shirt with blue stripes when he visits the Cunninghams; uses a fake ID card to see Bubbles the stripper (Barbara Rhoades) at Eddie's Pink Palace; attempted (but failed) to join the Demons motorcycle gang; purchased (with Richie and Ralph) a $175 car whose best feature was the chrome hood ornament. His parents own a garage and have a car with the license plate BFJ 380.

JOAN "JOANIE" LOUISE CUNNINGHAM

Relationship: Richie's younger sister.

Education: Jefferson High School (where she was a cheerleader). She was also a member of the Junior Chipmunks Scout Troop.

Nicknames: "Shortcake" (as called by Fonzie) and "Pumpkin" (by Howard).

First Baby Word: Hardware (constantly hearing her father talk about the family store).

Favorite Meal: Baked macaroni and applesauce.

Pet Hamster: Gertrude.

Singing Group: The Suedes with Milly (Jan Bunker) and Lilly (Jill Bunker); they provided backup vocals for pop singer Leather Tuscadero (Suzy Quatro).

First Crush: Richie's friend Potsie. She would try to impress him by playing "Secret Love" (selection H-14) on the Seebring 100 Selecto-Matic Jukebox at Arnold's Drive-In.

First Date: Spike (Danny Butch), Fonzie's nephew.

Boyfriend: Charles "Chachi" Arcola (Fonzie's cousin). The spin-off *Joanie Loves Chachi* appeared on ABC (1982–1983). After joining a motley band but failing to achieve musical stardom, the characters returned to *Happy Days* and were married in the final episode. Chachi has the catchphrase "Wa Wa Wa" and played drums in Richie's band.

Best Friend: Jennifer "Jenny" Piccalo, a boy-crazy girl who considers herself "the object of mad desire." She calls Joanie "Joans" and reads *Passionate Romance* magazine. She memorized the Milwaukee phone book in an initiation attempt to join the Rondell's Girls Club at Jefferson High; 555-4242 is her phone number, and she believes that large breasts are the key to success (even investing $29.99 in the Ajax Bust Developer in a failed attempt to become voluptuous). Phil Silvers played her father, Roscoe Piccalo.

OTHER CHARACTERS

Arnold Takashashi is the owner of the hangout, Arnold's Drive-In (located at 2815 Lake Avenue). He mentions his real first name as being Mitsumo, but when he purchased the drive-in, he couldn't afford to change the name. It is later owned by Al Delvecchio (Al Molinaro). In the first episode, it is called Arthur's

Drive-In. When the drive-in is destroyed by fire, Fonzie becomes Al's silent partner when it is rebuilt by the Trans Allied Corporation and becomes known as Arnold's—Fonzie and Big Al Proprietors (Fonzie wanted to call it Fonzie's, while Al wanted Big Al's). Al Molinaro played Al's brother, Father Anthony Delvecchio, and Alice Nunn was Al's Mama Delvecchio.

Arnold's delivery truck license plate is B 9362; the soda machine at the drive-in dispenses Spring Time Cola; college banners seen on the drive-in walls represent Iona, State, Purdue, Yale, and Indiana.

Charles "Chuck" Cunningham (Ric Carrott, then Gavan O'Herlihy, then Randolph Roberts) is Richie's older brother (appeared to do nothing but bounce a basketball and was dropped; said to be attending college on a basketball scholarship). It can be heard in later episodes that Howard mentions he has only two children, Richie and Joanie.

Ralph Malph was best friends with Richie and Potsie. He shared the experiences listed above for Richie and Potsie and was noted for his joke telling or making fun of a situation (he would always remark, "I still got it!"). Donny Most also left the series and was said to have joined the army with Richie. Alan Oppenheimer, then Jack Dobson, played Ralph's father, Mickey Malph.

Note: The original pilot film, *New Family in Town*, aired on *Love, American Style* as "Love and the Happy Days" on February 25, 1972. While the overall theme remained the same, the Fonzie character did not appear, and the program was more sentimental in its approach to living in the 1950s (here the Cunninghams were expecting their first TV set). Ron Howard, Marion Ross, and Anson Williams played the same characters, but Harold Gould was Howard, and Susan Neher was Joanie.

During the opening theme, the record seen playing on the jukebox reads "Happy Days. Lyrics by Norman Gimbel. Music composed by Charles Fox." While this song is heard as the closing theme (later as the opening theme), the song "Rock around the Clock" by Bill Haley and the Comets is actually heard as the record spins.

SPIN-OFFS
Laverne and Shirley (friends of Fonzie), *Mork* (the alien befriended by Richie; see titles for information), and *Fonz and the Happy Days Gang* (ABC, 1980). Here Fonzie, Richie, and Ralph befriend Cupcake (voice of Didi Conn), a girl from the twenty-fifth century whose defective time machine has sent her to 1957 Milwaukee. As Cupcake demonstrates her time machine, it malfunctions, stranding the group (including Fonzie's dog, Mr. Cool) in time. Their adventures to return to 1957 are depicted.

Harry O
(ABC, 1974–1976)

Cast: David Janssen (Harry Orwell).

Basis: A police detective (Harry Orwell) shot in the back, disabled, and forced to retire, becomes a private investigator to occupy his time and pay expenses.

HAROLD "HARRY" ORWELL

Year of Birth: 1931.

Place of Birth: Nebraska.

Business: Harry Orwell: Private Investigations. As a police officer, Harry was attached to the Homicide Division of the San Diego Police Department.

Address: Originally an unidentified beach house in San Diego. When a case brings Harry to Santa Monica, California, and he learns his home has been destroyed to make way for a high-rise building, he lives at a beachfront home at 1101 Coast Road.

Telephone Number: 555-4647.

Beach House Neighbors: Lindsay (Loni Anderson), an airline stewardess, and Sue (Farrah Fawcett). Sue had a Great Dane named Grover that just didn't like Harry.

The Shooting: During an active case investigation in 1969, Harry was shot in the back during a robbery in progress at a drugstore.

The Prognosis: The bullet lodged too close to his spine to operate and vigorous activity (like police work) causes extreme pain.

The End Result: Forced retirement and an income based on a disability pension. Unable to just sit around and do nothing, he chose to become a private detective.

Hobby: Repairing a boat he calls *The Answer* ("which I'll have as soon as I put it back together. I'm going on the ocean where they have no telephones; telephones bug me").

Trait: Grouchy and stubborn.

Car: An antique Austin-Healy MG that requires numerous repairs ("I don't have the $300 needed to fix it"); thus, as he says, "I do a lot of walking." He also takes a bus or a cab, but only "if it's tax deductible."

Character: Likes to keep to himself and is not particularly friendly; he is, however, a good friend to those who are his friends.

Dislike: Politics and mentioning or talking about the shooting incident that disabled him.

Romance: As he ages, Harry realizes that his chances of finding a true romance have grown slim. "I wish I was 17 again because when I was 17, I once said,

'A woman is like a bus. They'll be another one along in a few minutes.' Now that was a long time ago."

Favorite Grocery Store: The Agryz Market.

Police Department Contacts: Lieutenant Manuel "Manny" Quinn (Henry Darrow) of the San Diego Police Department and Lieutenant K.C. Trench (Anthony Zerbe) of the Los Angeles Police Department. While Manny accepted Harry for who he was, Trench had mixed feelings and disliked Harry's casual mannerisms and ability to rely on intuition rather than hard facts.

Note: Two ABC pilots were produced: *Harry O* (1973), subtitled "Such Dust as Dreams Are Made Of" (explores how Harry is shot by Harlan Garrison [Martin Balsam]), and *Smile Jenny, You're Dead* (1974; Harry investigates the death of a friend's son-in-law).

Hart to Hart
(ABC, 1979–1984)

Cast: Robert Wagner (Jonathan Hart), Stefanie Powers (Jennifer Hart), Lionel Stander (Max).

Basis: A husband and wife (Jonathan and Jennifer) join forces to solve crimes—more as a hobby than as official law enforcement officers.

JONATHAN HART

Background: Born in California and orphaned at an early age. He grew up on the streets and was headed for a life of crime when a stranger named Max rescued him. Max oversaw Jonathan's high school and college education (for transportation, Max gave Jonathan a 1950 Ford convertible). He majored in business and with Max's help (a $1,500 loan) began a company in 1965.

Company: Hart Industries (Jonathan is chairman of the board; Jennifer is chief executive officer). First shares of stock were issued on March 30, 1969.

Business Address: 112 North Las Palmas in Los Angeles.

Business Phone Number: 555-1271.

Business Bank: City Trust and Savings.

Company Divisions: Hart Shipping Lines, Chem-O-Cal, and Hart Toy were mentioned; aerospace and electronic are other divisions.

Home Address: 3100 Willow Pond Drive in Bel Air, California (later said to be in Beverly Hills, California).

Home Telephone Number: 555-1654 (later 555-3223).

Pet Dog: Freeway (named as such after Jennifer found him near the side of a freeway).

Thoroughbred Racehorse: J.J. Hart

Cars: HART 1 (a Rolls-Royce), HART II (also seen as 2 HARTS; a Mercedes-Benz 380 SL convertible), and HART 3 (a 1970 Mercedes-Benz 300 TD wagon).

Favorite Breakfast: Pancakes (but only on Mondays).

Musical Ability: The trumpet.

Girlfriend before Jennifer: Dominique Stefanos (Christina Belford).

JENNIFER HART

Heritage: Scottish.

Maiden Name: Jennifer Edwards.

Birthday: November 2, 1946 (as seen on her driver's license).

Father: Steven Edwards (Ray Milland), a former CIA spy; now a ranch owner.

Place of Birth: Hillhaven, Maryland.

Favorite Ranch Horse: Sweet Sue.

Education: Gresham Hill Prep School (where she was a cheerleader for the Bulls football team); New York University (journalism major and theater arts courses).

Occupation: Freelance journalist.

Published Book: 21 Reasons for Living. She also wrote a play, *Ladies of Whitechapel,* that theorizes that Jack the Ripper could have been a woman.

Hobby: Amateur sleuth (like Jonathan); "Their hobby is murder" (as Max says).

First Meeting: In London (interviewing Jonathan at the Hotel Ritz for her newspaper, the *Herald*). They flew a kite on their first date; first kissed on a ferryboat, and Jonathan proposed to Jennifer near Tower Bridge with the banner "Will You Marry Me?" They honeymooned in San Francisco's Napa Valley (stayed at O'Berge Inn, room 7).

Favorite Holiday: Christmas.

Favorite TV Soap Opera: "Doctor's Hospital" (mythical).

Trait: Gets a bit tipsy from champagne, lunches at La Scala's, and has her hair done at Salvatore's on Wilshire Boulevard. She will never eat a hamburger without mayonnaise.

Favorite Restaurant: Robaire's (French cuisine).

Double: Stefanie Powers played the evil Dominique Bitten, a mobster's wife.

MAX

Position: Housekeeper, cook, chauffeur, dog walker. He answers the phone with "Hart Residence." He calls Jonathan "Mr. H" and Jennifer "Mrs. H."

Addiction: Gambling, especially playing the horses. He runs an illegal off-track betting parlor from the Hart's kitchen and never mentions his last name.

TV Role: He and Freeway did a commercial for Dog Gone It dog food.

Relaxation: Smoking a cigar and reading a book.

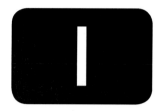

The Incredible Hulk
(CBS, 1978–1982)

Cast: Bill Bixby (David Banner), Lou Ferrigno (The Hulk), Jack Clovin (Jack McGee).

Basis: A scientist (Bruce Banner) is exposed to an accidental overdose of gamma radiation during an experiment that alters his DNA and transforms him into the Hulk, a green creature of incredible strength, when he becomes angered or enraged.

DR. DAVID BRUCE BANNER

Father: David W. Banner (John Marley); his late mother was named Elizabeth; they owned a farm in Grail Valley.

Sister: Dr. Helen Banner (Diana Muldaur).

Place of Birth: Treverton, Ohio.

Year of Birth: 1939.

Education: Treverton High School; State University.

Occupation: Physician and research scientist.

Marital Status: Widower. His first wife, Laura (Lara Parker), died in a car accident; Dr. Carolyn Fields (Mariette Hartley), his second wife (who learned of his secret), died shortly after their marriage due to an illness involving cellular degeneration. David's father and sister also discovered his secret.

Employment: The Culver Institute in Sacramento, California.

Lab Assistant: Dr. Elaina Marks (Susan Sullivan).

The Experiment: To discover how certain people can tap hidden resources of strength under stressful situations.

The Reason: David and Laura are riding in a car when a tire blowout causes it to go out of control and land in a ditch. David, thrown from the car, attempts to rescue Laura (trapped in the car) but is unsuccessful when it catches fire. Later, after reading accounts of people acquiring sudden strength in adverse situations, David believes there is a hidden factor that accounts for this, and gamma radiation could be the answer.

The Accident: David, experimenting on himself, is exposed to 300,000 units of gamma radiation for 15 seconds.

The Result: A change to David's DNA chemistry. When he becomes angered or enraged, he transforms into a creature called the Hulk.

First Transformation: While attempting to fix a flat tire, David injures his hand, becomes angered, and transforms into the Hulk.

The Cure: None. When David relaxes, the metamorphosis is reversed, and he again becomes himself. He now travels across the country seeking a way to reverse the process.

The "Crime": A fire breaks out while David and Elaina are conducting an experiment. David, unable to battle the flames, transforms into the Hulk. At this same time, Jack McGee, a reporter for the *National Register*, arrives for a scheduled interview with David. Jack witnesses the Hulk carrying Elaina to safety (the chemicals later claim her life) and mistakenly believes the creature killed her and David perished in the fire. Jack vows to bring the killer to justice and expose the creature he saw. The Hulk, however, will not kill because David Banner will not kill.

Jack McGee: Based in Chicago, where he is said to be with the news division. His ID number is 554 (seen on his employee card), and J. Smith is the editor. The *Register* sells for 50 cents and has offered a $10,000 reward for the capture of the Hulk.

First Mention of the Hulk: The second-season episode "The Disciple" (wherein David refers to his transformation as the Hulk; he previously called it the Creature).

David's Catchphrase: "Don't make me angry; you wouldn't like me when I'm angry."

Aliases: To survive, David takes various jobs and assumes numerous aliases (all using his first name but with a made-up last name beginning with the letter B). Names and jobs include David Bellars (lumberjack), David Bernard (scientist), David Burns (stage manager), David Bowman (building caretaker), and David Barton (bartender).

Longest Time between Transformations: 32 days (from the episode "A Solitary Place").

The Hulk: Green and muscular with white eyes during the transformation from human to creature. The Hulk appears frightening but will not harm humans unless absolutely necessary (he actually risks exposure by helping people in trouble). Acquiring clothes often becomes a problem for David due to the transformation's ripping his clothes.

The Wanted Poster: To avoid a public panic if it were known that a green creature exists, only police departments receive posters that state "For Circulation among Police Officers Exclusively." It is impossible to read its contents, as it is purposely blurred.

Episode Close: David is seen alone, walking or hitchhiking.

License Plate: 823 CE (David's car in the pilot).

1949 Flashbacks: Elizabeth, David's mother (Claire Malis); young David (Reed Diamond); young Helen (Juliana Tutak). Elizabeth was born in 1917 and passed away in 1949 from an illness.

UPDATES

The Incredible Hulk Returns (1988) finds David seeking to use a newly developed gamma transporter in an effort to rid himself of the Hulk.

The Trial of the Incredible Hulk (1989) is actually an unsold pilot film for a series based on the superhero character Daredevil. David, accused of robbery, hires Matt Murdock (Rex Smith), a blind attorney who is secretly Daredevil, to defend him.

The Death of the Incredible Hulk (1990) concludes the TV series in an involved story about David's efforts to test a DNA formula that can accelerate human healing and possibly cure him. Jack McGee is strangely absent (thus giving him no closure). David, becoming involved with terrorists seeking the formula for military applications, transforms into the Hulk to stop them by destroying their plane. Seconds before the aircraft explodes, the Hulk jumps out. As he falls to the ground below, he begins to transform from Hulk to human. Jasmin (Elizabeth Gracen), the Russian spy who became a part of David's life, witnesses the final seconds of the transformation (as David lies on the ground) and hears his final words: "Jasmin, I'm free."

The Jeffersons
(CBS, 1975–1985)

Cast: Sherman Hemsley (George Jefferson), Isabel Sanford (Louise Jefferson), Mike Evans, then Damon Evans (Lionel Jefferson), Franklin Cover (Tom Willis), Roxie Roker (Helen Willis), Berlinda Tolbert (Jenny Willis).

Basis: All in the Family spin-off about an African American family and their experiences moving from Queens, New York, to Manhattan to experience a better life.

OVERALL SERIES INFORMATION

Louise Jefferson (Isabel Sanford), her son Michael (Michael Evans), and Louise's brother-in-law Henry (Mel Stewart) were originally the neighbors of Archie Bunker (from 1971 to 1975). George, Louise's husband, was mentioned but not seen until 1973 (when Sherman Hemsley was cast in the role).

GEORGE JEFFERSON

Mother: Olivia (Zara Cully), called "Mother Jefferson" by Louise. His father was struck and killed by a bus when George was 10; Olivia's favorite drink is a Bloody Mary.

Place of Birth: Georgia.

Military Service: The Navy (U.S. Seventh Fleet; served in the galley on an aircraft carrier).

Address: Colby East, Apartment 12D, in Manhattan. Before marriage, George lived at 984 West 125th Street, Apartment 5C, in Harlem.

Occupation: Owner of the Jefferson Cleaners (stores in Manhattan, Harlem, Queens, the Bronx, and Brooklyn). He established his first store in 1971 and wanted to call his business the Handy Dandy Cleaners; Louise suggested Jefferson Cleaners.

Competition: Feldway Cleaners and Cunningham Cleaners.

Trait: Wealthy (but cheap) and snobbish. His stinginess is a result of growing up in poverty in Harlem. Christmas was an especially bad time, and George made a vow: if he ever made it big, he would do something for the people who moved into that same apartment. He now anonymously sends that family $100 a month. George has a tendency to label people of other races by derogatory terms (as he did with his white neighbor, Tom Willis, whom he called "Honky") and is always on the offensive, as he believes people talk about him behind his back.

Biggest Fear: Losing his hair.

Favorite Meal: Possum stew (it is actually rabbit stew, as Louise is unable to buy possum meat in Manhattan; George apparently cannot tell the difference).

Charities: "Send a Boy to Camp" and "Send a Girl to Camp" projects.

Pets: A dog named Wilma (on *All in the Family*).

Relatives: Aunt, Emma (Lillian Randolph).

LOUISE JEFFERSON

Parents: Howard (Leonard Jackson) and Maxine Mills (Josephine Premice).

Occupation: Housewife (married for 25 years when the series begins). Louise knows living with George means accepting his peculiar ways and agreeing

The Jeffersons. *CBS/Photofest.* ©*CBS*

with what he says (even if he is wrong). George believes he is the glue that keeps their marriage together "because I put up with all her faults" and can't be broken of his habit of calling women "girls" (as George explains, "They aren't boys"). Louise is now a counselor at the Help Center (phone number 555-2341) and shares office 102 with her friend Helen Willis. When things get rough, Louise and Helen resort to munching on "that bag of potato chips."

Nicknames: Called "Weez" and "Weezie" by George.

Maiden Name: Louise Mills.

Childhood: Louise mentions living on 13th Street and Amsterdam Avenue in Manhattan and growing up in a bad neighborhood where crime and hookers were prevalent. It was here that she developed the tough persona she now displays.

Blood Type: O-negative.

Activity: Den mother to the Red Robbins Girl Scout Troop.

Book: Ghetto Recipes (soul food recipes that Pelham Publishing rejected when it was discovered that the recipes came from a book her mother used, *Mrs. Kirby's Kitchen*).

Relatives: Louise mentions an older unwed sister who became pregnant and moved to France (where she became a singer).

LIONEL JEFFERSON

Relationship: George and Louise's son.

Nickname: "Diver" (his street name when he lived in Harlem).

Character: On *All in the Family*, Lionel was best friends with Archie Bunker's daughter, Gloria, and her husband, Mike. It was an established fact that Archie did not like black people (whom he called "colored"), but he did like Lionel (much of the humor stems from Archie making fun of blacks in front of Lionel without realizing what he is doing). Lionel likes Archie and knows he is not vicious. He realizes that Archie gives people of different races stereotyped labels simply because he does not know any better. Lionel later married Jenny Willis, the daughter of his upstairs penthouse neighbors (14th floor) Tom (white) and Helen (black) Willis. They eventually had a daughter named Jessica (Ebonie Smith) but later separated and divorced.

Middle Initial: "W" (Lionel never mentioned what it stood for).

Nickname for Jenny: "Honey Babes."

TOM AND HELEN WILLIS

They have been married for 23 years and are incorrectly said to be television's first interracial couple (Lucille Ball [white] and Desi Arnaz [Latin] from *I Love Lucy* in 1952 are the first such couple; this was followed by Mary

Alice [black] and Allan Drake [white] on *Sanford and Son* in 1975—seven months before *The Jeffersons* premiered). Tom is an editor for the Pelham Publishing Company. Helen's maiden name is Helen Douglas.

Relatives: Tom's father, Henry Willis (Leon Ames); Tom's Uncle Bertram (Victor Killian); Helen's father, "Grandpa Douglas" (Fred Pinkard).

OTHER CHARACTERS

Harry Bentley (Paul Benedict) is George's across-the-hall neighbor (Apartment 12E). He was born in England, attended Oxford University, and works as a Russian interpreter at the United Nations in Manhattan. To help Harry overcome his constant back problems, George kindly volunteers to stand on his back.

Florence Johnston (Marla Gibbs) is George's sassy maid and one of the few people who can insult (and stand up to) George. She left to become the housekeeper to Lyle Bock (Larry Linville), the manager of the St. Frederick Hotel in Manhattan (on the 1981 spin-off *Checking In*). Roseanna Christiansen as Carmen replaced her; Florence returned to *The Jeffersons* when *Checking In* was canceled after four episodes (the explanation being that the St. Frederick Hotel caught fire and was destroyed).

Kojak

(CBS, 1973–1978)

Cast: Telly Savalas (Theo Kojak), Kevin Dobson (Bobby Crocker), Dan Frazer (Frank McNeil), George Savalas (Detective Stavros), Vince Conti (Detective Rizzo), Mark Russell (Detective Saperstein). George Savalas originally worked under the name Demosthenes.

Basis: A tough, no-nonsense New York detective (Theo Kojak), based in a cold-in-the-winter and hot-in-the-summer precinct, uses determination to solve crimes.

THEO KOJAK

Heritage: Greek (the son of immigrant parents).

Year of Birth: 1922.

Place of Birth: Manhattan (a Greek community on the Lower East Side).

Sisters: Sophie (Penny Santon) and Mary Drosinis (Eunice Christopher).

Childhood Dream: To become a police officer (his only obsession).

Occupation: Plainclothes detective (lieutenant) with the New York Police Department; later promoted to chief of detectives. He was previously a patrol officer with the 26th Precinct.

Precinct: Manhattan South (attached to the 13th Precinct).

Precinct Address: 220 East 17th Street.

Home Address: 215 River Street.

Car: A 1973 bronze (then 1975) Buick Regal.

License Plate: 383 JDZ (also seen as 394 AFL).

Favorite Restaurant: Stella's (owned by Marie Stella, played by Carole Cook).

Trademark: Pencil thin cigars and Tootsie Roll lollipops. He is bald and wears a black Fedora hat with a silver band above the brim.

Catchphrase: "Who loves ya, baby" (he can also be heard saying "Baby" with numerous other dialogue exchanges).

Steadfast Rule: Women are not to be a part of his squad. He feels that, because of the gruesome nature of cases, female officers would not be able to handle the situation.

Exception: Jo Long (Joan Van Ark; from the 1977 episode "Lady in the Squad Room"), who teamed with Theo to test the possibilities of women investigating homicide cases.

Romantic Interest: Irene Van Patten (Diane Baker).

Favorite Game: Pool (frequents the Excelsior Pool Hall). He also mentions liking poker.

Pet Peeve: The law itself. He believes that high-profile criminals, with their expensive lawyers, beat the system and, even on murder charges, make bail.

Least Favorite Food: Red onions.

Favorite Drink: Coffee (even though he complains that the squad room coffee "is one step ahead of suicide").

Kojak. *CBS/Photofest.* ©CBS

Superior: Captain Francis "Frank" McNeil (married for 22 years to Lillian, played by Jean LeBouvier). Shelley Winters played Frank's sister-in-law Evelyn McNeil.

Squad: Crocker, Stavros, Rizzo, and Saperstein, whom he often calls "yo-yos," sometimes comparing them to the comedy teams of Laurel and Hardy and Abbott and Costello for all the arguments they have. Theo is famous for just yelling their names when he needs them (for example, "Crocker!" "Saperstein!" "Rizzo!"). Crocker is the only one he calls by a first name ("Bobby"). Theo has a reason why his squad acts as they do: "These guys don't know what they'll find out there. It could be a killer with a .357 Magnum or a body chopped up in pieces. They gotta get their laughs when they can."

Relatives: Niece, Elena (Gigi Semone); uncle, Constantino (Nick Dennis); Mary's children are Alexandra (Janice Hayden) and Johnny Drosinis (Michael Mullins).

Note: Telly Savalas first played Theo Kojak in the 1973 TV movie *The Marcus-Nelson Murders* (wherein he helps a teenager falsely convicted of murder); he then appeared in the 1985 TV movie *The Belarus File*, where he is teamed with FBI agent Dana Sutton (Suzanne Pleshette) to find a killer, and finally in the 1987 TV movie *Kojak: The Price of Justice*, wherein Theo helps a woman accused of murdering her two children.

UPDATES/REBOOTS

Kojak (ABC, 1989): Theo is now an inspector with the 74th Precinct in Manhattan while Crocker has become an assistant district attorney. He now uses sugar-free lollipops and drives a sedan with the license plate NRV 171, and Detective Warren Blake (Andre Braugher) is his partner.

Kojak (USA, 2005): Ving Rhames as Lieutenant Theo Kojak, Chazz Palminteri as Captain Frank McNeil, Michael Kelly as Detective Bobby Crocker, and Sybil Temple as Detective Emily Patterson. Here, Theo is African American but is still bald and addicted to lollipops (to help break his smoking habit).

Kolchak: The Night Stalker
(ABC, 1974–1975)

Cast: Darren McGavin (Carl Kolchak), Simon Oakland (Tony Vincenzo).

Basis: Reporter Carl Kolchak's encounters with and efforts to expose supernatural happenings and creatures through his newspaper stories.

CARL KOLCHAK

Heritage: Polish.

Place of Birth: Chicago on May 7, 1922.

Occupation: Reporter for INS (Independent News Service) in Chicago (a low-budget wire service that supplies stories to newspapers). Carl previously worked as a reporter for the Las Vegas *Daily News*, then the Washington, D.C., *Daily Chronicle*.

Education: Chicago School of Journalism. After graduating in 1950, he became a cub reporter for an unnamed newspaper but covered normal stories.

Character: Fast-talking and wisecracking. He is, if nothing else, relentless. If he feels there is a story to be had, he will go to all lengths to tell it.

Best Friend: Dumb luck, which, when combined with his persistence and wits, enables him to overcome bizarre situations.

The Change: 1972 as a reporter in Las Vegas when he attempted to prove that Jonas Skorzeny (Barry Atwater) was a vampire and responsible for a series of showgirl killings.

Dress: Clothes that are a bit wrinkled and seemingly out of style. He wears off-white tennis shoes, battered seersucker suits, and a straw boater hat.

Greatest Fear: The dentist (he also shows signs of being frightened by some of the creatures he encounters, such as a mummy, a werewolf, and a succubus).

Cars: Mustang (license plate UG 8806) and a 1968 Chevrolet Camaro Rallye Sport convertible.

OTHER CHARACTERS

Anthony "Tony" Vincenzo is Carl's easily exasperated, always yelling editor. Tony is forever assigning Carl to cover stories of general interest, not the bizarre stories he manages to stumble on. Tony mentions that in college he played the drums in a band called Tony Vincenzo's Neapolitans.

Ron Updike (Jack Grinnage) is an INS reporter seeking to become the paper's number one reporter; he mentions being born in San Francisco.

Emily Cowles (Ruth McDevitt) is the INS advice columnist ("Dear Emily"). She is called "Miss Emily" but was also referred to as "Edith Cowles" and "Edith Fenwick"; she was also said to be the INS "Riddle Columnist" and the crossword puzzle page editor.

Gordon Spangler (John Fiedler), called "Gordie the Ghoul," is Carl's contact at the morgue.

Note: The original pilot film, *The Night Stalker*, aired on ABC on January 1, 1972, and its follow-up TV movie, *The Night Strangler*, aired on January 16, 1973.

Kung Fu
(ABC, 1972–1975)

Cast: David Carradine (Kwai Chang Caine).

Basis: A Shaolin priest of the 1870s roams the American frontier seeking a half brother (Danny) but also battling the evils that exist. Flashbacks of Caine's strict training are interspersed with his adventures.

KWAI CHANG CAINE

Place and Year of Birth: China, 1850s; orphaned at the age of six.

Parents: An American father and a Chinese mother.

Shelter: With apparently no relatives, Kawi Chang wandered onto the grounds of (and is accepted into) the Temple of Whonon (a training school for future Shaolin priests).

Mentor: Master Po (Keye Luke), a wise but blind teacher.

Nickname: "Grasshopper" (as called by Master Po. When Master Po asked Caine to describe what he heard around him, he mentioned everything but a grasshopper. "How is it that you hear these things," asks Caine. "How is it that you do not," responds Master Po [and thus his nickname]).

Training: The art of kung fu, the medieval Chinese science of disciplined combat developed by Buddhist and Taoist monks.

First Training Lesson: The Inner Strength ("To discover a harmony of mind and body in accord with the flow of the universe").

Final Training Exercise: Walking across very delicate rice paper without damaging it.

Graduation Ceremony: To approach a cauldron of burning coals and place his arms around it, branding his skin with the symbols of a tiger and a dragon.

Parting Words: "Remember the wise man walks always with his head bowed, humble like the dust" (as said to Caine by Master Teh [John Leoning]).

Prized Possession: A pebble taken from the hand of Master Po in a training exercise.

Fugitive: After graduating, Caine recalls Master Po's dream to make a pilgrimage to the Forbidden City in the fifth month in the Year of the Dog and joins him. En route, they are accosted by guards of the Royal Nephew, and Master Po is shot. At the request of his mentor, Caine takes a spear from a guard and kills the Royal Nephew. Before he dies, Master Po warns Caine to leave China and begin a new life elsewhere.

Reward Posters: "Wanted for Murder. Kwai Chang Caine. $10,000 Alive; $5,000 Dead." Issued by the Royal Family; the Imperial Police (later the Order of the Avenging Dragon) seek Caine on their behalf. He is most wanted alive to face a beheading.

Character: Humble and just with a profound respect for human life (he is seen killing only in the pilot film). He carries with him a wooden flute and a pouch of medicines given to him by Master Po. When asked about his travels and where he is going, Caine responds, "I may never know."

Relatives: Half brother, Danny Caine (Tim McIntire); grandfather, Henry Raphael Caine (Dean Jagger). Through an affair that Henry had with Sara Kingsley (Patricia Neal), Caine has two blood relatives born out of wedlock: Margaret (Season Hubley) and John (Edward Albert) McLean.

Flashbacks: Caine, age six (Stephen Manley); teenage Caine (Radames Pera).

Note: In *Kung Fu: The Movie* (CBS, 1986), David Carradine again plays Kwai Chang Caine, roaming the American frontier of 1885 and battling the Manchu (Mako), a mysterious Samurai who has sworn to kill him.

The 1987 CBS TV movie *Kung Fu: The Next Generation* finds David Darlow as a 1980s Kwai Chang Caine, a descendant of the original Kwai Chang, struggling to raise his son, Johnny Caine (Brandon Lee).

Kung Fu: The Legend Continues is a 1993 syndicated series wherein David Carradine plays Kwai Chang Caine, a descendant of the original character. He is living in San Francisco and helps his son, Peter Caine (Chris Potter), a police detective, battle crime.

Laverne & Shirley

(ABC, 1976–1983)

Cast: Penny Marshall (Laverne DeFazio), Cindy Williams (Shirley Feeney), Michael McKean (Lenny Kosnowski), David L. Lander (Andrew Squigman), Eddie Mekka (Carmine Raguso), Phil Foster (Frank DeFazio), Betty Garrett (Edna Babish), Leslie Esterbrook (Rhonda Lee).

Basis: Two single women (Laverne and Shirley), living in Milwaukee during the 1960s, struggle to survive the daily aggravations of life, including menial jobs, nonlasting romantic relationships, and rather strange, if not unique, friends (Lenny and Squiggy).

OVERALL SERIES INFORMATION

Close friends Laverne and Shirley live at 730 Knapp Street, Apartment A (also given as 730 Hampton Street). They moved into the building in 1956, work in the bottle-capping division of the Shotz Brewery (from 10 a.m. to 6 p.m.), earn $1.35 an hour, and shop at Slotnick's Supermarket. They are teammates on the company bowling team, the Big Shotz (originally called the Hot Shotz), and were members of a club called the Angora Debs. In high school, Laverne (called "Gutsy"), Shirley ("Klutzy"), and their friend Ann Marie ("Nutsy") were known as "The Three Musketeers." When the series switched locales (to California), the girls acquired jobs in the gift wrapping department of Bardwell's Department Store. They now live at 113½ Laurel Vista Drive. Laverne and Shirley also joined the army (did their basic training at Camp McClellan and played prostitutes in the army training film *This Can Happen to You*). Vicki Lawrence was their tough sergeant Alvinia P. Plout (called "The Frog").

Lenny and Squiggy, Laverne and Shirley's uncouth friends and upstairs neighbors, work as beer truck drivers for the Shotz Brewery. In California episodes, they are co-owners of the Squignowski Talent Agency of Burbank and owners of an ice cream truck called Squignowski's Ice Cream. To acquire clients, especially girls, for their talent agency, they wrote a movie script called *Blood Orgy of the Amazon*. When they enter a room or meet someone, they say "Hello" (together) and are members of a lodge called the Fraternal Order of the Bass (fish parts adorn their hats).

The four characters are all 28 years old (when the series begins) and attended Fillmore High School. The program is a spin-off from *Happy Days*.

LAVERNE MARIE DEFAZIO
Father: Frank DeFazio. Her mother is deceased.
Place of Birth: Wisconsin.
Religion: Catholic.
Heritage: Italian.
Fears: Being in public alone; small places.
Shameful Secret: Her cousin Vito took her to the Junior Prom.
Favorite Sandwich: Sauerkraut on raisin bread.
Favorite Drink: Milk and Pepsi Cola.
Favorite Snack: Scooter Pies.
Trademark: Wears a large capital "L" on her clothing, even her lingerie.
Occupation (without Shirley): The Ajax Aerospace Company in California (at which time Shirley married and Cindy Williams left the series).
Nickname: Called "Messy Pants" as a little girl; her father calls her "Muffin."

Laverne and Shirley. *ABC/Photofest.* ©*ABC*

Boyfriend: Randolph Carpenter (Ted Danson), a fireman (killed in the line of duty).

Favorite TV Show: Ben Casey (of which she has trouble figuring out the plots).

SHIRLEY WILHELMINA FEENEY

Heritage: Irish.

Religion: Protestant.

Political Party: Democrat.

Money: Shirley hides her and Laverne's money in the Bible (usually between the Old and New Testaments).

Plush Cat: Boo Boo Kitty (its picture is even painted on her bedroom wall).

Catchphrases: "Hi-Yooo" for her hello; "Bye-Yooo" for good-bye.

Idol: Ringo Starr. She has what she calls the "Ringo Dream" (imagines that Ringo is in love with her).

Famous For: The Shirley Feeney Scarf Dance.

Favorite Foods: Barbecued chicken (but without extra barbecue sauce; "It's too messy and gets under my fingernails"), pizza with pepperoni and onions, and fish sticks.

Favorite Novel: Black Beauty (she read it eight times).

Favorite Reading Matter: "Dick Tracy Crime Stoppers" from the "Dick Tracy" newspaper comic strip.

Favorite Christmas Song: "O Come All Ye Faithful."

Favorite Prayer: "Now I Lay Me Down to Sleep."

Favorite Soap: Ivory.

Author: Wrote of her army experiences under the pen name S. Wilhelmina Feeney.

Performer: At the annual Shotz Brewery Talent Show, Laverne and Shirley perform as Jack and Jill (singer/dancers).

Least Favorite Childhood Memory: On the first day of kindergarten, the class bully, Candy Zarvakas, made her eat a box of Crayola crayons.

Boyfriend: Dr. Walter Meaney (when they married, she became Shirley Feeney Meaney).

Siblings: Four unseen brothers: Bobby, Christopher, Michael, and Timothy.

ANDREW "SQUIGGY" SQUIGMAN

Father: Helmut Squigman (Wynn Irwin).

Sister: Squigelyn Squigman (David L. Lander).

Religion: Lutheran.

Favorite Food Dressing: Bosco chocolate syrup (which he puts on everything).

Most Prized Possession: His moth collection.

Family "Blessing": The famous Squigman Birthmark (a large red blotch shaped like Abraham Lincoln).

Favorite Things: Old sandwiches and toenail clippings.

Relatives: Squiggy's unseen Uncle Elliott, the owner of a wax museum.

LEONARD "LENNY" KOSNOWSKI

Religion: Lutheran.

Heritage: Polish (his last name translates as "Help, there's a hog in my kitchen").

Military Service: Army Reserves.

Pet Turtle: Unnamed (it killed itself trying to scratch Lenny's name off its back).

Only "Toy" as a Kid: Sauerkraut.

Favorite Things: Horror movies and sports.

Home Away from Home: As Lenny states, "The gutter."

Business: Dead Lazlo's Place (a diner, called Lazlo's Place, that he renamed after inheriting it from his late uncle Lazlo). He hired Shirley (who worked as Betty the waitress) and Shirley (who cooked the meals).

OTHER CHARACTERS

Frank DeFazio, Laverne's father, owns a combination pizza parlor and bowling alley called the Pizza Bowl. He sells it when he also moves to California (Burbank) to operate a Cowboy Bill's Western Grub franchise ("Stuff your face, western style").

While in Milwaukee, Frank becomes romantically involved with Edna Babbish, Laverne and Shirley's five-times-married landlady. They married before Frank gave up the Pizza Bowl after 12 years in business. Linda Gillin played Edna's daughter, Amy.

Carmine Raguso, called "The Big Ragoo," is Shirley's boyfriend (before Warren). He calls her "Angel Face" and works as a singing messenger.

Rhonda Lee is Laverne and Shirley's Hollywood neighbor, an aspiring actress who starred in the play *Bono Mania* (the life of singers Sonny and Cher).

Note: The animated spin-off *Laverne and Shirley in the Army* (ABC, 1981) finds Laverne and Shirley stationed at Camp Fillmore, where Sergeant Squeely (voice of Ron Palillo), a talking pig, is their superior.

Little House on the Prairie
(NBC, 1974–1982)

Cast: Michael Landon (Charles Ingalls), Karen Grassle (Caroline Ingalls), Melissa Gilbert (Laura Ingalls), Melissa Sue Anderson (Mary Ingalls), Lindsay and Sidney Greenbush (Carrie Ingalls), Wendi and Brenda Turnbeaugh (Grace Ingalls), Victor French (Mr. Edwards), Richard Bull (Nels Oleson), Katherine MacGregor (Harriet Oleson), Alison Arngrim (Nellie Oleson),

Jonathan Gilbert (Willie Oleson), Linwood Boomer (Adam Kendall), Dean Butler (Almanzo Wilder), Merlin Olsen (Jonathan Garvey), Hersha Parady (Alice Garvey), Matthew Laborteaux (Albert Quinn), Allison Balson (Nancy), Patrick Laborteaux (Andy Garvey), Ketty Lester (Hester Sue Terhune), Jason Bateman (James Cooper), Missy Francis (Cassandra Cooper).

Basis: A pioneering family (the Ingalls) and their struggles to establish a life for themselves on the harsh frontier of the 1870s.

OVERALL SERIES INFORMATION

Charles and Caroline Ingalls are the parents of Laura, Mary, Carrie, and Grace. Their fifth child, Charles Frederick, died of an illness as an infant. Charles and Caroline later adopt Albert Quinn, an orphan living off scams, and siblings James and Cassandra Cooper following their parents' death in a wagon accident.

Charles, Caroline, Mary, and Laura first live in Wisconsin's Big Woods but give up their "Little House" (as Laura called it) for a better life in Kansas when Charles is given 160 acres of land to homestead. It is 1868 (Grace is now a part of the family) when the government moves their boundaries to protect the land for the Kansas Indian tribe, and the family must move. They journey north and establish a home in Plum Creek near the town of Walnut Grove in Minnesota. Their first crop (wheat) is destroyed by a hailstorm.

With Walnut Grove falling into ruin, Charles moves to Winoka, Dakota Territory. He secures a job as the manager of the Dakota Hotel while Caroline becomes head of the kitchen and dining room (each earning $45 a month). When he feels uncomfortable, he returns to Plum Creek and organizes its citizens to restore the town.

Charles first met Caroline Holbrook when his family purchased the former Barton Place farm in the Big Woods and the two families became neighbors. They were both 12 years old at the time and attended the Big Woods School (later Concord College, Class of 1856). Caroline first mentions that she fell in love with Charles when he gave her cornflowers picked from a field ("I fell in love with him at that moment"). She later states that the gift was a necklace made out of seeds from a plant called Job's Tears.

CHARLES PHILIP INGALLS

Parents: Lansford (Arthur Hill) and Laura Colby Ingalls (Jan Sterling).
Siblings: Brother, Peter Ingalls (David Considine, then Mark Lenard); sisters, Amelia Ingalls (Carlena Gower) and Molly Ingalls (Robin Muir).
Place of Birth: Wisconsin's Big Woods.
Birthday: January 10, 1835.
Musical Ability: The fiddle and harmonica.

Laura's Nickname for Charles: "Pa." She calls Caroline "Ma."

Occupation: Farmer (estimates that his 160-acre farm is worth $100; he also works for the Hanson Lumber Company and later owns a lumber mill and freight-hauling business).

Work Horses: Patty (also called "Pat") and David.

Trait: A man of his word. Always believes in telling the truth.

Membership: The Grange Association.

Relaxation: Smoking a pipe.

Skill: Making elegant furniture (worked in Minneapolis at Sven's Furniture-Guns). On each table he created, he carved the initials "CI" (for "Charles Ingalls").

Affliction: Damp weather causes Charles's left leg to stiffen up.

Flashbacks: Young Charles (Mathew Laborteaux); young Lansford (Nicholas Coster).

CAROLINE INGALLS

Parents: Frederick (Barry Sulivan) and Charlotte Holbrook (Virginia Kiser).

Siblings: Eliza Holbrook (Kristi Jill Wood, then Hersha Parady; she later married Charles's brother, Peter Ingalls); brother, Henry Holbrook (Gregg Forrest).

Place of Birth: Wisconsin's Big Woods.

Year of Birth: 1835.

Maiden Name: First given as Caroline Holbrook, then Caroline Kleiner.

Trait: Does what is necessary to provide for her family (like trading eggs for necessities at the general store). She is a woman of strong Christian beliefs and fiercely dedicated to her children. Caroline also has an uncontrollable desire to help people in dire situations.

Occupation: Housewife. Caroline mentions that she was a teacher but not where. She was then a cook/waitress in Nellie's Restaurant and Hotel (later known as Caroline's Restaurant and Hotel).

Ability: Crocheting and sewing (makes her and her daughters' clothes).

Flashbacks: Young Caroline (Katy Kurtzman).

LAURA ELIZABETH INGALLS

Year of Birth: 1867.

Place of Birth: Wisconsin's Big Woods.

Character: Laura, the second-born child, was originally a tomboy and shared a special bond with her father. She showed little interest in schoolwork as a child and preferred to do boy things like fishing (which she claims is her expertise). She also keeps what she calls her "Remembrance Book," wherein she records her experiences.

Ambition: To become a teacher. When Laura wins a writing contest held by the Broxton Publishing Company of Minneapolis, her entry *Little House in the Big*

Woods (based on her childhood memories) wins and is about to be published when Laura, dissatisfied over editorial changes, rejects the prize. This episode, "Once upon a Time" encompasses a unique ending. The scene dissolves from Laura's time to the modern day where a young girl (Shawna Landon) is seen in a library and scanning the books on a shelf. As she spots the one she is seeking, the camera moves in for a close-up of the title: *Little House on the Prairie* by Laura Ingalls Wilder (published 40 years after that story won).

Pets: Jack, then Bandit (dogs); Jasper (raccoon); Bunny (horse); Fred (billy goat); Rosebud (milk cow).

Favorite Perfume: Lemon Verbena.

Quirk: Going to the mountaintop to pray (believed that her prayers would be closer to God).

Education: The Plum Creek School (Walnut Grove); the Livery School (Dakota).

Charles's Nickname for Laura: "Half Pint."

Occupation: Teacher at the Plum Creek School (considered very strict and a tough grader). Laura is actually the school's third teacher. Eva Beadle (Charlotte Stewart) was the first teacher; she was replaced by Eliza Jane Wilder (Lucy Lee Flippen), and Laura replaced her when Eliza Jane married Harve Miller (James Cromwell) and left town.

First Love: Schoolmate Johnny Johnson (Mitch Vogel), whom Laura felt was not interested in her because she had not yet developed her breasts (what she called "bumps"; she attempted to fix the problem by placing two apples in her dress, but after embarrassing herself [the "bumps" slipping out of place], she realized that being herself was the key to impressing him).

Husband: Almanzo Wilder, Eliza Jane's younger brother. Almanzo, older than Laura, works at the Walnut Grove Feed and Grain supply store (he and Charles later establish Ingalls and Wilder, a freight-hauling business). In real life, Almanzo Wilder had a sister named Laura. To make it clear that when Almanzo mentioned Laura (meaning his wife), he would call her "Beth" (as a nickname for her middle name, "Elizabeth").

Child: Rose. In real life, Laura had two children: Rose and an unnamed boy who died 12 days after birth (she and Almanzo were undecided on a name at the time). Rose married, divorced, and then remained single in real life.

Relatives: Almanzo's brother, Perley Wilder (Charles Bloom).

MARY INGALLS

Birthday: January 10, 1865 (same day as her father).

Place of Birth: Wisconsin's Big Woods.

Character: Mary, the firstborn child, was more of a lady (feminine and gentle) compared to Laura when first introduced. She is closer to her mother than her father and helps her mother care for her sisters. Mary was also held hostage by the notorious outlaws, Frank and Jesse James, when they sought refuge in Walnut Grove.

Affliction: Lost her sight at the age of 15 due to a prior bout with scarlet fever.

Education: The Plum Creek School. After her loss of sight, she attended the Burton School for the Blind in Burton, Iowa. Here, she learned to adjust to her situation and befriended her blind teacher, Adam Kendall (later to become her husband and with whom she had a child named Adam Charles Kendall).

Occupation: Schoolteacher. Mary first taught at the Willow Ferry School in Whisper County (earning $15 a month). She also worked for three weeks (at 50 cents a week) at the general store to help pay for barn repairs. After marriage, Mary joined Adam as a teacher at the Winoka Academy for the Blind. When the building is sold and the school closed, they establish their own school in Walnut Grove at the Harriet Oleson Institute for the Advancement of Blind Children. Tragedy strikes when Charles's son Albert, secretly smoking a pipe in the school's cellar, causes a fire that claims the life of Mary's infant son, Adam Jr., and the wife (Alice) of Charles's friend Jonathan Garvey. The school is rebuilt by Adam's father as the Alice Garvey-Adam Kendall Jr. School for the Blind. It is also called the Sleepy Eye School when Mary and Adam relocate to the town of Sleepy Eye. Adam was previously awarded the Louis Braille Award for Excellence in teaching the blind.

Adam's Miracle: Adam was blinded as a child during a fishing trip when he slipped on rocks attempting to cross a stream. He hit his head, causing severe trauma and eventual blindness. Years later, Adam accidentally knocks over a box of nitroglycerin while searching for Braille books in Jonathan Garvey's freight house. The ensuing explosion restores Adam's sight when he recovers from a concussion. With an interest in the law, Adam enrolls in a Missouri law school to acquire his license. He graduates in the top 1 percent of his class and establishes a practice in Walnut Grove (Adam Kendall, Attorney-at-Law) with Mary becoming his secretary. With few clients, Adam feels he cannot make a living in Walnut Grove, and he and Mary move to New York City to join his father's law firm. In real life, the Adam Kendall character never existed, and Mary never married or had children.

Mary's Favorite Book: Paradise Lost by John Milton.

Relatives: Adam's estranged father, Giles Kendall (Philip Abbott).

CARRIE AND GRACE INGALLS

Carrie was the youngest daughter (born in Wisconsin) until the birth of Grace (in Walnut Grove). In real life, Carrie married and raised two stepchildren; Grace married but had no children. Carrie had a pet turkey she called "Tom."

ISAIAH EDWARDS

Commonly called "Mr. Edwards," he is the mountain man the Ingalls family befriended as they journeyed west. He became Charles's best friend and partner in a lumber mill. He is married to Grace Snider (Bonnie Bartlett, then Corinne Michaels) and the father of John (Radames Pera), Alicia (Kyle Richards), and Carl (Brian Part).

THE OLESON FAMILY

Parents: Nels and Harriet.

Children: Nellie and Willie.

Character Information: Nels and Harriet are owners of the town's general store, Oleson's Mercantile (the store's icehouse served as the jail). Harriet is also a reporter for the town newspaper, *The Pen and the Plow* (she writes the "Harriet's Happenings" column), and was the first to bring the telephone to the town through a franchise she purchased.

Nellie and Willie attend the Plum Creek School. Nellie, while very pretty, is rather nasty (Harriet calls her "mean, spoiled, and conniving"), while Willie is very mischievous. Nellie relishes the fact that her family is wealthy and continually brags about having the best of everything (much to Harriet's delight but Nels's chagrin).

Harriet tried to reform Nellie by giving her the responsibility of running the restaurant section of the store (called Nellie's Restaurant; it later became Nellie's Restaurant and Hotel, run by Harriet, when Nellie fell in love with [and married] Percival Cohen [Steve Tracy], a Jewish accountant. This especially upset Harriet, as she is Protestant). Nellie and Percival became the parents of twins (Jenny and Benny) and moved to New York to help Percival's mother ("Mama Kelly") run the family business (hotel and store) after the death of his father ("Papa Kelly"). It is at this time that Caroline Ingalls becomes the owner and changes the name to Caroline's Restaurant and Hotel (with help from Hester Sue, the former teaching assistant to Adam and Mary).

Without Nellie, Harriet fell into a state of depression until she and Nels adopted a girl (from the county orphanage) named Nancy, a pretty Nellie look-alike who was twice as obnoxious, selfish, and mean. Willie also settled down and married Rachel Brown (Sherri Stoner). Ann Hall appeared as Harriet's cousin Miriam.

OTHER CHARACTERS

Jonathan Garvey, married to Alice and the father of Andy, is Charles's friend. He and Charles began a freight-hauling business, but after the death of Alice,

Jonathan moved to Sleepy Eye to start a receiving-and-shipping business called Garvey's Freight.

The Reverend Robert Alden (Dabbs Greer) preaches at the Community Church of Walnut Grove; Ebenezer Sprague (Ted Gerhring) is the banker; Lars Hansen (Karl Swenson) founded Walnut Grove 50 years ago and owns the lumber mill; and Hiram Baker (Kevin Hagen) is the town doctor.

SPIN-OFF
Little House: A New Beginning (NBC, 1982–1983). Charles, unable to make a living in Plum Creek, sells his "Little House" to John and Sarah Carter (Stan Ivar, Pamela Roylance), the parents of Jeb (Lindsay Kennedy) and Jason (David Friedman). Charles, Caroline, Carrie, and Grace move to Fir Oak, Iowa (where Charles is said to have acquired a job in "a fine men's store"). John is a blacksmith, and Sarah becomes the editor of the town newspaper, the Walnut Grove *Gazette*. Laura relinquishes her job as a schoolteacher to care for Rose, while Almanzo and Mr. Edwards, their friend, run a lumber mill started by Charles. When Almanzo's widowed brother, Royal Wilder (Nicholas Pryor), dies from a heart attack, Laura and Almanzo take on the responsibility of raising his daughter, Jenny. Etta Plumb (Leslie Landon) becomes the new schoolteacher. Laura and Almanzo later establish their own business, the Wilder Boardinghouse.

UPDATES
Little House: Look Back to Yesterday (1983) reveals that Charles had become a purchasing agent for J.R. Bennett and Company in Iowa and that Albert, who hopes to become a doctor, had been diagnosed with an incurable disease.

Little House: The Last Farewell (1984) finds the citizens of Walnut Grove uniting to protect their homes from Nathan Lassiter (James Karen), an unscrupulous mining engineer seeking to buy their land. In the closing scene, the town is destroyed by dynamite, but two buildings remain standing: the church and the schoolhouse.

Little House: Bless All the Children (1984) is set during the Christmas season of 1896 and deals with Laura and Almanzo's efforts to find their daughter Rose, who has disappeared and whom Laura fears has been kidnapped.

Note: The NBC series is based (loosely) on the *Little House* books by Laura Ingalls Wilder. Laura was born in a log cabin on the edge of the Big Woods in 1867 and based her stories on her travels with her family by covered wagon through Kansas, Minnesota, and the Dakota Territory. The books were first published in 1935 when Laura was 68 years old (she passed away in 1957 at the age of 90).

Little House on the Prairie is a 2005 ABC series that closely follows the books and presents a very harsh look at the life of the pioneering Ingalls family. Joining Charles (Cameron Bancroft) are his wife, Caroline (Erin Cottrell); their two young daughters, Laura (Kyle Chavarria) and Mary (Danielle Ryan Chuchran); and Laura's dog, Jack. The one stranger they meet and befriend, Mr. Edwards (Gregory Sporlander), becomes their neighbor. The Indians, the intense heat, the bitter cold, the wildfires, and the struggle for survival are realistically portrayed and captivating.

CBS presented two TV movies based more realistically on Laura's life: *Beyond the Prairie: The True Story of Laura Ingalls Wilder* (2000) and *Beyond the Prairie II: The True Story of Laura Ingalls Wilder* (2002). The first story introduces Laura Ingalls (Alandra Bingham, Meredith Monroe, and Tess Harper) as a teenager living on the South Dakota prairie with her father, Charles (Richard Thomas); mother, Caroline (Lindsay Crouse); and sisters, Mary (Barbara Jane Reams), Grace (Courtnie Bull and Lyndee Probst), and Carrie (Haley McCormick). The sequel follows Laura (Meredith Monroe); her husband, Almanzo Wilder (Walt Goggins); and their daughter, Rose (Skye McCole Bartusiak), as they move to Missouri to begin an apple farm.

Lou Grant
(CBS, 1977–1982)

Cast: Edward Asner (Lou Grant), Linda Kelsey (Billie Newman), Robert Walden (Joe Rossi), Daryl Anderson (Animal), Mason Adams (Charlie Hume), Nancy Marchand (Margaret Pynchon), Jack Bannon (Art Donovan).

Basis: Dramatic spin-off from a sitcom (*The Mary Tyler Moore Show*) about a former newsman turned TV producer (Lou Grant) who reestablishes himself as a newsman after a 10-year absence. Lou's trivia information from *The Mary Tyler Moore Show* has been included here.

OVERALL SERIES INFORMATION

The newsroom setting first showed staff members using typewriters, then switching to video display terminals (brand name unreadable).

The Los Angeles *Tribune* (offices on the fourth floor of an unidentified office building) sells for 25 cents a copy and has a circulation of 404,000. In the first-season opening theme, a bird chirps while a tree is cut down (to be made into paper), and a paper boy is seen delivering the *Tribune* to homes: one is thrown and lands in muddy water, another finds its way to a roof, and one becomes the bottom cage liner for a canary. From the second season on, the opening visuals change to reflect the cast members in the newsroom. "A Free Society

Needs a Free Press" is the *Tribune's* slogan. The paper was established in 1916, and Mrs. Pynchon, the paper's owner, angered readers when she decided to no longer run the *Little Orphan Annie* comic strip.

Flo Meredith (Eileen Heckart), a respected newspaper reporter (Mary Richards's aunt on *The Mary Tyler Moore Show*), was the only character from that series to appear on *Lou Grant*. Lou resented Flo for her remarks that he had given up reporting to become a TV producer; her opinion changed somewhat when she congratulated him on returning to his roots (although she believed the *Tribune*, which was the second-largest paper in Los Angeles, was not the most respected publication). Strange as it may sound, the newspaper staff members make bets about when an earthquake will strike and its magnitude.

While all sources state that *Lou Grant* "is the only dramatic series in American TV history to originate from a comedy series," this may be incorrect. *Trapper John, M.D.* was also a dramatic spin-off, but controversy exists from where: the TV series or the feature film *M*A*S*H*.

LOUIS "LOU" GRANT

Place of Birth: Goshen, Michigan. He spent his summers on a farm where his duties included disposing of rats caught in traps.

Year of Birth: 1927 (50 years old when the series begins).

Parents: John Simpson Grant (1887–1956) and Helen Hammersmith Grant (1890–1961). John was an office supplies salesman.

Religion: Episcopalian.

Height: 5 feet, 9 inches tall.

Occupation: City editor of the Los Angeles *Tribune*. Lou first worked as a delivery boy for the Goshen *Leader* (which sold for five cents a copy). He later became the editor of that paper, then the Detroit *Free Press*. In San Francisco, he worked as a reporter (with Charlie Hume) on *The Bulletin*. After an illustrious career, he ventured into television news, where he became the producer of *The Six O'Clock News* on WJM-TV, Channel 12, in Minneapolis (mentioned on *Lou Grant* as beginning in 1967 and on *The Mary Tyler Moore Show* as beginning in 1961). When new management took over WJM-TV in 1977, Lou was dismissed and returned to the newspaper game, where he joined the staff of the Los Angeles *Tribune* as its city editor (and reuniting with Charlie Hume, the managing editor, who convinced Lou to join the staff). Lou saw his first copy of the *Tribune* in a street vending machine with the headline "Energy Shortage Critical." The first story Lou covered was a sex scandal involving an underage girl.

Marital Status: Divorced (from Edie due, in part, to his lack of affection; role played by Priscilla Morrill). Edie, who is Ukrainian, and Lou were married for 23 years.

First Romantic Interest: High school girlfriend Carol (Georganne Johnson), a Catholic (disliked by Lou's parents due to her religion), who Lou considered marrying.

Children: Janie (Nora Heflin, then Barbara Dirickson), Ellen, and Sarah. Ellen (Ann Sweeny) is married to Burt Peters (Robert Pine) and the mother of Nick (Meeno Peluce). They live in Phoenix, Arizona. Janie is single and lives in Chicago; Sarah is not seen.

First Car: 1934 Plymouth (purchased with the help of his aunt).

Education: Goshen High School (a member of the Hornets football team. On *The Mary Tyler Moore Show* episodes, a picture of Lou in his Hornets uniform can be seen on his office wall).

Weight: Lou mentions he lost 40 pounds since moving to Los Angeles.

Residence: A home at Silver Lake.

Bank Account Balance (1977): $280.

Favorite Los Angeles Eateries: Tamales (Mexican) and Mario's Tracatoria (Italian).

Bar/Restaurant Hangout: McKenna's (Los Angeles), the Happy Hour Bar (Minneapolis).

Dream: To open a bar and call it Lou's Place. In Minneapolis episodes, Lou was depicted as having a slight addiction to alcohol, as it was apparently the only way he could cope with a dead-end job. The drinking aspect is virtually ignored on the spin-off. He also disliked having kids in the newsroom because he can't "cuss" (as he says).

Medical Condition: Diagnosed with thyroid cancer in 1978 (successfully removed following an operation).

Military Service: Master sergeant in the army during World War II. Later, when Lou mentions he has written an unpublished novel about his army experiences in Iwo Jima and Guadalcanal, he refers to the year as 1958.

Favorite Actor: John Wayne.

Unusual Activities: Has what he calls his "Christmas list" (writes down the names of people who annoy him); uses a police scanner to monitor crimes.

Dislikes: Waiting in line for anyone or anything; injustice. He did serve several hours in jail for disorderly conduct in a courtroom and was arrested for driving drunk (his blood alcohol level of 0.12 percent exceeded the allowable 0.10 percent).

Relatives: Cousin, Connie (not seen); aunt, Jane Howell Grant (1890–1961).

OTHER CHARACTERS

Information on staff members of the *Tribune* is very limited to just passing remarks during episodes.

Billie Newman, a Metro reporter, was born in Bismarck, North Dakota (although she mentions Rapid City, South Dakota, as her hometown in another episode). She is the daughter of Betty (Allyn Ann McLerie) and Paul Newman (Marshall Thompson. Slight comedy stems from the fact that Paul doesn't realize he has the name of a famous actor). Billie is divorced (since 1970) from Greg Serantino (Vincent Baggetta), who left her for another woman (Jeanette). She later (1982) marries Ted McCoviny (Cliff Potts), a scout who recruits new players for Major League Baseball teams. Billie, a vegetarian, had an older brother who was stillborn at seven months (it is mentioned that during her pregnancy, Betty took DES, a drug that is now known to cause cancer).

Billie replaced Carla Mardigian (Rebecca Balding), a general assignment reporter, in the fourth episode. In the fifth-season episode "The Wedding," Billie's official name is given as Billie Victoria Newman.

Margaret Pynchon, the owner of the *Tribune*, is often called "Mrs. Pynchon" or "Mrs. P." She is a widow (Matthew, her late husband, previously operated the paper on behalf of its owner, Margaret's father). Due to their inability to have children, Margaret has sort of "adopted" one in the guise of her Yorkshire terrier, Barney (for whom she paid $30 as a puppy); she later has a Yorkie named Mac. Mrs. P. is not particularly fond of modern technology (even television) and writes her memos to her staff on napkins. In addition to the *Tribune* (where she started working as a copy girl; she took over ownership after the death of her husband in 1961), she also owns a chain of taco stands and 7,000 acres of land (through Matthew's holdings) that he purchased after World War II (before it was used for the internment of Japanese Americans). Matthew attended Whitman High School (where he set up a scholarship). Margaret's car license plate reads 7U 741, and after suffering a stroke, she is seen walking with a cane.

Margaret's relatives include her niece, Tiffany (Maureen McCormick), and her nephews, Freddy (Jerry Fogel), Fred Hill (Alan Fudge), and Colin (William Bogert). Her Uncle Roger and Elena, her housekeeper from El Salvador, are not seen.

Charles "Charlie" Hume has been a newspaperman all his life. He previously worked with Lou on the San Francisco *Bulletin* before becoming the managing editor of the Los Angeles *Tribune*. He is married to Marian (Peggy McKay) and the father of Joanie (Laurette Spang) and Tommy (David Hunt Stafford), who joined the Hare Krishnas. Charlie is also a member of the Western States News Conference, and he and Marian were married in Las Vegas. Charles Lane plays Charlie's 76-year-old father, Rupert Hume; W.K. Stratton is Scott Hume, Charlie's nephew; James Callahan is Charlie's brother, Steven Hume; and Bonnie Bartlett is Charlie's sister, Claire.

Joseph "Joe" Rossi is a general assignment reporter who often worked with Billie Newman. He was born in New Jersey but raised in California, where his father, Carmine, a recovering alcoholic, earned a living as a barber. His home phone number is 555-4711.

Dennis Price is an award-winning photographer whose appearance (a slob) earned him the nickname "Animal" (as he is mostly called). He was born in Tacoma, Washington; served with the army during the Vietnam War; and studied painting in Paris. He has a brother named Kenneth, who works as a lawyer in Tacoma. It is mentioned that Animal and Billie worked on a hit-and-run story together in 1976; this is a continuity problem, as Billie began working at the paper in 1977.

Arthur "Art" Donovan was born in Honolulu, Hawaii, and worked as a wire service reporter for AP (Associated Press) before the *Tribune*. He temporarily left the *Tribune* to work as the campaign manager of a female senator in 1972. Geraldine Fitzgerald played his mother, Peggy (suffering from leukemia; his father died of emphysema); Barbara Barrie was his aunt, Edna, and Bruce Davison his cousin, Andrew.

The Love Boat
(ABC, 1977–1986)

Cast: Gavin MacLeod (Merrill Stubing), Bernie Kopell (Adam Bricker), Ted Lange (Isaac Washington), Fred Grandy (Burl Smith), Lauren Tewes (Julie McCoy), Jill Whelan (Vicki Stubing), Patricia Klous (Judy McCoy), Ted McGinley (Ashley Covington-Evans).

Basis: Brief incidents in the lives of the passengers who book passage aboard a luxury cruise ship, the *Pacific Princess*, affectionately called the *Love Boat*.

OVERALL SERIES INFORMATION

The *Pacific Princess*, owned by the Pacific Cruise Lines, became the *Royal Princess* in honor of the program's 1,000th guest star, Lana Turner, on May 4, 1985. It has nine decks (such as the Promenade, the Fiesta, and the Aloha decks). Pirate Cove is the barroom (restrooms are called "Pirates" and "Damsels"); dinner is served in the Coral Room at 8 p.m.; entertainment dominates the Acapulco Room and the Terrace Lounge.

In 1985, the *Love Boat* Mermaids were added to spice up the cruise in song-and-dance numbers: Susie (Deborah Bartlett), Maria (Tori Breno), Amy (Teri Hatcher), Patti (Deborah Johnson), Sheila (Macarena), and June (Nancy Lynn Hammond).

CAPTAIN MERRILL STUBING

Father: Merrill Stubing Sr. (Phil Silvers).
Brothers: Milo and Marshall Stubing (Gavin MacLeod).
Year of Birth: 1931.

Place of Birth: Upstate New York.

Ex-Wife: Stacy Stubing Scoggstaad (Bonnie Franklin). In 1986, Merrill marries Emily Haywood (Marion Ross), a wealthy widow who becomes the special events director.

Daughter: Vicki (by Stacy).

Cabin: Not numbered, but "Captain Merrill Stubing" is seen on his door.

Character: Merrill served in the navy and has captained several cruise ships over the years; he considers his current position as the best job of his career. He is never seen on the bridge, as he is more involved with the lives of his passengers. He is relaxed and married in a way to the sea, and it is mentioned that he wears a size 16 shirt collar.

Relatives: Uncle, Cyrus Foster (Red Buttons); aunt, Hilly (Olivia de Havilland); nephew, L. Courtney Stubing IV (Peter Isacksen).

BURL "GOPHER" SMITH

Parents: Rosie (Ethel Merman) and Elliott Smith (Bob Cummings), a former show business couple.

Sister: Jennifer Smith (Melissa Sue Anderson). She was nicknamed "Chubs" as a kid and is now attending Oakland State College.

Place of Birth: Oakland, California.

Date of Birth: June 29, 1948.

Occupation: Assistant purser, then purser. He received the nickname "Gopher" for his dedication to the job. Politics fascinated Gopher, and he left to pursue a political career.

Education: Oakland State College, where he earned a degree in business and finance. He had been fascinated by the sea since he was a child and signed aboard the *Love Boat* to partially live a dream.

JULIE MCCOY

Parents: Father (Norman Fell), mother (Betty Garrett).

Occupation: Cruise director.

Place of Birth: Pennsylvania.

Year of Birth: 1953.

Sister: Judith "Judy" McCoy.

Residence: Crews quarters cabin C-125. She sets her clock radio alarm to ring at 7:30 a.m., and in high school Julie had the nickname "Monkey McCoy."

Quirk: Although pretty, Julie feels she is not as attractive as the female guests who book passage. She attempted to become a platinum blonde but returned to her natural strawberry blonde color after the dye turned her hair green.

Replacement: Judy McCoy, Julie's younger sister (born in Philadelphia in 1955), became the cruise director when Julie left to pursue a different career.

Relatives: Aunt, Sylvia (Carol Channing); cousin, Carter Randall (Richard Dean Anderson); Carter's wife, Muffy (Linda Blair).

ADAM BRICKER

Occupation: Ship's doctor. He was previously in private practice with an office on the Upper East Side of Manhattan.

Place of Birth: Manhattan in 1933.

Original Career Goal: At the age of 14, Adam set his mind on becoming a sports-writer (no mention is made as to what changed his mind).

Trait: Fancies himself as a ladies' man, although he has been married and divorced three times. He married Cheri Sullivan (Heidi Bohay), his fourth wife, in 1986.

Relatives: Ex-wives, Samantha (Juliet Prowse), Nancy (Elizabeth Ashley), and Elaine (Stephanie Beacham); ex–mother-in-law, Connie Carruthers (Cyd Charisse).

ISAAC WASHINGTON

Mother: Millie Washington (Pearl Bailey).

Occupation: Bartender.

Place of Birth: Chicago.

Education: While a high school was not named, he was called "Freight Train" as a member of the football team. He became a bartender to give him the resources to pursue his writing career. He penned the book *Pacific Passions* (about life on the *Love Boat*) and a science-fiction thriller called *Invasion from a Forgotten Galaxy*.

Crew Quarters Cabin: C-30.

Relatives: Aunt, Tanya (Isabel Sanford); uncle, Charles (Mel Stuart).

VICTORIA "VICKI" STUBING

Parents: Merrill and Stacy Stubing (divorced; it appears that Vicki is in Merrill's custody).

Position: Assistant cruise director.

Date of Birth: September 19, 1966.

Age: 11 years old. She resides in a cabin adjoining her father and calls him "Captain Merrill." It is hinted that Vicki receives tutoring as opposed to attending school.

Pet Frog: "Frog."

Trait: Unsure of herself. Vicki looks up to Julie for guidance as she progresses into womanhood (when she first signed on, Vicki believed she was unattractive and feared she would have small breasts).

ASHLEY COVINGTON-EVANS

Occupation: Photographer.

Character: The son of a wealthy society couple, Ashley, called "Ace," found enjoyment in romancing the ladies. When Gopher left, Ace was promoted to purser.

ABC PILOT FILMS

The Love Boat (1976). *The Crew:* Ted Hamilton, the captain (Thomas Allenford); Dr. Adam O'Neill (Dick Van Patten); Jeri Landers, the cruise director (Terri O'Mara); Gopher, the purser (Sandy Helberg); Isaac, the bartender (Theodore Wilson).

The Love Boat II (1977). *The Crew:* Thomas Madison, the captain (Quinn Redecker); Dr. Adam Bricker (Bernie Kopell); Sandy Summers, the cruise director (Diane Stillwell); Burl "Gopher" Smith, the purser (Fred Grandy); Isaac Washington, the bartender (Ted Lange).

UPDATES

The Love Boat: A Valentine Cruise (CBS, February 12, 1990). The *Love Boat* was now called the *Sky Princess.* Gavin MacLeod (Captain Merrill Stubing), Bernie Kopell (Dr. Adam Bricker), Ted Lange (Isaac Washington, now the chief purser), and Jill Whelan (Vicki Stubing, now a travel agent) repeated their roles. Kim Urlich (as Kelly Donaldson, a former English literature major, was the new cruise director). It was mentioned that Emily, Merrill's wife, had passed away.

The Love Boat: The Next Wave (UPN, 1998 series). The *Love Boat* is now a cruise ship named the *Sun Princess.* It is captained by James "Jim" Kennedy III (Robert Urich), a 48-year-old ex–navy man. Camille Hunter (Joan Severance) is the security chief, John Morgan (Corey Parker) is the ship's doctor, Suzanne Zimmerman (Stacey Travis) is the cruise director, Paolo Kaire (Randy Vasquez) is the bartender, Will Sanders (Phil Morris) is the purser, and Danny Kennedy (Kyle Howard) is Jim's son.

Mary Hartman, Mary Hartman

(Syndicated, 1976–1977)

Cast: Louise Lasser (Mary Hartman), Greg Mullavey (Tom Hartman), Claudia Lamb (Heather Hartman), Debralee Scott (Cathy Shumway), Dody Goodman (Martha Shumway), Phil Bruns (George Shumway), Mary Kay Place (Loretta Haggers), Graham Jarvis (Charlie Haggers).

Basis: Soap-opera spoof that focuses on Mary Hartman, a very pretty housewife and mother, and the daily incidents that disrupt her secluded but complicated life.

MARY HARTMAN

Parents: George and Martha Shumway.

Full Name: Mary Penelope "Penny" Hartman.

Maiden Name: Mary Shumway.

Birthday: April 8, 1945 (32 when the series begins). In real life, Louise Lasser was born on April 11, 1939.

Sister: Catherine "Cathy" Shumway.

Husband: Tom Hartman, an assembly line plant worker at the Fernwood Auto Plant.

Daughter: Heather Hartman.

Address: 343 Bratner Avenue in the Woodland Heights section of Fernwood, Ohio.

Education: Woodland Heights Elementary School; Fernwood High School.

Biggest Worry: The waxy yellow buildup on her kitchen floor. She often ponders the situation for hours on end, hoping to figure out a way to solve the problem.

Background: A typical girl who enjoyed playing with dolls and helping her mother around the house. She was good in school and planned to work with her father at the auto plant. Her life changed when she became a high school freshman and, at 14, immediately began a steady relationship with Tom (an 18-year-old senior). When Tom graduated and acquired a job at the auto plant, he continued to date the now 15-year-old Mary. They married two years later and moved in with her parents. She became pregnant and quickly settled into her dreary existence as a housewife.

Trait: Totally dependent on Tom and lives for the time they can spend together. She feels she is no longer attractive and rarely dresses to be alluring or sexy. She has created a shell around herself and believes she is not capable of being anything more than a housewife. She has sex with Tom only because she knows she will lose him if she doesn't.

Fear: Heather will not live up to her expectations and, strange as it sounds, fail to develop large breasts (she believes small breasts are not appealing to men); she doesn't seem to worry that Heather is a poor student in school. Even though 12-year-old Heather has not physically begun to develop, Mary bought her a first bra "to show her I have faith in her."

Quirks: Mary has become mesmerized by television soap operas (she believes the characters are real), lights up a cigarette from the filter tip end, and constantly talks and often rambles. When she gets upset, she says, "I need a glass of water."

Favorite Magazine: Woman's World.

First Traumatic Incident: The mass murder of the Lombardi family, their two goats, and eight chickens. The family lived on Mary June Street.

Second Traumatic Incident: Being held hostage by a killer in the Chinese laundry at 414½ Miler Road.

Third Traumatic Incident: Heather's kidnapping when it is leaned she witnessed the Lombardi family slayings and was kidnapped by the killer, Davy Jessup (Will Seltzer).

Real-Life Revelation: Discovering that Tom has been unfaithful but herself realizing that she has romantic feelings toward Dennis Foley (Bruce Solomon), a sergeant with the Fernwood Police Department.

Mary's Sister: Cathy, born on June 6, 1955, is 10 years younger than Mary (in real life Debralee Scott was born on April 2, 1953). She is very sexy and pretty but promiscuous. She is a graduate of Fernwood High School and is almost always unemployed (she held a job in a beauty parlor for a short time). Mary constantly worries about Cathy's numerous affairs and tries to be her guiding light, but with her real lack of experience with other men (Tom was her first everything) she is often puzzled at what to do.

Mary's Parents: George and Martha Shumway have been married for 36 years. They live (with Cathy) at 4309 Bratner Avenue, and George works alongside Tom at the auto plant. Also living with them is Martha's father, Raymond "Grandpa" Larkin (Victor Killian), a senile 83-year-old who is forever asking,

"Where's the peanut butter?" George and Tom are members of the Glorious
Guardians of Good fraternity.

Mary's Neighbors: Charlie and Loretta Haggers. They live at 345 Bratner Avenue,
and Charlie works with Tom and George. Loretta is an aspiring country-and-
western singer, very sweet and trusting, and much younger than Charlie (she is
22; Charlie is 43). The age difference is not a problem for Loretta, but Charlie,
who is also Loretta's manager, sees that younger men have eyes for his wife.

Loretta's Occupation: Singer at the Capri Lounge.

Pet Goldfish: Conway and Twitty (named after singer Conway Twitty).

First Recorded Song: "Baby Boy" (reflects Loretta's term of endearment for Charlie).

Final Episode: Mary left Tom for her lover, Sergeant Dennis Foley. George Shumway fell asleep on a conveyor belt and was dumped into a vat of Rustoleum.
Extensive plastic surgery changed the original George (Phil Bruns) into the
new George (Tab Hunter). Several months later, after being burned in a car
accident, surgery was again performed, and the old George (Bruns) reemerged.

When the series returned for its second season as *Forever Fernwood*, it
was life as usual but without Mary. Tom was now a single parent, and his
interactions with the people of Fernwood were depicted; these include Eleanor Major (Shelley Fabares), his romantic interest; Garth Gimble (Martin
Mull), the preacher; Mac Slattery (Dennis Burkley), the truck driver; Jerry
Hubbard (Fred Willard), Loretta's new manager; Barth Gimble (Martin
Mull), the local TV talk show host; and Annabelle Kearns (Renee Taylor),
the girl who believes she is Mary Hartman.

Producer Norman Lear explained that the series title is based on real
TV soap operas that often repeat lines. Dody Goodman is the voice in the
opening theme saying, "Mary Hartman, Mary Hartman."

SPIN-OFF

America 2-Night (Syndicated, 1978). Unable to raise the necessary funds to continue his local talk show in Ohio, Barth Gimble (Martin Mull) relocates to Alta
Coma, California, where he becomes the host of *America 2-Night* over U.B.S.
(the United Broadcasting System)—"The Network That Puts U before the B.S."
Jerry Hubbard (Fred Willard) is Barth's announcer; Happy Kyne (Frank DeVol)
is the leader of the show's orchestra, the Mirth Makers.

The Mary Tyler Moore Show
(CBS, 1970–1977)

Cast: Mary Tyler Moore (Mary Richards), Ed Asner (Lou Grant), Gavin
MacLeod (Murray Slaughter), Ted Knight (Ted Baxter), Valerie Harper

(Rhoda Morgenstern), Cloris Leachman (Phyllis Lindstrom), Lisa Gerritsen (Bess Lindstrom), Betty White (Sue Ann Nivens), Georgia Engel (Georgette Franklin).

Basis: After a breakup with her boyfriend (Bill), Mary Richards, a single, 30-year-old woman working as a secretary, leaves Manhattan to begin a new life as a television news producer in Minneapolis.

MARY RICHARDS

Parents: Walter (Bill Quinn) and Dotty Richards (Nanette Fabray). Walter is a doctor, and Dotty, a housewife, was first called "Marge."

Place of Birth: Roseburg, Minnesota. As a child, she attended Camp Sunshine (five years) and Camp Anwack (summer of 1950).

Year of Birth: 1940 (30 years old when the series begins).

Religion: Presbyterian.

Education: Leif Erickson High School (Class of 1959. She was a cheerleader and voted Most Popular Girl in School; in a later episode, she says she was not a cheerleader but a pom-pom girl); the University of Minnesota (for two years; she was a member of the Gamma Gamma Delta sorority; her alumni newsletter is called *The Gopher*).

IQ: 128.

Height: 5 feet, 7 inches tall.

Hair: Brunette.

Character: Sweet, trusting, and unable to tell a lie (causes inner conflict). She speaks her mind but becomes nervous and stammers. Mary keeps a complete record of everything she does and helps support her grandmother. She does volunteer work for the local YWCA (Young Women's Christian Association) and was a Big Sister to a delinquent teenage girl named Francie (Mackenzie Phillips).

Residence: A Victorian apartment house at 119 North Weatherly (Apartment D) in Minneapolis (four miles from her parents' home). In 1975, Mary moves to a new apartment (932), but the address is not given.

Monthly Rent: $125 (then $145, and finally $175 at the first address).

Occupation: Associate producer of *The Six O'Clock News* on WJM-TV, Channel 12 (later promoted to producer when her boss, Lou Grant, chose to make himself the executive producer). Mary also produces *The Sunday Show*, a weekend public affairs series that earned her a prestigious Television Editors Award (called the Teddie Award). Her first attempt at producing was a failed pilot called *Talk of the Town* (which she created with her friend Rhoda; she was also tempted to leave WJM for WKX-TV when she was offered the opportunity to produce her own series [*The Ladies Talk Show*] but declined when Lou gave her a much-needed raise). She also produced

"What's Your Sexual I.Q?," the most controversial special to air on WJM. Mary, who can type 65 words a minute, had originally applied for a job as a secretary, but the position was filled. Lou first mentions hiring Mary (at $10 a week less) for two reasons: he hates spunk (which Mary has), and she "has a nice caboose." He later mentions hiring her without TV experience because of a run in her stocking on her knee (her continual efforts to conceal it from him impressed him).

Salary: $280 a week. In 1969, Mary earned $8,000 a year as a secretary.

Favorite Drink: Vodka tonic.

Favorite Lunch: Chef's salad.

Favorite Movie: Gone with the Wind.

Least Favorite Color: Yellow.

Quirks: Makes chocolate chip cookies to impress guests; washes her hair before she goes to the hairdresser; fears that if she is in with a crowd of people and someone's stomach growls, people will think it is hers; buys a jar of asparagus tips once a year to see if she still hates them.

Plumbing Bill: $28.50 to unclog hair from the shower drain.

Exercise Routine: 100 run-in-place steps each day.

Shopping Routine: Does what she calls "weekend grocery shopping" on Friday.

Ford Mustang Car License Plate: 5FA 36H (as seen in the opening theme).

Apartment Decoration: A large plastic "M" on her wall.

Reputation: Throwing terrible parties. (As Lou says, "You give rotten parties. I've had some of the worst times of my life at your parties." It was at one of these parties that Lou broke up with his wife, Edie.) She is, however, the life of other people's parties.

Dating History: Mary estimates that in 20 years of dating, she has had 2,000 dates (based on her theory of two dates a week).

Nickname: Called "Mare" by Rhoda.

Jail Time: Mary is protective of her stories and spent time in jail (with two prostitutes) for refusing to reveal her sources.

Relatives: Aunt, Flo Meredith, a renowned journalist (Eileen Heckart).

Note: In 1977, Mary is fired and leaves Minneapolis. In a follow-up 2000 ABC-TV movie, *Mary and Rhoda*, it is learned that Mary is living in Manhattan, a recent widow and the mother of Rose (Joie Lenz), an English major at New York University. Her late husband, Steve Corwin, was a congressman who died in a rock-climbing accident. She lives at 415 84th Street and works as a segment producer for WNYT-TV, Channel 6.

LOUIS "LOU" GRANT

Mary's boss, the news producer (additional information can be found in the entry *Lou Grant*).

The Mary Tyler Moore Show. *CBS/Photofest. ©CBS*

Place of Birth: Goshen, Michigan. He spent his summers on a farm where his duties included disposing of rats caught in traps.

Year of Birth: 1927.

Parents: John Simpson Grant (1887–1956) and Helen Hammersmith Grant (1890–1961). John was an office supplies salesman.

Religion: Episcopalian.

Height: 5 feet, 9 inches tall.

THEODORE "TED" BAXTER

Father: Robert Baxter (Liam Dunn); he deserted Ted's unnamed mother 40 years ago.

Brother: Hal Baxter (Jack Cassidy), a male model and star of "The Cling Bag Man" TV commercials. As kids, Ted and Hal (who is two years younger than Ted) were in the same class in school (Ted being held back twice).

Residence: Apartment 1517 (address not given).

Occupation: Newscaster (anchorman) for the WJM-TV Channel 12 *Six O'Clock News.*

Salary: $31,000 a year; also mentioned as $750 a week.

Political Party: Republican.

Pet Dog: WJM (named after the station).

Trait: Incompetent. He has trouble pronouncing words (e.g., "Arkansas" becomes "Are-Kansas"), can't add numbers (unless a dollar sign is placed before them; he then becomes a computer), is very vain, and believes he is a ladies' man. Ted continually polishes his shoes because when his shoes shine, he shines; when his shoes are dull, he is dull. He is also very frugal and watches every cent he spends (e.g., he has hired a high school student to do his taxes [at $5 a year] and a prelaw student [at $2 an hour, plus two-cents-a-mile travel expenses] as his lawyer).

Hero: Newsman Walter Cronkite. He hopes to one day become an anchorman in New York City (his dream since a child).

Background: Information is limited to his constant rambling—"It all began at a 6,000-watt radio station in Fresno, California" (where he earned $65 a week). He later expands on this by saying that as a kid he listened to Lowell Thomas (a famous reporter and world traveler) on the radio and received his inspiration from him. He has a fake newspaper headline on his dressing room wall that reads "Ted Baxter Wins 3 Emmys" and is, on occasion, mistaken for CBS newsman Eric Sevareid (something Ted doesn't deny). Ted is in love with himself and believes he has many talents. He calls the station's control room the "Technical Place" and needs to read from cue cards (news writer Murray Slaughter calls them "idiot cards"). He once had an original idea for a TV series called *The Ted Baxter Show* (as Lou says, "He only submitted a title").

Coffee: Black with six sugars.

Favorite Disney Movie: Snow White.

Favorite Eatery: Antonio's Restaurant.

Contract: Nonexclusive, which allows Ted to work on other television projects (like commercials. Of all he did—for a tomato slicer, a woman's product, and a dog food product—only one was given a name: Ma and Pa's Country Sausage, where Ted was Farmer Ted, the spokesman). He also performs in plays at the Twin Cities Playhouse. He auditioned to become the host of a New York–based game show (*The $50,000 Steeplechase*) but elected to remain as a newsman in Minneapolis.

Business Venture: Ted Baxter's Famous Broadcasting School.

Award: The Teddie Award as "Best Newscaster."

Biggest Fear: Having to part with money.

Quirks: Ted likes to read other people's mail and has made it his goal to become a part of everyone's business. Plastic flowers bring back memories of Ted's childhood summers at the beach: "They smell just like my beach ball."

Ted's Program Closing: "Good night and good news."

The Birds and the Bees: Ted first mentions that he learned the facts of life on the street and later that he learned them from the book *God's Little Acre.*

Appearance Change: Believing that sporting a moustache would make him more distinguished, Ted grew one but soon encountered Lou's objections and eventually shaved it off when he learned that the audience reaction was negative.

Girlfriend, Then Wife: Georgette Franklin, a window dresser at Hemple's Department Store. Georgette is also said to have worked for a car rental agency and as an assistant to Rhoda at her plant store Rhodadendron.

Character: Shy, sweet and trusting, and very soft spoken. In a conversation with Rhoda, Mary mentions that she introduced Ted to Georgette; it is later seen that Ted meets Georgette in Mary's apartment at Rhoda's going-away party. Georgette is 5 feet, 6½ inches tall and with Ted hosted a failed variety pilot (*The Ted and Georgette Show*). Georgette later gives birth to a son in Mary's apartment (she goes into labor, but an ambulance arrives too late); they previously adopted a boy named David (Robbie Rist). Georgette married Ted in a plaid dress, as that was Ted's favorite color.

Ted's Prior Girlfriend: Betty Bowerchuck (Arlene Golonka), the daughter of WJM-TV personality Chuckles the Clown. The romance ended when Ted could not abide the idea that his prospective father-in-law was a clown.

RHODA MORGENSTERN

Relationship: Mary Richards's best friend and upstairs neighbor (additional information can be found in the entry *Rhoda*).

Sister: Debbie Morgenstern (Liberty Williams). Not seen are her sister Brenda and brother Arnold. Only Brenda became a part of the spin-off.

Age: 29 (when the series begins).

Address: 119 North Weatherly (an attic apartment).

Rent: $87.50 a month.

Occupation: Window dresser (later manager in charge of windows) at Hemple's Department Store. Rhoda mentions she also worked at Bloomfield's Department Store (but was fired) and turned down a job with Bloomingdale's in New York. Rhoda has a knack with plants and flowers and owned a floral shop called Rhodadendron.

Pageant Winner: Crowned "Ms. Hemple's Department Store."

Religion: Jewish.

Pet Goldfish: Goldie.

Relatives: Aunt Rose (Brett Somers).

MURRAY SLAUGHTER

Occupation: The station's lone news writer.

Quirks: Often complains about having to write for an idiot (Ted Baxter).

Note: He has an IQ of 125, earns $275 a week, and began his career as a news writer (and occasional newscaster) in radio. While Ted mostly approves of what Murray writes, he wishes he would include more statements about the president, as he likes to agree with what the president has to say.

Wife: Marie (Joyce Bulifant). They have been married since 1955 and are the parents of Bonnie (Sherry Hursey), Ellen (Tami Bula), and Laurie (Helen Hunt). After the birth of Laurie, Murray, who wanted a son, and Marie adopt a Vietnamese boy. Murray, the only staff member not to be nominated for a Teddie Award, hopes to become a playwright (his only attempt, *All Work and No Play* [about life in the newsroom], was performed by Ted at the Twin Cities Playhouse and received amazingly bad reviews). Doug Slaughter, Murray's father, was played by Lew Ayres.

OTHER CHARACTERS

Phyllis Lindstrom is first a tenant in Mary's apartment building, then its owner, and finally its manager (under the name Ellen P. Management). She later acquires a real estate license (working for Lakefield Realty) and became Mary's assistant when the news program expanded to an hour. She has been married to the never-seen Lars (a dermatologist) for 17 years and is the mother of a daughter named Bess.

Bess, an eighth grader, enjoys wearing outlandish makeup, calls her mother by her first name, and locks herself in the closet when she gets upset. She is best friends with Mary and calls her "Aunt Mary." Bess likes to drink milk from a German beer stein, and while she is a good artist, she can draw only flowers. Lars is a member of the Society of Concerned and Responsible Dermatologists, or SCARD (which Phyllis pronounces as "Scarred"). She claims that her greatest talent is "choosing the right wine for dinner." Robert Moore appeared as Phyllis's gay brother-in-law, Ben Lindstrom.

The Phyllis character was spun off into the series *Phyllis* (CBS, 1975–1977), wherein Phyllis and Bess begin new lives in San Francisco (they live at 4482 Bayview Drive, and Phyllis first works as an assistant to Julie Erskine at Erskine's Commercial Photography Studio, then as the administrative assistant to Dan Valenti of the San Francisco Board of Administration).

Sue Ann Nivens is the host of WJM-TV's *Happy Homemaker Show*. She has advice for everybody and has made it her goal to win Lou's affections (something he continually tries to avoid. She considers Lou "a big cuddly Teddy bear"). She dots her "i"s with little hearts and at six years of age won a baby beauty contest by impersonating Shirley Temple and singing the song "On the Good Ship Lollipop." She is very particular about everything and tries to implement her style onto everyone she knows (e.g., when packing her shoes for a trip, she places them "soles up for Heaven").

Sue Ann began her television career in Chicago with a cooking show called *Let's Talk about Meat*. She and Ted hosted *Talk of the Town*, an hour-long Sunday afternoon talk show pilot. She mentioned having a fast-food franchise called Sue Ann's Big Pink Bucket and was nominated as "Twin Cities TV Woman of the Year." When WJM cancels her show, Sue Ann works with Mary in the newsroom. Pat Priest appeared as her sister, Lila, the host of a TV cooking show in Georgia.

Note: The station's beloved performer, Chuckles the Clown (Mark Gordon, then Richard Schaal), suffered a horrible fate: while dressed as Peter Peanut (a character on his show) and serving as the grand marshal of a parade, a rogue elephant (Jocko) crushed him to death when it tried to shell him. Chuckles' credo was, "A little song, a little dance, a little seltzer down your pants."

In addition to *The Chuckles the Clown Show,* three other series are mentioned as running on WJM-TV: reruns of *My Mother the Car* (airs at 7 p.m. following the news), *Uncle Umbo, the Polka Prince,* and *The Uncle Bucky Show.*

In the final episode, Mary, Lou, and Murray are fired while Ted is kept on. The station's call letters, WJM, are the initials of the station owner, "Wild" Jack Monroe. Early episodes feature John Amos as Gordon "Gordy" Howard, the African American weatherman (a position taken over by Ted when Gordy left WJM to become a talk show host). Each episode normally ends with a cat meowing (spoofing the MGM movie logo of a lion roaring). In the episode "Put on a Happy Face," Mary is seen in place of the cat in the circular MTM logo doing her Porky Pig impression, "Th-Th-Th-That's all folks!"

*M*A*S*H*

(CBS, 1972–1983)

Cast: Alan Alda (Hawkeye Pierce), Wayne Rogers (Trapper John), Mike Farrell (B.J. Hunnicutt), Larry Linville (Frank Burns), Loretta Swit (Margaret Houlihan), McLean Stevenson (Henry Blake), Harry Morgan (Sherman Potter), Gary Burghoff (Radar O'Reilly), David Ogden Stiers (Charles Winchester), Jamie Farr (Maxwell Klinger), George Morgan, then William Christopher (Father Mulcahy).

Basis: Life during the Korean War as experienced by a group of army doctors and nurses attached to the 4077th, a Mobile Army Surgical Hospital (M*A*S*H).

OVERALL SERIES INFORMATION

During wartime, the medical corps fights for every life. Helicopters go right to the battlefields to return wounded soldiers to nearby M*A*S*H units (as roads are primitive and make ground travel by trucks very difficult). The 4077th is located five miles from the Korean War front in one of the most brutal climates on earth—unbearably hot in the summer, subzero temperatures in the winter.

The 4077th is anything but classy. Its doctors and nurses often operate under battle conditions, risking their lives to save others. In order to remain sane amid the insanities of war, the personnel act somewhat abnormally.

CAPTAIN BENJAMIN FRANKLIN PIERCE

Place of Birth: Crabapple Cove, Maine (in another episode, he mentions that his family home is in Vermont).

Father: Daniel Pierce (Robert Alda), a doctor in Crabapple Cove.

Nickname: "Hawkeye" (from the novel *The Last of the Mohicans.* "My father was crazy about that book"). He also named him after Benjamin Franklin.

Siblings: Questionable. Hawkeye first mentions he has a sister (unnamed), then in a later episode that he has no siblings. The same situation exists with his mother. He first says his mother passed away when he was a boy; he later mentions she is alive.

Dog Tag Number: 19095607.

Pay: $413.50 a month.

Position: Chief surgeon (called "the best cutter in the outfit" [certified in chest and general surgery]). He worked previously as a hospital surgeon before being drafted.

Trait: Totally opposed to the war and constantly defies authority. He will not carry a gun (even when he patrols as "officer of the day") and has a reputation as a nurse chaser. He thinks of himself as the "social director of the heart" for all the temporary relationships he has with nurses.

Tent Nickname: "The Swamp" (as he considers the unit a "cesspool").

Favorite Drink: Martini (which he makes from a still in his tent that he calls the "wellspring of life").

The Food: "We eat fish and liver day after day. I've eaten a river of liver and an ocean of fish." In civilian life, he ordered spareribs from Adam's Ribs (near Dearborn Station).

Misses Most: "A mattress thicker than a Matzo, my own bathroom and any woman out of uniform, and the entire state of Maine."

Favorite Magazine: The Joys of Nudity.

Film Role: Starred in the army documentary *Yankee Doodle Doctor* (as a wacky, Groucho Marx–like surgeon).

Relaxation: Collapses after a day of surgery and drinks. He also says, "At night I dream I'm awake." He also enjoys drinks at the local watering hole, Rosie's Bar.

CAPTAIN "TRAPPER" JOHN MCINTIRE

Occupation: Surgeon. He is also Hawkeye's tent mate.

Wife: Louise (but also called "Melanie").

Children: Becky and Cathy.

M*A*S*H. *CBS/Photofest. ©CBS*

Reputation: Called (by Hawkeye) "champion of the oppressed and molester of registered nurses."

Sport: A boxing champion in college. He now participates in the army's Inner Camp Boxing Tournaments as "Kid Doctor" (weighs in at 175 pounds).

Trait: Shares Hawkeye's love of playing practical jokes and chasing nurses. He would like to go AWOL (absent without leave) to see his wife and kids. When the locals need medical help, Trapper is the one they turn to.

Relaxation: Smoking cigars, drinking martinis, and playing poker with Hawkeye.

Favorite Magazines: Field and Stream and *Popular Mechanics.*

Film Role: Played a Harpo Marx–like surgeon in the *Yankee Doodle Doctor* army film.

Smuggling Operations: To help the nearby Sister Theresa's Orphanage, Trapper and Hawkeye "borrow" camp supplies for the children. As a kid, Hawkeye had an imaginary friend named Tuttle that he blamed for doing things that got him in trouble. To cover up their smuggling efforts, Hawkeye and Trapper say they are delivering supplies on orders from the nonexistent Captain Jonathan Tuttle.

The Good-Bye That Never Happened: Trapper and Hawkeye never had a chance to say good-bye (Hawkeye, returning from rest and relaxation in Tokyo with the "Mount Rushmore of hangovers," learns that Trapper was transferred stateside two hours earlier).

CAPTAIN B.J. HUNNICUTT

Occupation: Surgeon (replaced Trapper John to become Hawkeye's new tent mate).

Place of Birth: Mill Valley, California.

Wife: Peggy (May 23 is their wedding anniversary); Erin is their daughter.

Full Name: Never revealed; always called "B.J." Official army records list his first name as B.J. (B.J. does mention that his parents' names are Bea and Jay, thus his first name?).

Education: Stanford Medical School (top 10 in his class).

Award: The Bronze Star (saved a soldier under fire).

Trait: A clean-cut, even-tempered family man who is tempted by nurses but avoids their advances ("I'm hopelessly and passionately in love with my wife").

Relaxation: "Horseplay—taking your frustrations out on other people" (as B.J. says).

Nickname: Called "Beej" by Hawkeye.

Misses Most: The company of his wife and her cooking.

MAJOR FRANK BURNS

Wife: Louise (they have three unnamed daughters).

Occupation: Doctor (shares a tent with Hawkeye and B.J.). Hawkeye believes that Frank became a doctor for the money ("He married money and is crazy about money"). Frank claims that he became a doctor when his mother, who is "the guiding light of my life," asked him to (her picture is in a silver frame by his bed). Frank brags about his $35,000 house and two cars and keeps in touch with patients with his "What's Up Front Doc" letters.

Nickname: "Ferret Face" (which was given to Frank by his brother and which he let slip out when drinking with Hawkeye and Trapper John).

Fear: His wife will discover he is having an affair with Margaret Houlihan.

Favorite Dinner: Pork chops ("with extra fat").

Brokerage House: Sanders, Landers, and Flynn in New York City.

Misses Most: His country club and 30-foot yacht.

Goal: To expose Hawkeye for defying military rules (Hawkeye would like to see Frank transferred to another base—"preferably an enemy base").

MAJOR MARGARET HOULIHAN

Father: Lieutenant Colonel Alvin F. Houlihan (Andrew Duggan). Her mother, whom Alvin calls "Buttercup," is not seen.

Occupation: Head nurse. She has been a nurse for 10 years and has a spotless record.

Salary: $400 a month.

Nickname: "Hot Lips." While not explained in the TV series, the feature film on which the series is based (*M*A*S*H*) finds Margaret (Sally Kellerman) and Frank Burns (Robert Duvall) sharing a passionate moment, but both are unaware that a microphone has been placed under their cot and that what they are saying is being broadcast over the PA system. Margaret's words to Frank, "Oh Frank, my lips are hot. Kiss my lips," branded her with the nickname "Hot Lips."

Fault: A stickler for following the rules (makes her appear all-military and harsh; she often feels alienated because her nurses "never make me a part of their activities").

Hope: For the doctors and nurses to behave in a military manner (but they won't; "They're terribly unruly and undisciplined, and I thank God for each and every one of them when those casualties roll in").

Trait: Tries to be beautiful and alluring and uses her sex appeal to get her way; when the shelling starts, she becomes frightened ("I don't like being afraid; it scares me").

Misses Most: "The beauty parlor in Tokyo and a sense of order and discipline."

Most Treasures: Brushes her father gave her (she brushes her hair 100 times a night).

The Relationship: Margaret feels that Frank, whom she calls "Tiger," is not overly romantic. She becomes turned on when he flares his nostrils ("I get so excited") and knows that "he thinks of me as a bag of desirable bones, not a girl with a mind and a brain." Their relationship ended when Margaret married Major Donald Penobscott (Beeson Carroll, then Mike Henry), the man of her dreams. Frank suffered a nervous breakdown, was transferred to a hospital in Indiana, and was promoted to lieutenant colonel.

COLONEL HENRY BLAKE

Occupation: Doctor (and the first commander of the 4077th). In one episode, Henry mentions, "I left a growing practice and a wife with a fistful of credit cards at home."

Place of Birth: Bloomington, Illinois (he later says he is from the twin cities of central Illinois called Bloomington–Normal).

Wife: Lorraine (but also called "Mildred").

Children: Jane, Molly, and Andy. Only Molly was seen in a home movie.

Education: Illinois State University (he is often seen wearing a blue sweater with an orange "I" [the college colors] and drinking from a mug with the same colors).

Favorite Sport: Fishing (he is often seen wearing his green fishing cap).

Character: More like "one of the guys" as opposed to being a leader (e.g., he found Hawkeye's antics amusing). Although in charge, he was actually lost without the help of the company clerk (Radar). Henry tries to run a responsible medical unit, but his true lack of authority found him sending notices to various personnel, as nobody listened to him when he spoke. Although married, Henry tries to impress the nurses with stories about fishing. He believes that Frank "is the biggest horse's patootie on this post" and that "the only thing GI about him is athlete's foot."

The Farewell: Henry's joyous transfer stateside turns to sadness when the 4077th learns that his transport plane has been shot down over the Sea of Japan and there are no survivors. Frank becomes the temporary commanding officer and tries to introduce order and discipline "to make this a more enjoyable war for all of us."

COLONEL SHERMAN POTTER

Occupation: Doctor (replaced Henry as commander of the 4077th). He established a practice in 1932.

Place of Birth: Riverbend, Missouri (he later mentions he is from Hannibal, Missouri, then Nebraska).

Wife: Mildred (no relation of Henry Blake's wife), who calls him "Puddin' Head."

Career: At the age of 15, Sherman joined the cavalry (lied about his age). He fought in World War I, then World War II (stationed in England), and now the Korean War.

Favorite Animal: Horses (he had one at the 4077th called "Sophie." When the war ended, he gave Sophie to the Sister Teresa's Orphanage, as he couldn't take her home).

Favorite Movie Star: Doris Day.

Safe Combination: 43-36-42 (mentioned as being his wife's measurements).

Character: Sherman finds Hawkeye's antics a rule violation but realizes why he is doing it and never punishes him. He paints pictures of horses (seen on his office wall) by sitting on a saddle and wearing a cowboy hat. He shares drinks with Hawkeye and B.J., wears a Hawaiian shirt when he relaxes, and considers his troops at the 4077th "the best group of people I ever worked with." Harry Morgan originally played General Bartford Hamilton Steele, a spit-and-polish officer in the episode "The General Flipped at Dawn."

Note: The picture of Sherman's wife on his desk is Harry Morgan's real wife, Eileen.

CORPORAL WALTER EUGENE O'REILLY

Occupation: Farmer; he was drafted and is now the company clerk.

Place of Birth: Iowa.

Nickname: "Radar" (for his ability to perceive what others think).

Serial Number: 3911880.

Security Blanket: His teddy bear (never given a name).

Favorite Drink: Grape Nehi.

Pets: Daisy (mouse), Fluffy and Bingo (rabbits), and Bongo, Babette, Mannie, Moe, and Jack (guinea pigs).

Character: Writes the announcements heard over the PA system and manages to acquire items without the hassle of red tape (through bartering) over the shortwave radio with his contact Sparky. When Henry Blake is out of his office, Radar smokes his cigars and drinks his brandy. He also sent a Jeep home piece by piece through the mail.

Childhood: As a kid, Radar had an imaginary friend named Shirley.

Hobby: Peeking through the hole in the nurses' shower tent.

The Farewell: Radar received a hardship discharge when his Uncle Ed died and he became his family's sole support. He left behind his cherished possession, his teddy bear (which he placed on Hawkeye's bed). In a follow-up letter, we learn that Walter O'Reilly, gentleman farmer, also works in the local general store to pay the bills.

Note: Gary Burghoff plays Radar's mother when Radar's home movies are shown.

MAJOR CHARLES WINCHESTER III

Occupation: Surgeon. Frank's replacement and Hawkeye and B.J.'s new tent mate. He was working at Tokyo General Hospital before his transfer to the 4077th.

Place of Birth: Boston.

Education: Harvard Medical School.

Favorite Music: Classical (especially fond of composer Gustav Mahler).

Favorite Drink: Wine.

Favorite Newspaper: The Boston *Globe* (sent to him by his sister).

Nickname: "Major Windbag" (as called by Margaret, for he constantly talks about himself). His middle name is Emerson.

Character: Pompous. He believes that he is an extraordinary surgeon, but "the meatball surgery that is performed in the OR is causing my skills to deteriorate; they're wasting away." He is a gourmet and says that "breakfast at the 4077 makes you look forward to lunch." He sends tape-recorded "letters" to his parents and says that "classical music reminds me that there is still some grace and culture in the world." He carries a picture of himself dining with actress Audrey Hepburn in his wallet. He met her, a friend of the family, at a luncheon but had never seen any of her films.

MAXWELL KLINGER

Rank: First a corporal, then a sergeant (replacing Radar as the company clerk).

Heritage: Lebanese American.

Middle Initial: Q (what it stands for is not revealed).

Place of Birth: Toledo, Ohio.

Favorite Home Town Restaurant: Tony Packo's.

Favorite Baseball Team: The Toledo Mud Hens.

Character: Seeks a Section 8 psychiatric discharge and pretends to be insane (he is called the company's "resident loon"). He dresses in women's clothes, hoping to convince his superiors "that I'm nuts." He patrols in a skirt, wore a special Carmen Miranda dress for Henry Blake's farewell, and purchases his gowns from Mr. Syd of Toledo. He calls the trucks that bring in the wounded the "bad humor trucks" and "hates the damned army, but I love these people." He doesn't relax ("If I do, someone will think I like it here").

Side Job: Prints the camp newsletter, *M*A*S*H Notes* ($2 monthly subscription fee; 10 cents newsstand price per issue), and writes the advice column "Dear Aunt Sadie" (Margaret writes "About Faces," a beauty column).

Final Episode: Klinger marries Soon-Lee (Rosalind Chao), a migrant farmworker. Prior to this, Maxwell married his childhood sweetheart, Laverne Esposito (by shortwave radio), while he was in Korea and she was stateside in Toledo (it is assumed that they later divorced). Both ceremonies were performed by Father Mulcahy.

FATHER FRANCIS MULCAHY

Occupation: The unit's chaplain (first a lieutenant, then a captain).

Character: Raises money for the Sister Theresa Orphanage and finds his faith in God challenged every day by the horrors he sees. He relaxes by playing poker ("Shearing the flock," as he says); all his winnings go to help Korean children. He mentioned that the only thing he will miss after the war "is the Korean children and all their smiles." He suffered a hearing loss from an explosion while evacuating prisoners of war.

Note: First-season episodes feature Spearchucker Jones (Timothy Brown), a doctor who worked with Hawkeye and Trapper John. When the show's producers learned that African American surgeons did not serve in Korea at the time, he was dropped.

Gary Burghoff, Jamie Farr, Todd Susman, and Sal Viscuso are the voices heard over the unit's PA system.

Visiting generals call the 4077th "a nut house, a mad house." The unit is nearest to Kimpo Airfield in Seoul. Rosie's Bar is the local watering hole (where Klinger sometimes works as a bartender). There is a signpost on the grounds with arrows pointing to Coney Island, San Francisco, Tokyo, and Burbank. When Margaret decided to make a time capsule "so future generations will know we were here," Hawkeye contributed Radar's teddy bear; Charles, a bottle of cognac; Klinger, the Scarlett O'Hara dress he wore (from the film *Gone with the Wind*); and B.J., a broken helicopter fan belt. Fox Movietone News did a documentary on the 4077th on October 9, 1952.

While the TV series ran for 11 years, the Korean War lasted only three years.

SPIN-OFFS
Sherman Potter, Maxwell Klinger, and Father Mulcahy reunite in the 1983–1984 CBS series *After-M*A*S*H*. With the war ended, Potter returns to his hometown to become the chief of staff of the General Pershing VA Hospital with Klinger and Father Mulcahy assisting him. Rosalind Chao is Klinger's wife, Soon-Lee, and Barbara Townsend (then Anne Pitoniak) is Sherman's wife Mildred.

In the 1984 CBS unsold pilot *W*A*L*T*E*R*, Gary Burghoff reprises his role as Walter "Radar" O'Reilly in an attempt to feature the character as a police officer.

The 1979 CBS series *Trapper John, M.D.* features Pernell Roberts as a doctor at San Francisco Memorial Hospital. Controversy exists as to whether this dramatic spin-off from a comedy is from the TV series or the movie version of *M*A*S*H*. *Lou Grant* is considered to be the only drama that evolved from a sitcom (*The Mary Tyler Moore Show*).

Matt Helm
(ABC, 1975–1976)

Cast: Anthony Franciosa (Matt Helm), Laraine Stephens (Claire Kronski), Jeff Donnell (Ethel).

Basis: A former government intelligence agent (Matt Helm) turned private detective uses his training as a spy to solve complex crimes.

MATTHEW "MATT" HELM
Former Organization: The Company.
Partner at the Time: Karen Ashley (played by Marlyn Mason).
Business: Matt Helm Private Investigations.
Business Address: 11 Melrose Drive, Los Angeles.
Home Address: The McGuire Beach House at 2001 Postal Road in Malibu Beach, California.
Telephone Number: 555-2040.
Car: Red Thunderbird convertible.

License Plate: 258 8PP.

Police Department Contact: Lieutenant Hanrahan (Gene Evans) of the Parker Division of the Los Angeles Police Department.

Character: Handsome, suave, and sophisticated ladies' man with a keen interest in helping people who are facing difficult circumstances.

Fee: $200 to $500 a day plus expenses (based on the complexities of a case).

Telephone Service: Ethel's Answering Service (Ethel calls Matt "Matthew").

CLAIRE KRONSKI

Occupation: Lawyer and Matt's live-in girlfriend.

Place of Birth: Texas.

Birthday: July 24, 1941.

Education: Tulane University; Harvard Law School.

Office Address: 36 Primrose Lane.

Telephone Number: 555-1333.

Nickname: Called "Kronski" by Matt (her first name is rarely said).

Character: Very pretty, dedicated to her job, and, as Matt says, "The most honest lawyer who ever lived—but one of the sneakiest people I have ever known."

Maude

(CBS, 1974–1978)

Cast: Bea Arthur (Maude Findlay), Bill Macy (Walter Findlay), Adrienne Barbeau (Carol Traynor), Conrad Bain (Dr. Arthur Harmon), Rue McClanahan (Vivian Harmon).

Basis: A free-spirited middle-aged woman (Maude Findlay) struggles to cope with the incidents that creep in and threaten to destroy her latest marriage (to Walter) and her relationship with her beautiful daughter (Carol).

MAUDE FINDLAY

Age: 47 (when the series begins); Walter is 49.

Mother: Florence Chadburn (Audrey Christie).

Address: 30 Crenshaw Street in Tuckahoe, New York (also given as 271 Elm Street). Maude and Carol (at age three) previously lived in Everett, Massachusetts; they moved to Tuckahoe after Maude's divorce from her first husband (Barney Traynor) in 1951. Chester Claiborne was Maude's second husband and Albert Hilliard her third husband (married for seven months); she dated Russell Asher before meeting Walter. She arranges her wedding albums alphabetically by husband.

Telephone Number: 555-9060.

Award: "Mother of the Year" (voted by the Tuckahoe PTA in 1951).

Catchphrase: "God 'ill get you for that" (which she says when upset).

Political Party: Democrat.

Favorite President: Franklin Delano Roosevelt.

Education: Our Lady of Chastity High School (where she was nicknamed "Chunky" and became the first girl to be elected class president).

Trait: Liberated, compulsive, stubborn, opinionated, and must have her own way. She often needs a glass of wine to calm her nerves (but often overindulges and passes out). She hates war toys and gave up martinis for six months to breast-feed Carol.

Goal: Let the world know that "women are not only sex symbols."

Occupation: Housewife. She worked as an agent, then office manager, at the Ace Realty Company at $7,000 a year; she later becomes a U.S. congresswoman (at which time the series ended and she and Walter moved to Washington, D.C.).

TV Show: Appeared on the game show *Beat the Devil*.

Maids: Florida Evans (Estelle Rolle), African American; Nell Naugatuck (Hermione Baddeley), Cockney Brit; and Victoria (Victoria Butterfield), West Indian. Florida was spun off into the series *Good Times* (see the entry *Good Times* for information).

TV First: Maude's decision to have an abortion when she felt she was too old to have another child.

Relatives: Cousin, Marshall Keebler (John Byner), who believes he is Captain Hero; aunts, Tinkie (Bella Bruck) and Lola Ashburn (Eve Arden); uncle, Henry (Charles White). Unseen are Maude's cousin Darryl, Aunt Rhoda, and two unnamed sisters.

WALTER FINDLAY

Occupation: Owner of Findlay's Friendly Appliance Store (also called Friendly Findlay's Appliances; he established it by selling merchandise from the back of his car). He is said to be a Maytag salesman and the 28th-largest appliance dealership in Westchester. When the business fails, Walter becomes a nail (hardware) salesman, then reopens the store as the New Findlay's Friendly Appliances (on Mohawk Street).

Award: "Tuckahoe Businessman of the Year."

Political Party: Republican.

Claim to Fame: Has seen the original 1933 film *King Kong* 153 times.

First Meeting: Walter met Maude in October 1968 at the height of the Nixon–Humphrey political campaign. His friend Arthur Harmon made the introductions.

Military Service: Army (private first class) during World War II. It was at this time that Walter met actress Jane Russell (star of the film *The Outlaw*) at a

Stage Door Canteen show and received a kiss from her. He transferred the lipstick to a napkin and keeps that memento in a secret compartment in his wallet (and away from Maude).

Addiction: Alcohol. He is said to be a recovering alcoholic, and too much drinking causes Walter to revert to his childhood (which Maude can't stand).

Catchphrase: When Maude gets out of hand, he yells "Mauuuude. SIT!"

Favorite Song: "Spanish Eyes."

Shoe Size: 9½B.

Relatives: Ex-wife, Marta (Carole Cook).

CAROL TRAYNOR

Birthday: June 11, 1949 (27 when the series begins). Maude's first husband, Barney Traynor, is her father.

Marital Status: Divorced (from Vernon).

Son: Philip (Brian Morrison, then Kraig Metzinger).

Occupation: Office secretary at Lambert Industries.

Measurements: 36-25-36 (Carol mentions wearing Maidenform bras). She accentuates her figure in low-cut blouses and short skirts (which Maude despises). She has brown eyes and hair; stands 5 feet, 3 inches tall; and wears a size 8 shoe.

Trait: A feminist who stands up for what she believes in. She calls her mother "Maude" or "Mother" and inherited her father's dimples. Carol was seven years old when her father passed and would like to live her own life without Maude's interference.

Final Episode: Carol moves to Denver, Colorado, when she acquires a better job.

ARTHUR AND VIVIAN HARMON

Occupation: Arthur appears to be both a private practice physician and a doctor at an unnamed hospital. Vivian is a housewife (Arthur opposes married women working and believes they do not deserve pay that is equal to men). When Arthur comes home "from a messy operation," he would like to have dinner ready for him.

Arthur's First Wife: Agnes (deceased).

Vivian's Former Husbands: Chick Cavendish and Jimmy Cavender.

Vivian's Character: Rather demure and naive at times. She and Maude have been friends since college.

Vivian's Dog: Chuck (also called "Rufus").

Arthur's CB Handle: Silver Scalpel.

Relatives: Arnold, Arthur's twin brother (Conrad Bain).

Final Episode: Arthur and Vivian move to Red River, Idaho, when Arthur decides to begin a new practice.

Note: The "Cousin Maude's Visit" episode of *All in the Family* (December 11, 1971) introduced Edith's cousin, Maude (Bea Arthur). Here, Marcia Rodd played Carol.

McMillan and Wife
(NBC, 1971–1976)

Cast: Rock Hudson (Stewart McMillan), Susan Saint James (Sally McMillan), Nancy Walker (Mildred), John Schuck (Charles Enright).

Basis: The wife (Sally) of a police commissioner (Stewart) turns detective to help her husband solve crimes.

STEWART MCMILLAN

Mother: Beatrice McMillan (Mildred Natwick).

Occupation: Lawyer turned commissioner of the San Francisco Police Department.

Direct Business Phone Number: 922-3299.

Limo License Plate: 589 ODQ.

Address: 345 Melrose (originally 250 Carson Street).

Nickname: "Mac" ("Everybody calls me Mac").

Telephone Number: 555-8600.

Sedan License Plate Number: 835 CRO.

Military Service: Naval intelligence during the Korean War (he is now in the Naval Reserves and serves two weeks a year at the navy's Legal Service Office).

Favorite Newspaper: The *Daily Post.*

Favorite Breakfast: English muffins broken apart ("One breaks an English muffin; one does not cut it").

Lunch: Mac is rarely home and eats at a health food store called the Grainery.

Health Club: Sam's, where Mac enjoys a steam and a rubdown.

Uncanny Ability: An exceptional liar (he can pass any lie detector test).

Ancestors: Mac's grandfather, John P. McMillan, created a company called Kenamack Alfalfa in 1903; it failed when he could not devise new uses for alfalfa.

College Sport: Member of the football team.

SALLY MCMILLAN

Mother: Emily Hull (Linda Watkins).

Maiden Name: Sally Hull.

Occupation: Housewife. She also works with deaf children at Century Hospital.

Station Wagon License Plate: 376 QK6.

Hope: To surpass her mother in the cooking department and become a gourmet. Mac hates Saturday brunch with Sally's mother because "she's a terrible cook." Sally is taking cooking classes at the local high school and believes she may soon achieve her goal—"Mac loved my rattlesnake béarnaise and walnut casserole in goat butter."

Quirk: When Sally becomes upset, she meditates. Each time she and Mac move, they must have dinner at a table set with her Aunt Sophie's chairs.

Character: Bright, pretty, and bubbly and, since marrying Mac, believes she has the mind of a detective. She is easily frightened and always finds she needs Mac's help when she stumbles on a mystery. Sally doesn't mean to find trouble: "it sort of finds me." She gathers evidence "by peeking" ("It's not nice to be sneaky"). She often wears a football jersey (number 18) as a nightgown (from the San Francisco 49ers).

Halloween Tradition: Displaying her life-size skeleton.

Favorite Sport: Baseball.

OTHER CHARACTERS

Mildred is Mac and Sally's housekeeper. She has a slight drinking problem and calls herself "a Jill of all trades." She has cooking utensils set for her 5-foot height, although Mac would like them a bit higher, as he likes to cook but hates to bend over for the utensils. Mildred stores eggs in the meat-keeper section of the refrigerator.

Sergeant Charles Enright is Mac's assistant; 261 058 is his squad car license plate.

Note: In 1976, when a contract dispute forced Susan Saint James to leave the program, her character was killed off in a plane crash, and the title became simply *McMillan.* Nancy Walker also left the series (to star in *The Nancy Walker Show*), and Martha Raye replaced her as Agatha Thompson, Mildred's sister. Mac was now a widower, and Enright became a lieutenant and more closely involved in Mac's investigations.

Mork and Mindy
(ABC, 1978–1982)

Cast: Robin Williams (Mork), Pam Dawber (Mindy McConnell), Conrad Janis (Fred McConnell), Jonathan Winters (Mearth), Tom Poston (Frank Bickley), Ralph James (voice of Orson), Shelley Fabares (Cathy McConnell), Robert Donner (Exidor).

Basis: A view of Earth life as seen through the eyes of an extraterrestrial (Mork) as he begins a mission to observe customs and report back to his superior (Orson).

MORK

Home Planet: Ork (200 million miles away with three moons; its capital is Fizbot).

Ork Life: Inhabitants, who resemble humans, evolved from the chicken. They are hatched from eggs, their spaceships resemble eggs, and they drink through their fingers.

Ork Occupation: Earth observer. Mork reports to Orson via his Scorpion Reports (which are preserved on microwire cassettes). He is later promoted to master sergeant, and only Orson can contact Mork because, as Mork says, "I have an unlisted brain." He previously worked as a dinner diver in a lobster tank and an explorer who charted 16 galaxies. He claims that Venus is a backward planet (their latest technology is the invention of the garbage can) and that no one wants to visit Pluto, as "it is a Mickey Mouse planet" (referring to the Disney character Pluto the dog).

Earth Occupation: Counselor at the Pine Tree Day Care Center. He also became the first male cheerleader for the Denver Broncos cheerleading team, the Pony Express; Lieutenant Mork Formork when he joined the air force (thinking it was a travel club); and Father Mork when he attempted to become a priest at St. Peter's Church.

Terms of Endearment for Orson: Orson is apparently overweight, and Mork refers to him as "Your Immenseness," "Your Fatitude," and "Your Magnitude." Mork contacts Orson by concentrating and saying, "Mork calling Orson, Mork calling Orson."

Place of Birth: A laboratory test tube (there are no parents on Ork).

Guarantee: Mork is covered for rusted skin and ankle blowouts.

Education: Ork Prep School.

Footwear: Size 8 red sequined Time Traveling Shoes.

Pets: Beebo (an Orkan Nauger Chump); Bob (an Earth caterpillar).

Orkan Enemies: The Necotons, especially Captain Nevana (Raquel Welch) of the Necoton Black Army.

Earth Ally: Mindy McConnell (befriends Mork when he lands in Boulder, Colorado).

Favorite Orkan Holiday: National Backwards Day.

Catchphrase: "Shazbut" (says when he gets angry).

Greeting: "Na-Nu, Na-Nu."

Relaxation: Standing on his head.

Life without Mork: When Mork felt he caused Mindy nothing but trouble, Orson used the Plasma Essence Reversifier to show him that if he were not present, Mindy would have married a loser (Cliff) and worked two jobs (cocktail waitress and salesgirl) to not only support them but also pay off Cliff's gambling debts.

MINDY MCCONNELL

Birthday: October 18, 1951, in Boulder, Colorado.

Parents: Fred and Beth. Fred is a widower when the series begins.

Bra Size: 34C. She stands 5 feet, 6 inches tall; has brown hair; and wears a size 7½ shoe.

Address: 1619 Pine Street in Boulder, Colorado. Mork resides in the attic.

Education: Boulder High School (her locker combination was 33-17-3); University of Colorado (majored in journalism).

Occupation: Salesgirl at her father's business (McConnell's Music Store); "Miss Lonely Hearts" advice columnist for the *Boulder Journal*; newscaster at KTNS-TV, Channel 31; and finally the host of the morning show *Wake Up Boulder*.

Jeep License Plate: ML 29H.

Orkan Name: Through Mork's reports, Mindy is known as the "Soft-Lapped One" to Orson. She was also the first Earthling to eat Fleck, an Orkan food that brings out strange behavioral qualities.

As a Child: The first girl to play Little League baseball in Boulder.

Teddy Bear: Mr. One Eye.

The Marriage: Love eventually developed between Mork and Mindy, and they married on October 5, 1981. They spent their honeymoon on Ork, where Mindy won fourth place in a pet show, as Orkans consider Earthlings pets.

The Baby: Mork becomes pregnant and lays an egg that hatches and produces an elderly baby they name Mearth (for "Mork, Mindy, and Earth"). Orkan babies are born old and become young with time. Mearth has a teddy bear (Teddy) and attends Ork Prep School one day a month (via the Orkan school bus—the 828 Transport Beam).

Relatives: Grandmother, Cora Hudson (Elizabeth Kerr); she calls Fred "a wiener"; cousin, Nelson Flavor (Jim Staahl); uncle, Dave McConnell (Jonathan Winters); aunt, Caroline McConnell (Beverly Sanders).

Flashbacks: Young Mindy (Missy Francis).

OTHER CHARACTERS

Fred McConnell is Mindy's father, a widower, and owner of McConnell's Music Store. He later marries (Cathy) and becomes a conductor with the Boulder City Orchestra. Exidor is Mork's offbeat friend who is considered the local loon. He has an invisible dog (a Doberman) named Brutus, an invisible aide named Pepe, and a business called Exidor T-Shirts. Frank Bikley is Mindy's downstairs neighbor, a greeting card writer with a dog named Bikley. Remo (Jay Thomas) and Jeanie DaVinci (Gina Hecht), friends of Mork and Mindy, are a brother and sister who own DaVinci's Restaurant (later called the New York Delicatessen).

SPIN-OFF

Mork and Mindy (ABC, 1982) finds an animated Mork and Mindy as teenagers and attending Mt. Mount High School.

Nancy Drew
(ABC, 1977–1979)

Cast: Pamela Sue Martin, then Janet Louise Johnson (Nancy Drew), William Schallert (Carson Drew), Jean Rasey, then Susan Buckner (Georgia "George" Fayne).

Basis: The crime-solving adventures of Nancy Drew, a beautiful young woman who fancies herself as a private investigator.

NANCY DREW

Birthday: June 6, 1956 (she is 21 when the series begins).

Place of Birth: River Heights, a small New England town.

Address: 8606 Bainbridge Street (lives with her widowed father, Carson).

Education: River Heights High School; River Heights University.

Measurements: 36-26-34 (Pamela Sue as Nancy Drew).

Background: Raised by her father since she was three years old (at which time her mother died of a heart attack). She grew up admiring her father and experienced firsthand how the criminal justice system works. Her childhood was spent solving small neighborhood mysteries, and this led Nancy to set her goal to become a detective.

Occupation: Carson's office assistant (researches legal files and checks driving records; later Carson's part-time investigator: "The day she began part-time investigative work for me was the start of my gray hairs").

Character: Dislikes being told she is wrong about something and does not think like a typical detective: "I don't consider what I do prying. I just observe." Even though Nancy carefully calculates each move and is very thorough, she often takes chances. She looks beyond the obvious and seeks the clues that others have overlooked and may be the key to solving a crime. She can also ride a motorcycle and trick ride.

Favorite Charity: The Children's Hospital Toy Fund.
Relatives: Aunts, Ruby (Irene Tedrow) and Lea (Queenie Smith).

CARSON DREW
Place of Birth: River Heights.
Year of Birth: 1922.
Occupation: Private-practice attorney.
Education: River Heights High School; Boston University.
Business Address: The Municipal Building at 9068 Main Street (next to the Essex Smoke House).
Character: Careful about what cases he accepts. If it is too controversial, he tends to back down (unless Nancy convinces him otherwise).

GEORGIA "GEORGE" FAYNE
Relationship: Nancy's best friend and assistant.
Place of Birth: River Heights.
Nickname: "George."
Education: Same as Nancy (they have been friends since grade school).
Address: 16 River Street.
Occupation: Nancy's assistant (Nancy mentions that she is grooming George to become a detective, but the time has not yet come to let her act alone).
Character: Frightened of everything she feels is dangerous and often paints a graphic picture of what will happen if she and Nancy go any further. George seems to come up with the clues "that do not mean anything except to Nancy."

NED NICKERSON
Position: Carson's assistant (when played by George O'Hanlon Jr.); investigator for the Boston district attorney's office (when played by Rick Springfield).
Character: Ned was originally Nancy's boyfriend and Carson's legman, although Nancy was never quite sure of his intentions. Ned was very indecisive and was replaced by a more forceful version (who did have an eye for Nancy, but the intent was for more diversified stories involving big-city criminals).

UPDATES
The characters, based on the novels by Carolyn Keene, next appeared in syndication in 1995 as *Nancy Drew*. Here, Nancy (Tracy Ryan) is 21 years old and lives on her own in Apartment 603 of the Caillisto Hotel at 306 Marsh Avenue (the locale is not identified). She works in a temp agency and is studying criminology.

Georgia "George" Fayne (Joy Tanner), Nancy's friend, and Beth Marvin (Jhene Erwin), George's cousin, share Apartment 3 over the Phillips Shoes store. They also attend college: George for film editing and Beth for journalism.

George works as a messenger for Quick Draw Couriers and Beth as a writer for *The Rag*, the city's alternative newspaper. Carson Drew does not appear, and Ned (Scott Speedman) is seen only occasionally.

In 2002, ABC aired *Nancy Drew*, an unsold pilot that found an 18-year-old Nancy (Maggie Lawson) attending River Heights University. Lauren Birkell played George Fayne, and Jill Ritchie was Beth Marvin (George's cousin), also college students. They live on campus at the Kelly Hall dorm.

The program was originally broadcast on an alternating basis with *The Hardy Boys* (as *The Hardy Boys/Nancy Drew Mysteries*). Here, Frank (Parker Stevenson) and Joe Hardy (Shaun Cassidy), the sons of world-renowned detective Fenton Hardy (Edmund Gilbert), solve crimes as unofficial detectives in their hometown of Bayport.

Nanny and the Professor
(ABC, 1970–1971)

Cast: Juliet Mills (Phoebe Figalilly), Richard Long (Harold Everett), David Doremus (Hal Everett Jr.), Kim Richards (Prudence Everett), Trent Lehman (Bentley Everett).

Basis: A mysterious woman (Nanny) uses her mystical powers to help a widowed college professor (Harold) raise his three children (Hal, Prudence, and Bentley).

PHOEBE FIGALILLY
Place of Birth: England.

Year of Birth: April 18, 1864 (as seen on her passport).

Character: Phoebe is 106 years old when the series begins and has a British accent. She can "make things happen" for the good, and it is assumed that she is just magical (although it appears she may be a guardian angel or a witch). She magically appears to people in need (such as her employer, Harold Everett, who desperately needed a nanny for his three children) and assumes the role of a nanny (hence her nickname "Nanny").

Everett Address: 10327 Oak Street in Los Angeles, California.

Ability: "To spread love and joy" (as "nice things happen around her"). She can communicate with animals, read people's minds, and solve situations by implanting thoughts that allow people to resolve their own dilemmas.

Car: A 1930 Model A that she calls Arabella (its radio broadcasts only the music of the time in which it was made).

Relatives: Aunts, Henrietta, a psychic (Elsa Lanchester); Justine (Ida Lupino); and Agatha (Marjorie Bennett), who travels by air balloon; uncles, Horace (Ray Bolger) and Alfred (John Mills).

THE EVERETT FAMILY

Harold is a mathematics and related fields professor at Clinton College (also called Collier University) in Los Angeles. He occasionally dates but cannot seem to connect with the right woman to become a mother to his children (it is hinted that a romantic spark had been ignited between Harold and Nanny, but the series was canceled before developing the idea). Van Johnson played Harold's uncle, Bob Everett.

Harold Jr., called "Hal," is 12 years old; Bentley, called "Butch," is eight years old, and Prudence, age five, is the youngest of Harold's children. Nanny addresses Harold Sr. as "Professor." Eileen Baral plays Francine Fowler, the girl with a crush on Hal. She has a French poodle named Fifi.

The Everett family pets are Waldo (sheepdog), Mike and Myrtle (guinea pigs), Sebastian (rooster), and Jerome and Geraldine (baby goats).

In 1973, ABC aired an animated pilot film that was to relate various adventures with Nanny and the Everetts called *Nanny and the Professor and the Phantom of the Circus*. The original cast repeated their roles and found Nanny helping her Aunt Henrietta solve the mysterious disappearances of performers from her traveling circus.

The New Avengers
(CBS, 1978–1979)

Cast: Patrick Macnee (John Steed), Joanna Lumley (Purdy), Gareth Hunt (Mike Gambit).

Basis: Update of *The Avengers* (ABC, 1966–1969) that follows three secret agents as they battle the enemies of the British government.

JOHN STEED

Occupation: Ministry agent. He was previously captain of an ex–naval launch (mid-1940s) in the Mediterranean that dealt with illegal cigarette trafficking; civil servant in London; then economic adviser to a sheik in the Middle East.

Address: 3 Stable Mews in London. He also owns a country estate he calls "Steed's Stud" (where he entertains the ladies, breeds horses, and issues assignments).

Telephone Number: Whitehall 1819 (originally Whitehall 00-001).

Belief: Britain rules, and he has sworn to defend it against all its enemies.

Abilities: Trained to withstand brainwashing and torture and is an expert on poisons, firearms, and breaking codes.

Award: The Medal of Honor.

Place of Birth: England.

Education: Eton College.

Military Service: The Royal Navy during World War II (he enlisted in 1939 and soon became a lieutenant in command of a torpedo boat).

Trademark: His Edwardian-style wardrobe. He is debonair and a purveyor of Old World charm and courtesy.

Weakness: The opposite sex.

PURDY

Birthday: May 1, 1946.

Place of Birth: India.

Name: Her father, a brigadier in the British army, named her after the Purdy, the most respected and expensive shotgun in the world (she is not known by any other name).

Measurements: 34-24-34. She stands 5 feet, 8 inches tall.

Education: International. She and her family were constantly uprooted, and she attended such prestigious schools as La Sorbonne and Roedean.

Languages: English and Russian.

Occupation: Ministry agent. While Purdy had aspirations to become a high-fashion model, her father's death (shot as a spy after joining the Secret Service) set her on a path to avenge his death by becoming an agent to "even up the score." She attempted to become a ballerina but was discharged from the Royal Ballet for being too tall.

Ability: Well versed in the martial arts, especially a French technique called "panach" (using her feet as weapons); an expert on firearms (learning to handle guns from her father).

Car: A TR7 sports car.

Home: A basement flat in London that is decorated in the 1930s art deco style.

Trait: Very meticulous when on a case. She studies every detail and carefully plots each move to lessen the risk factor.

MICHAEL "MIKE" GAMBIT

Occupation: Ministry agent. He previously worked as a crocodile wrestler in the Congo, then as a professional race car driver.

Place of Birth: England.

Heritage: Hails from a long line of distinguished military officers and was groomed to become a soldier.

Military Service: The British army (served in the Parachute Regiment); he later served with Special Air Services and gained knowledge of guerilla warfare when he worked as a mercenary in the Middle East and Africa. He mentioned joining the Royal Navy when he was 14 years old.

Car: A Jaguar XJS.
Abilities: Expert in unarmed combat; skilled shot, archer, and pilot.
Wake-Up Call: Every morning, as the sun begins to rise, a sparrow he named Charlie flies on his windowsill "to sing his heart out and wake me up."

The New Dick Van Dyke Show
(CBS, 1971–1974)

Cast: Dick Van Dyke (Dick Preston), Hope Lange (Jenny Preston), Angela Powell (Annie Preston), Michael Shea (Lucas Preston).
Basis: Incidents in the life of Dick Preston, a talk show host turned actor.

RICHARD "DICK" PRESTON
Mother: Marge Preston (Mabel Albertson); she hates Dick's talk show.
Wife: Jenny Preston.
Children: Annie and Lucas Preston.
Sister: Michelle Preston (Fannie Flagg). She is called "Mike" and works as Dick's booking agent and secretary.
Address: A ranch-style house on Hayes Creek Road in Carefree, Arizona.
Occupation: Host of *The Dick Preston Show*, a 90-minute talk-variety program.
Program Closing: Dick ends his show with "Bye. Have a nice rest of the day."
Station: Aired and produced by KXIU-TV, Channel 2, in Phoenix, Arizona.
Station Owner: The Compton Broadcasting Company.
Agent: Bernard "Bernie" Davis (Marty Brill), Dick's friend and business manager. Nancy Dussault plays Bernie's wife, Carol.
Hobby: Collects old 78-rpm records. Jack Sena playing "Bumble Boogie" is his most treasured record (took him 20 years to find it).
The Change: Dick moves to California to play Dr. Brad Fairmont, a surgeon at Pleasant Valley Hospital, on the TV soap opera *Those Who Care*. Margot Brighton (played by Barbara Rush) is his costar as Dr. Susan Allison.
Address: 747 Bonnie Vista Road in Tarzana, California.
Show Personnel: Maxwell "Max" Mathias (Dick Van Patten), the producer; Alex Montez (Henry Darrow), the director; and Dennis Whitehead (Barry Gordon), the writer.
Neighbor: Richard Richardson (Richard Dawson), the star of a TV series called *Harrigan's Hooligans* (a spoof of Dawson's time on the series *Hogan's Heroes*). Chita Rivera plays Richard's wife, Connie.

JENNIFER PRESTON
Nickname: Jenny.
Education: Carefree High School; Arizona State College.

Occupation: Housewife. She was previously an executive office secretary.

Dream Home: The Historic Morgan House in Carefree.

Business: Delicatique (sold clothes made by the local Sioux Indian tribe in the Phoenix Mall). She painted the store (the former Moskowitz Butcher Shop) in her high school colors of green and purple. The rent is $200 a month.

Pet Cat: Mr. Rosenbloom (named after Annie's third-grade teacher).

Third Child: While working as the secretary for Planned Parenthood, Jenny became pregnant and gave birth to a son she and Dick named Chris (Tiffany Graff).

ANNIE AND LUCAS PRESTON

Annie is nine years old and attends the Camelback Grammar School. She is called "Pumpkin" by Dick and Jenny and "Sweetness" by Bernie. She has a hand puppet named Nosey, enjoys Puffed Wheat Flakes cereal for breakfast, and did a TV commercial for Cicely's Instant Oatmeal.

Lucas is 16 years old and attends an unnamed high school that is presumably some distance from their house (as he lives on campus). He believes he is a ladies' man and appears to have a never-ending supply of girlfriends. One such girl, Judy Williams (Ta-Tanisha), was African American and the 1971 episode "Interracial Dating" was quite controversial for its time. The family's acceptance of Judy was made easier when Annie wrote a poem: "Roses are red, violets are blue, why can't people be colors too."

Note: Carl Reiner is heard as the studio director of Dick's first series; Barry and Stacy Van Dyke, Dick's real-life children, play various roles.

The Odd Couple
(ABC, 1970–1975)

Cast: Jack Klugman (Oscar Madison), Tony Randall (Felix Unger).
Basis: A perfectionist photographer (Felix Unger) and an untidy sportswriter (Oscar Madison) attempt to live together "without driving each other crazy."

OVERALL SERIES INFORMATION
It is first mentioned that Oscar met Felix when they were jurors for the trial of Leo Garcey (a man accused of driving his roommate crazy); it is next said that Oscar and Felix met as children in Chicago and, finally, in the 1950s, on a double date.

OSCAR TREVOR MADISON
Parents: Father, Blinky Madison (Jack Klugman); mother (Elvia Allman, then Fran Ryan). Blinky worked in a speakeasy (later said to have been a bookie and a restaurant owner).
Address: 1049 Park Avenue (at 74th Street and Central Park West), Apartment 1102, in Manhattan. The spare key is hidden in the fire hose next to the front door; Oscar acquired the apartment by checking the obituary columns to see who died and where they lived.
Occupation: Sportswriter for the New York *Herald* (previously worked as a copywriter for *Playboy* magazine, then as a sportswriter for the New York *Times*).
Broadcasting Career: Hosts the radio program *The Oscar Madison Sports Talk Show* (later called *Oscar Madison's Greatest Moments in Sports*).
Place of Birth: Philadelphia (born at Our Lady of Angels Hospital); he later mentions being born in Chicago, then the Bronx, New York.
Education: James K. Polk High School (later says Bayonne High School); he also attended the Langley Tip-Toes Dancing School as a child.

College Roommate: Monty Hall (the TV show game host). Oscar appeared on Monty's show, *Let's Make a Deal* in a horse costume (Felix was the head, Oscar the rear). Oscar and Felix also appeared on Allen Ludden's game show *Password.*

Childhood Nickname: "Chicky" (as called by his mother).

Military Career: Served in the army, where he was cited as the perfect example of what not to do—"In any other army in the world, he would have been shot on sight."

Favorite Drink: Beer.

Favorite Eateries: Edible Eddie's, April Fools Tacos, and Heidi's Nautical Nosh.

Favorite Dinner: Lasagna and French fries.

Favorite Sandwich: Salami and jelly on white bread.

Favorite Dessert: Boston cream pie.

Favorite Food Topping: Ketchup (which he puts on virtually everything).

Favorite Baseball Team: New York Mets.

Bowling Team: Member of the Bon Vivants.

Shoe Size: 11D.

Favorite Song: "Reckless."

Favorite Singer: Jaye P. Morgan (for whom he and Felix wrote the song "Happy and Peppy and Bursting with Love").

Vices: Gambling (betting on the horses and playing poker); smoking cigars.

Ex-Wife: Blanche (Brett Somers). They married on Christmas Day in Abnerville, Connecticut, and went to a Rangers–Red Wings hockey game on their honeymoon. They divorced due to their constant arguing. Blanche was born in Kew Gardens, New York, and was previously engaged to Cecil Panch.

Relatives: Niece, Martha (Hilary Thompson).

Flashbacks: Oscar as a boy (Adam Klugman).

FELIX ALEX UNGER

Father: Morris Unger (Tony Randall), an optometrist; mother not mentioned.

Brother: Floyd Unger (William Redfield). He also mentions having a sister. Felix was called "Little F," while Lloyd was called "Big F" (Floyd now runs the Unger Bubble Gum factory in Buffalo, New York).

Place of Birth: Felix first mentions Chicago, then Buffalo, Oklahoma, and Toledo, Ohio.

Occupation: Photographer (owner of Felix Unger Photography—Portraits a Specialty; also seen as F.U. Enterprises). Felix also worked as a photographer for *Playboy* magazine (under the name Spencer Benedict ["I'm going to use my real name to shoot nudes?"]); a boxer; and a singer/dancer (in an act with Richard Dawson).

Business Address: 380 Madison Avenue (next to the Pottery Barn).

The Odd Couple. *ABC/Photofest. ©ABC*

Awards: The Silver Nipple Award (for his portraits of babies); the Dink Award (for his TV commercial for Fat-a-Way Diet Pills); a home economics medal in high school; and a grammar school spelling bee (spelled "zeppelin" correctly).

Ex-Wife: Gloria (Janis Hansen). They met on a blind date, and she was a Bunny at the Manhattan Playboy Club at the same time Felix worked for *Playboy* magazine. After seven years of marriage, they divorced when she could no longer stand his perfectionist ways. Felix then became Oscar's roommate. Edna (Pamelyn Ferdin, then Doney Oatman) and Leonard (Leif Garrett, then Willie Aames) are their children. Gloria called Felix "Honey Bear" and

"Mr. Clean"; "Just One More Chance" was their song. Gloria, her maiden name given as both Schaefler and Fleener, lived at 145 Central Park West. She measures 38-26-34, and 212-724-7069 is her phone number.

Felix's IQ: 186.

Childhood: As a youngster, Felix frequently visited his grandmother in Glenview, New York (she owned a farm, and he became fond of a cow named Alice). He was a neat child and a perfect student and acquired the nicknames "Felix the Pest" and "Felix the Cat" (after the 1920s cartoon character). He was also voted "Cutest Boy," "Most Likely to Succeed," "Most Limber Boy," and "Most Likely to Interrupt" at school.

Expertise: Knowledgeable on radio theme song trivia.

Acting: Felix is a member of the Radio Actors Guild and as a teenager appeared on the actual radio series *Let's Pretend* (reflecting Tony Randall's real career). In college, he hosted his own radio show, *Felix*.

Military Career: Army private during World War II. He was stationed in England (with the 22nd Training Film Platoon, Educational Division of the Special Services) and starred in the army training film *How to Take a Shower* (where he originated the line "Men, don't let this happen to you"). He won the Silver Canteen Award for his song about Hitler ("To a Sour Kraut") and was transferred to Greenland (where he became a lieutenant). He retired as a captain and now serves two weeks a year in the Army Reserves.

Allergies: Allergic to mayonnaise, sour cream, flamingos, fog, and plush animals (as a kid, "I curled up with a sponge"); he later says he had a plush bear named "Mr. Friend."

Pets: Albert (parrot); Spot (dog).

Medical Condition: An annoying and loud sinus problem and a trick back.

Quirks: A fascination with ghosts (resulting from his role as Hamlet in the play); changes the kitchen cabinet shelf paper when upset and makes ladyfingers from scratch.

Favorite Eatery: Nino's Italian Restaurant.

Favorite Music: Opera. He is a member of the Edward Viella Ballet Appreciation Club and the Lexington Avenue Opera Club. He subscribes to *Opera News* magazine and becomes embarrassed in public because he cries at operas.

Classical Music Band: The Sophisticates. When hired to play country music, Felix renames the band Red River Unger and His Saddle Sores.

Ability: Prides himself on knowing the best French restaurants in Manhattan.

Favorite Sport: Squash.

Boyhood Friend: Orville Kruger ("the boy with the odd-shaped head"); his first girlfriend was "Big Bertha."

Hobby: Stamp collecting.

Relatives: Grandmother, unnamed (Madge Kennedy).

Flashbacks: Felix as a boy (Johnny Scott Lee, then Sean Manning); grandfather, unnamed (Tony Randall).

OTHER CHARACTERS

Dr. Nancy Cunningham (Joan Hotchkis) became Oscar's ladylove in later episodes. Before meeting her, Oscar dated "Crazy" Rhoda Zimmerman. She loves boxing and hockey and has a mole on her left hip; she works "out of Dr. Melnitz's office."

Miriam Welby (Elinor Donahue) became Felix's romantic interest (although in the final episode, Felix and Gloria remarry).

Myrna Turner (Penny Marshall) is Oscar's awkward secretary (she calls him "Mr. M"). She studied tap dancing for 12 years and danced at the Alabama–Mississippi football game half-time. Her siblings are Verna and Werner Turner, while her boyfriend is named "Sheldn" ("they forgot the 'o' on his birth certificate"). Myrna feels she will never be a lady ("I talk nasal, I have an unproud bust, and I sit like a frog"). She was born in November (a Scorpio) and quit smoking after joining the Smoker's Institute.

Murray Greschner (Al Molinaro) is a police officer with the New York Police Department. He is married to Mimi (Jane Dulo, then Alice Ghostley) and has a rather poor arrest record (he has tried for 11 years to become a sergeant). He loves animals, plays with Felix's band (piano and harmonica), and considers his policeman's nightstick his magic wand (as he is a big fan of magicians). He has a style of handwriting he calls the "Murray Curl."

UPDATES

An African American version appeared as *The New Odd Couple* (ABC, 1982). Oscar Madison (Demond Wilson) and Felix Unger (Ron Glass) were said to be college buddies during the 1950s who become roommates following their divorces. Telma Hopkins appeared as Felix's ex-wife, Frances.

The 1993 CBS TV movie *The Odd Couple: Together Again* finds Felix and Gloria (Barbara Barrie) still married and preparing for their daughter Edna's (Toni Kalem) wedding. As a favor to Gloria, Felix moves in with Oscar (recovering from throat surgery) when she finds his efforts to arrange Edna's wedding a total nuisance.

REBOOT

Apartment 21A of the Royal Arms Apartments is home to Oscar Madison (Matthew Perry) and Felix Unger (Thomas Lennon) in the CBS 2015 version of *The Odd Couple*. Oscar hosts *The Oscar Madison Show* (on satellite radio); Felix owns Unger Photography. Ashley (Christine Woods) is Felix's ex-wife; Gaby (Lauren Graham) is Oscar's ex-wife; Emily (Lindsay Sloane) is Felix's girlfriend, a waitress at Langford's, Oscar's favorite sports bar. Garry Marshall played Oscar's father, Walter Madison.

One Day at a Time
(CBS, 1975–1984)

Cast: Bonnie Franklin (Ann Romano), Valerie Bertinelli (Barbara Cooper), Mackenzie Phillips (Julie Cooper), Pat Harrington Jr. (Dwayne Schneider), Michael Lembeck (Max Horvath), Shelley Fabares (Francine Webster), Howard Hesseman (Sam Royer), Boyd Gaines (Mark Royer), Mary Louise Wilson (Ginny Wroblinki).

Basis: A divorcee (Ann Romano) with two daughters (Barbara and Julie Cooper) struggles to begin a new life as a single mother.

ANN ROMANO

Parents: Kathryn (Nanette Fabray) and Michael Romano (Jeff Corey). Kathryn calls Barbara "Muffin" and Julie "Pumpkin."

Age: 34 (when the series begins).

Place of Birth: Logansport, Indiana.

Education: Logansport High School. She later attends City College, taking a course in English literature. She has a degree from the Evelyn Wood Speed Reading School and yearned to attend Northwestern University.

Ex-Husband: Ed Cooper (Joseph Campanella). Ann married Ed when she was 17 years old and retains her maiden name; her daughters carry their father's last name.

Address: 1344 Hartford Drive, Apartment 402, in Indianapolis, Indiana.

Telephone Number: 555-4124.

Occupation: Account executive for the Connors and Davenport Advertising Agency. She later quits and joins with Nick Handris (Ron Rifkin) to form the Romano and Handris Advertising Agency (later called Handris and Associates). When the business fails, Ann teams with her former coworker Francine Webster to open the Romano and Webster Advertising Agency. In the final episode, Ann takes a job in London.

Employer: Claude Connors (also called "Al Connors" and played by John Hillerman) at Connors and Davenport. Ann insisted that she be addressed as "Ms. Romano." Claude did so by calling her "M. S. Romano" (saying the "M" and "S" as separate letters).

Connors and Davenport Phone Number: 555-7974.

Biggest Accounts: Rutledge Toys (at Connors and Davenport); Sunshine Ice Cream (at Romano and Webster).

Boyfriends: First-season episodes find Ann romantically involved with David Kane (Richard Masur), her divorce lawyer (with the firm of McInerney, Wollman, Kollman and Schwartz). She later marries Sam Royer, an architect, on May 16, 1983.

Address (When Married): 322 Bedford Street, Apartment 422.

Favorite Ice Cream Flavor: Almond mocha.

Bra Size: 34A. She stands 5 feet, 3 inches tall.

Bank Account: Ann and Julie have a joint checking account (1-222-1220-877-02453) at the First Security Bank.

As a Child: When Ann felt sad, she would watch *The Mickey Mouse Club*, as the Mouseketeers made her happy.

Nickname: Called "Shorty" by Max, Julie's husband in later episodes.

Relatives: Grandmother, Helen Romano (Elizabeth Kerr); mother-in-law, Estelle Cooper (Priscilla Morrill); cousin, Sophie (Gretchen Corbett); Sam's ex-wife, Marge Royer (Claudette Nevins). Not seen was Ann's cousin Phyllis.

JULIE LAURA COOPER

Relationship: Ann's eldest and most rebellious daughter.

Age: 14 (when the series begins). Because of Julie's ways, Ann calls her "My Harem-Scarem Daughter" ("One minute she is this way, the next that way").

Education: Jefferson High School (starred in her senior class play, *The Sound of Music*).

Bra Size: 32B.

Plush Teddy Bear: TuTu Bear.

Favorite Snacks: Celery and ice cream; bananas and pickles.

Occupation: Student, then receptionist at the Curran Animal Center (and the Free Clinic), freelance fashion designer, gofer to filmmaker Nick Jamison, waitress at Barney's Tavern, and student at the Berkum Management Institute in Ohio (training as the manager of an unnamed donut shop).

Cult: Julie joined (but later left) the LOGs (Lambs of God).

Boyfriend: Max Horvath, a flight attendant for PMA Airlines; they met on a ski trip, married one week later in a park, and had a daughter named Annie (J.C. and R.C. Dilley and Paige and Lauren Maloney). Max later works at the Gonigan Travel Agency.

BARBARA JEAN COOPER

Relationship: Ann's youngest daughter.

Age: 13 (when the series begins; in real life, Valerie and Mackenzie were the same age).

Original Trait: Tomboy (which she quickly sheds for boys and dating).

Bra Size: 34B.

Dress Size: 5.

Education: Jefferson High School (a member of the basketball team); City College (works part-time in its bookstore; she was originally accepted into the University of Wisconsin). Barbara was also said to attend Marshall High School.

Occupation: Student, then lifeguard at the Rego Park Kiddie Pool; cook at Quickie Burger; stock "boy," then sales clerk, at Olympia Sporting Goods (owned by Erickson Enterprises); agent with the Gonagin Travel Agency.

Expertise: Elizabethan poetry.

Favorite Ice Cream Flavor: Rocky Road.

Favorite Actor: Woody Allen.

Favorite Movie: Manhattan.

Favorite Composer: George Gershwin.

Nemesis: The never-seen, well-developed Trish the Dish, who was the dream of all the boys at Jefferson High School.

Boyfriend: Mark Royer, Sam's son (a dentist), whom she later married.

Biggest Disappointment: Her inability to conceive and have children (diagnosed shortly after she married).

Childhood Recollection: Ate a caterpillar when Julie told her it was a fuzzy Tootsie Roll.

DWAYNE F. SCHNEIDER

Occupation: Superintendent of Ann's first apartment building. He lives in Apartment 1 and has been working there for 12 years (in 1979). He calls himself a "maintenance executive" and had dreamed of becoming an archaeologist. At the age of two months, he was a diaper ad model. As an adult, he was offered the position of the Thorton Mills Company man of distinction by the Darvish Modeling Agency (but turned it down when it meant moving to France).

Place of Birth: Secaucus, New Jersey.

Education: Irvington High School.

Middle Name: Flo (after Broadway producer Florence "Flo" Ziegfeld).

Affiliation: I.B.M. (Indianapolis Building Maintenance).

Favorite Actor: John Wayne (whom he refers to by Wayne's nickname, "The Duke").

Favorite Magazine: The Super's Digest (for janitors).

Lodge: The Secret Order of the Beavers Lodge, North Central Chapter (as the activities director and entertainment chairman; nominated as "Supreme Grand Yak").

Bowling Team: The Wild Bunch; later called the Beavers Bowling Team.

Felony: At the age of eight, Dwayne stole a yo-yo from a five-and-dime.

Military Service: The navy's Sixth Fleet (as a torpedo repairman). After his hitch, he went to school to learn plumbing.

Best Friend: Harold, called "Beerbelly" (Chuck McCann). Beverly Sanders is Beerbelly's wife, Selma.

Musical Ability: Plays the organ.

Marriage: According to Dwayne, he married in 1957, but it lasted only one week (his wife got up one morning, hot-wired his truck, and just took off). In the pilot episode, Dwayne mentions that he is married; in another episode, he mentions that he was married for five days and got a divorce.

CB Handle: Super Stud (uses his CB radio to talk with truck drivers).

Favorite Pickup Joint: The Boom Boom Room of the Purple Pig Club.

Investment: $1,000 in Georgette Jeans (one of Ann and Francine's accounts).

Romantic Interest: Ginny Wroblinki, Ann's neighbor, a waitress at the Alibi Room Bar.

Trait: Carries a pack of cigarettes under the right sleeve of his white T-shirt (it can be seen in a rectangle outline).

Catchphrase: "Don't ever forget and please remember" (followed by a saying, for example, "The old Arab saying, 'It is the wise man who ducks before the camel spits'" or "It is better to not have been in love than not to have loved at all"). Ann calls these "pearls of wisdom."

Relatives: Son, Ronnie Baxter (Darrell Larson); nephew, Harvey (Mark Hamill). Mentioned are Uncle Harry ("collects rats"), Cousin Ethel ("mud wrestling judge"), and Great Aunt Josie ("waters the scotch down for a chain of midwestern hotels").

Note: On May 24, 1984, CBS aired *Another Man's Shoes*, a pilot in which Dwayne leaves Indianapolis for Daytona Beach, Florida, to care for his orphaned niece Lori (Natalie Klinger) and nephew Keith (Corey Feldman). He works as the maintenance man for Jackie Cahill (Candace Azzara), the owner of Jackie's Arcade at Morgan Beach.

Paper Moon
(ABC, 1974–1975)

Cast: Christopher Connelly (Moses Prey), Jodie Foster (Addie Loggins).

Basis: A young girl (Addie) and a traveling Bible salesman (Moses) team up to survive the difficult times of the early 1930s through elaborate schemes.

MOSES "MOZE" PRAY

Occupation: Con artist.

Cover: Salesman for the Dixie Bible Company.

Scheme: "The widow business" (Moze scours the obituary columns looking for widows to sell them a Bible, supposedly ordered for them by their late husbands).

Car: A 1931 roadster, license plate 681 132.

Marital Status: Single.

Gimmick: A fake gold tooth to help sell Bibles. He also has a deluxe edition available that has the person's name printed in gold lettering.

Questionable Daughter: Addie (see below).

ADELAIDE "ADDIE" LOGGINS

Date of Birth: November 19, 1922.

Mother: Essie Mae Loggins (born in Oak View, Kansas).

Address: 47 Bridge Corner in Ophelia, Kansas.

Father: Addie's father deserted the family after her birth, and she suspects that Moze is her father because "I look like you." Moze admits that he knew Essie (met in a bar) but says, "I don't look like you. I'm not your father." When Moze returned in 1933 to attend Essie's funeral, Addie first saw him and made the connection.

The Change: It had been arranged for Addie to live with her Aunt Bessie in St. Joseph, Missouri. Moze had agreed to take Addie, but en route, Addie convinces Moze to let her stay with him when he learns her aunt dislikes her.

The Partnership: Although he continually insists that he is not Addie's father, Moze finds that he cannot get rid of her. He then lays down the law: "I make all the decisions. You just have to look like a pretty little girl" (her part in scams).

Addie's Role: The treasurer ("If it wasn't for me," Addie says, "we'd be broke all the time"; she keeps an emergency $10 in a cigar box that contains her treasured items). Addie now calls herself "Addie Pray."

Destination: The back roads of the Midwest during the Great Depression.

Note: The series is based on the feature film of the same title (wherein Moses was a Bible salesman for the Kansas Bible Company and Addie was nine years old).

The Partridge Family
(ABC, 1970–1974)

Cast: Shirley Jones (Shirley Partridge), David Cassidy (Keith Partridge), Susan Dey (Laurie Partridge), Danny Bonaduce (Danny Partridge), Suzanne Crough (Tracy Partridge), Jeremy Gelbwalks, then Brian Forster (Chris Partridge), Dave Madden (Reuben Kincaid).

Basis: A widow (Shirley) attempts to live a normal life while performing with her children (Keith, Laurie, Danny, Tracy, and Chris) as the singing Partridge Family.

OVERALL SERIES INFORMATION

Family Address: 698 Sycamore Road in San Pueblo, California (also given as "the 700 block on Vassario Road").

Pet Dog: Simone.

First Professional Job: Caesar's Palace in Las Vegas (as openers for Johnny Cash).

Billing: "America's Newest Singing Sensation."

First Song Performed: "Together."

Agent: Reuben Kincaid.

Transportation: A yellow 1957 Chevrolet school bus (psychedelically repainted).

License Plate: NLX 590.

Warning Posted on the Bus: "Careful. Nervous Mother Driving."

SHIRLEY PARTRIDGE

Maiden Name: Shirley Renfrew.

Parents: Amanda Renfrew (Rosemary DeCamp). Shirley's father is first called "Walter Renfrew" (Jackie Coogan), then "Fred Renfrew" (Ray Bolger). They are first said to be married for 44 years, then 40 years.

Marital Status: Widow (husband's name is never mentioned).

Occupation: Mother; she previously worked as a teller at the Bank of San Pueblo.

Education: While childhood schools are not mentioned, Shirley enrolled at San Pueblo Junior College to complete courses in psychology (she married after beginning college and had to drop out when she became pregnant with Keith).

Trait: Very neat, tidy, and organized. When someone arrives at the family home unexpectedly, she worries about how the house looks. She is very sweet and caring, and performing with her children makes her feel like a kid again.

Award: Voted Mother of the Year by *Women's Journal* magazine.

KEITH DOUGLAS PARTRIDGE

Age: 16 (the eldest child). He plays guitar, sings, and writes the songs for the band.

Education: San Pueblo High School; San Pueblo Junior College.

School Activities: Member of the high school band and basketball team (wore jersey 15).

Favorite Foods: Meatloaf, steak, and potatoes.

Favorite "Reading" Matter: The girlie *Playpen* magazine (not for the pictures "but for the short stories").

Ambition: To become a filmmaker. With the help of younger brother Danny, Keith produced a film called *16½* (originally called *A History of the World*, "but we ran out of film during the sixteenth century," says Danny), which depicted events in his family's life and was publicly shown at the Royal Theater. Keith and Danny were paid $100 by the theater owner. Keith also mentioned that he wanted to become a lawyer.

Film Audition: Keith auditioned for (but lost) the role of Vito, the baby-faced gangster in an unnamed movie to be produced by World International Pictures.

Popularity Problems: Girls who never liked Keith before now want to date him.

Make-Out Spot: Muldoon's Point.

LAURIE PARTRIDGE

Age: 15 (the second-born child).

Date of Birth: December 10, 1954.

Education: San Pueblo High School (voted Homecoming Queen); San Pueblo Junior College.

Hangout: The Taco Stand (also frequented by Keith).

Height: 5 feet, 7 inches tall.

Favorite Color: Blue.

Worst Day: Getting braces on her teeth (due to a condition called Pybolt syndrome, the metal in Laurie's mouth picked up radio signals, and songs by the Rolling Stones could be heard coming out of her mouth).

Jealous Streak: Sometimes becomes upset by all the attention girls bestow on Keith (she later realizes that "girls are a fringe benefit of the business of becoming a rock star").

Trait: Very liberal. She believes in equal rights for women and often complains that Keith's songs are all about love and girls and degrade women.

Favorite Magazine: Liberal Outlook.

Popularity: Surprisingly, Laurie, as pretty as she is, never faced a situation where boys were eager to date her because of who she now was.

Thoughts about Keith: She is not concerned about Keith's becoming involved with anything dangerous (like drugs) because "all he thinks about is girls."

Band Standing: Sings and plays keyboard; it is also strange that although Laurie opposes the songs Keith writes, she never attempts to write one that expresses her beliefs.

DANIEL "DANNY" PARTRIDGE

Age: 10 (the third-born child).

Trait: A schemer. It was actually Danny who organized the family into a band. He borrowed recording equipment from school and talked Shirley into becoming their lead singer when the original singer became ill. He then convinced Reuben Kincaid to represent the group.

Obsession: Money.

Favorite Reading Matter: U.S. Finance and Monetary Report magazine.

Favorite Colors: Dollar green and 14-karat gold.

Bank: An Old West–like safe in his bedroom.

Stock: One share of preferred AT&T stock.

Hobby: Collecting stamps.

School: While a school name is not mentioned, Danny feels it is a waste of time. He attempted (but failed) to become a songwriter, then a (horrible) stand-up comedian (using decades-old jokes), and finally a business tycoon.

Sports: Pitcher for the Dodgers Little League team.

Hangout: The Sweet Shop (later the Taco Stand).

Girls: Danny did have a friend who was a girl (Gloria Hickey, played by Patti Cohoon), but he generally didn't like to associate with them. One 11-year-old girl, Julie Lawrence (Jodie Foster), became fascinated by him and attempted (but failed) to get close to him.

TRACY AND CHRIS PARTRIDGE

Virtually nothing is presented. Tracy (the youngest child) sang and played the tambourine, while Chris (the fourth-born child) played drums. Tracy has a doll called "Patti Partridge" and started a Christmas tradition wherein she places mistletoe over her head to receive a kiss by each member of the family. Tracy is also Reuben's spy: he pays her 10 cents to call him each time Shirley bakes his favorite dessert, apple pie.

OTHER CHARACTERS
Reuben Kincaid (middle name Clarence) is the band's manager. The company for which Reuben works is never revealed, nor is the record label for the Partridge Family albums. Reuben believes Danny is "a 40-year-old midget in a kid outfit" for how he wheels and deals. Reuben's girlfriend, Bonnie Kleinschmidt (Elaine Giftos), is an airline stewardess. His mother (Margaret Hamilton) called him "Ruby."

SPIN-OFF
Partridge Family: 2200 A.D. (CBS, 1974). Shirley (Sherry Alberoni), Laurie (Susan Dey), Keith (Chuck McLennon), Danny (Danny Bonaduce), Tracy (Suzanne Crough), and Chris (Brian Forster) appear in animated form as they perform on various planets.

Police Woman
(NBC, 1974–1978)

Cast: Angie Dickinson (Pepper Anderson), Earl Holliman (Bill Crowley), Ed Bernard (Detective Joe Styles), Charles Dierkop (Detective Pete Royster).

Basis: The lone policewoman (Pepper Anderson) in an all-male squad risks her life to solve crimes associated with murder, kidnapping, and robbery. (See also *Get Christie Love*.)

PEPPER ANDERSON
Real Name: Suzanne Anderson. She first mentions her name as Lee Anne. She chose the nickname "Pepper" "because I like it."

Occupation: Sergeant with the Criminal Conspiracy Division of the Los Angeles Police Department. She was originally a patrol car officer with the Westside Division and moved her way up to the Juvenile Division. After six months, she was transferred to the Vice Squad Division (where she often served as "hooker bait" for perverts). Pepper was groomed by her mother to become a model and eventually became a high-fashion print and runway model. The income was good, but it was not the life she wanted. She quit for more excitement as a police officer.

Sister: Cheryl Anderson (Nicole Kallis). Pepper's parents are not seen or mentioned, and it appears that Pepper cares for Cheryl, who is much younger and attends the Austin School for Learning Disabilities (suffers from autism).

Address: 102 Crestview Drive (the word "Pepper" can be seen on her bedroom wall).

Telephone Number: 514-7915.

Bra Size: 38C ("Pepper needs a pair of 45s [guns] to protect her 38s" was an inside joke).

Partners: Bill Crowley, Joe Stiles, and Pete Royster.

Education: University of California, Los Angeles; the Los Angeles Police Academy.

Sedan Car License Plate: 635 CIN.

Police Woman. *NBC/Photofest.* ©NBC

Character: Her beauty seems to attract seedy characters, and she often acts as bait when working on a case. She does take chances and risks her life to apprehend criminals. She does get shot, punched, and roughed up—"It comes with the territory," she says.

Least Favorite Assignments: Posing as Bill's wife (as Bill tells her, "It was either you and Joe or you and Pete").

OTHER CHARACTERS

William "Bill" Crowley is a career cop and Pepper's superior. He tends to let Pepper do things her way, as he believes that her feminine intuition is a powerful weapon against crime. But he also tells her, "If you work for me, it's 24 hours a day." Bill is divorced from Jackie (Bebe Besch) but still deeply loves her. Although Pepper believes that Bill is Irish, he continually tries to convince her that he is Italian and that as a child his grandmother called him "Cattivone," which he says is Italian for "Bad Boy." Bill often calls Pepper "Pep." Joe Styles was a medic during the Vietnam War.

Note: The original pilot, broadcast as a segment of *Police Story* (NBC, March 26, 1974), found Angie Dickinson playing policewoman Lisa Beaumont with Bert Convy as Bill Crowley and Ed Bernard and Charles Dierkop as Detectives K.C. Styles and Royster. "Flowers of Evil," the episode of November 8, 1974, was very controversial at the time, as it dealt with a trio of lesbian killers. It was withheld from syndication until Decades TV broadcast it on June 24, 2016. In this episode, Pepper mentions that in college she shared a room with a girl who was a lesbian (but they were not lovers).

Rhoda
(CBS, 1974–1978)

Cast: Valerie Harper (Rhoda Morgenstern), David Groh (Joe Gerard), Julie Kavner (Brenda Morgenstern), Lorenzo Music (voice of Carlton).

Basis: The Mary Tyler Moore Show spin-off about Mary Richards's best friend, Rhoda Morgenstern, as she leaves Minneapolis to begin a new life in New York City.

RHODA FAYE MORGENSTERN

Parents: Ida (Nancy Walker) and Martin Morgenstern (Harold Gould). Ida's maiden name is Ida Nissel.

Siblings: Sisters, Debbie Morgenstern (Liberty Williams); Brenda (see below); unseen brother, Arnold.

Date of Birth: December 1941, in the Bronx, New York.

Religion: Jewish.

Address: Apartment 4G at 3517 Grand Concourse near Fordham Road in the Bronx (as a child); 119 North Weatherly (Minneapolis; an $87.50 a month attic apartment). In Manhattan: 332 West 46th Street, Apartment 9B (when married; rent $200 a month); later Apartment 4G ($175 a month rent when single).

New York Education: P.S. 7 grammar school (won the science fair with a model of the human brain); Evander High School (a member of the Sharkettes gang).

Minneapolis Occupation: Window dresser (later Manager in Charge of Windows) at Hemple's Department Store (where she won the beauty pageant title Ms. Hemple's Department Store). She also worked at Bloomfield's Department Store, turned down a job with Bloomingdale's in New York and owned a floral shop called Rhodadendron.

New York Occupation: Editor's assistant at Waterman Publishing Company (1974); Windows by Rhoda, an interior decorating business (1974-1976); designer for the Doyle Costume Company (1976–1978, where she earns an extra $2.50 an hour as the bookkeeper).

Husband (1974–1976): Joe Gerard, owner of the New York Wrecking Company. Joe is divorced from Marian (Joan Van Ark) and the father of Donny (Todd Turquand then Shane Sinutko). After leaving Minneapolis, Rhoda returned to New York for a two-week vacation and met Joe through one of Brenda's baby sitting jobs (watching Donny). After she and Joe divorce, Rhoda is wooed by Johnny Venture (Michael DeLano), a nightclub performer, known as Mr. Microphone, at Club 77.

Unpublished Book: "How to Eat Anything You Want Whenever You Want—And Get Very Very Fat."

Pet Goldfish: Goldie (Minneapolis episodes).

Favorite Eatery: The Duke of Pizza (New York episodes).

Favorite Doll: Wendy (until her head fell off and Rhoda banished her to a trash can).

Most Embarrassing Childhood Moment: "When I played a salt shaker in a school play and wet my pants."

New York Tradition: Rhoda and Brenda gather at their parents' house every two weeks for dinner (Friday nights); Ida always complains that Rhoda doesn't wear a bra.

Character: A bit rough around the edges, not afraid of confrontation, and able to care for herself. She feels she has a weight problem and constantly diets (she is tempted by sweets and says, "I should just apply it to my hips"). Her one success story was joining Calorie Cutters and losing 20 pounds.

Relatives: Aunt Rose (Brett Somers); Joe's Parents: Paul (Robert Alda) and Ruth Maginnes-Gerard (Paula Victor).

BRENDA MORGENSTERN

Middle Name: Faye (her mother loved the name and gave it to her and Rhoda).

Education: Evander High School; an unnamed night school (taking bookkeeping courses as a part of the bank's Earn While You Learn program).

Occupation: Teller at the First Security Bank.

Beauty Pageant: Contestant at the First Security Bank's annual Favorite Teller Pageant (wherein the winner would appear in an ad campaign); she lost.

New York Address: The same building as Rhoda but in Apt. 2D, later 6G.

Monthly Expenses: Rent: $175; phone: $25; utilities: $20; laundry: $15; beauty and cosmetics: $30; miscellaneous: $30.

Boyfriends: Benny Goodwin (Ray Butenica), works in a highway toll booth; Gary Levy (Gary Silver), the owner of a clothing store called Gary Levi (specializes in selling jeans), Nick Lobo (Richard Masur), a struggling musician (plays accordion) who walked away from the family trash business to pursue his dream.

Jealous Streak: Envious of Rhoda as she feels she is not as pretty. To improve her looks she adopted a blonde wig (she is a brunette) and lost weight (abandoning junk food).

CARLTON, YOUR DOORMAN

Occupation: The apartment house doorman (never seen; only heard).

Catch Phrase: "Hello, this is Carlton, your Doorman" (which he says when he is buzzed by a tenant).

Fault: Alcohol (as he most often sounds intoxicated, although he insists he has stopped drinking and can speak clearly). Has a tendency to mix up tenant's mail.

Words of Wisdom: "It's not drinking that causes hangovers, it's stopping"; "If it is raining and you walk through that storm, you'll get wet"; "If the weather's crummy and you feel crummy, then you fit right in"; "If you are in a room with no windows and turn off the light, you will be in the dark."

Relatives: Unnamed mother (Ruth Gordon).

Note: An attempt was made to spin the character off in an animated series called *Carlton, Your Doorman* (CBS, 1980) that found Carlton (voice of Lorenzo Music) attempting to better his position in life.

UPDATE

The 2000 ABC-TV movie *Mary and Rhoda* reveals that Rhoda is now a professional photographer and the mother of Meredith (Marisa Ryan), a medical student at Barnard College.

The Rockford Files
(NBC, 1974–1980)

Cast: James Garner (Jim Rockford), Stuart Margolin (Angel), Joe Santos (Dennis Becker), Gretchen Corbett (Beth Davenport).

Basis: An ex-con turned private detective solves cases he calls the "Rockford Files" (those that are considered unsolvable or labeled inactive by the police).

JAMES SCOTT "JIM" ROCKFORD

Business: The Rockford Private Detective Agency (also called the Rockford Agency). He began the agency in 1968 and has a Yellow Pages phone book ad, but a phone number does not appear. Jim also solves cases for the Boston

Casualty Insurance Company and worked temporarily as a reporter for a gossip sheet called the *National Inquisitor*.

Fee: $200 (then $250) a day plus expenses.

Home: The Paradise Cove Trailer Colony in Malibu Beach, California.

Address: 29 Palm Road (also given as 29 Cove Road, 2354 Pacific Coast, and 2354 Ocean Boulevard).

Telephone Number: 555-2368 (later 555-9000).

Car: A bronze Pontiac Firebird Esprit.

License Plate: 853 CNG (later OK 6853 and 853 OKG).

Military Service: Army corporal with the Fifth Regimental Combat Team (part of the 24th Infantry) during the Korean War. His bravery earned him the Silver Star.

The Crime: Falsely convicted of armed robbery and sentenced to 20 years at San Quentin. He was given a full pardon after five years when new evidence cleared him.

The Aftermath: Bitter and refuses to talk to anyone about his conviction.

Height: 6 feet, 2 inches tall.

Weight: 200 pounds.

Favorite Drink: Scotch.

Relaxation: Fishing.

Rockford Files. *NBC/Photofest.* ©*NBC*

Favorite Eatery: Casa Tacos (he always leaves a 10 percent tip "because it seems like 10 percent is enough").

Favorite Orchestra Leader: Count Basie.

Favorite Singer: Ella Fitzgerald.

Weapon: A gun that he rarely uses (he keeps it in a coffee can or cookie jar in his home).

Theory: Bending the law to fit his needs "because I don't like the alternatives."

Alias: Jerry Vanders, reporter for the Los Angeles *Sun* (allows him to get into places his private investigator license can't).

Fault: Difficulty remembering a license plate number even after seeing it.

OTHER CHARACTERS

Joseph "Rocky" Rockford (Noah Beery Jr.) is Jim's father, a 68-year-old retired big-rig truck driver. He drove for 45 years and is a member of Truckers Union Local 214. His favorite TV show is *Falcone* (mythical) and he calls Jim "Sonny." He drives a two-tone gray-and-maroon 1975 GMC K-15 Sierra Classic pickup truck (license plate IE 49901). Robert Donley played Rocky in the pilot episode.

Evelyn Martin, called "Angel" (his street name), is a con artist who often assists Jim. While he can be trusted (at times), Jim calls him a "Transformer" ("Someone who rats on someone to save his own neck"). Angel mentioned that he once wrote the Miss Lonely Hearts column for his brother's newspaper. He first drove a 1969 Cadillac, then a white 1965 Cadillac DeVille convertible that he nicknamed Lucille.

Dennis Becker is a sergeant (then lieutenant) with the Homicide Division of the Wilshire branch of the Los Angeles Police Department. He has a desk in the squad room (418) and hopes to make lieutenant (but fears his association with an ex-con is preventing him from achieving that goal; he believes that Jim enjoys visiting crime scenes and other human disasters). He calls Rockford "Jimbo." Dennis is married to Peggy (Pat Finley), who is attending evening classes at the University of California, Los Angeles.

Elizabeth "Beth" Davenport is Jim's romantic interest, a lawyer with the firm of Hardcort and Lowe. She calls Rockford "Jim" and drives a yellow Porsche 914 (first season), then a red Mercedes-Benz 450 SL.

SPIN-OFF

Richie Brockelman, Private Eye (NBC, 1978). Here Richie Brockelman (Dennis Dugan) is a young private eye who emulates Rockford, but has little success in acquiring cases. He has office 24 in the Bromley Building at 4th and Alameda in Los Angeles and charges (but rarely gets) $200 a day. He lives at 8410 Turtle Dove Drive and drives a sedan with the plate 238 PCE. Barbara Bosson plays his secretary, Sharon Peterson.

The Ropers
(ABC, 1979–1980)

Cast: Norman Fell (Stanley Roper), Audra Lindley (Helen Roper), Jeffrey Tambor (Jeffrey Brookes III), Patricia McCormick (Anne Brookes), Evan Cohen (David Brookes).

Basis: Three's Company spin-off that follows former landlords Stanley and Helen Roper as they begin new lives in an exclusive community where their lower-class standing is anything but appealing to their snooty neighbor, Jeffrey Brookes III.

STANLEY ROPER
Address: 46 Peacock Drive at the Royal Condominium Town House Complex in Chevia Hills, California.

Telephone Number: 555-3099.

Occupation: Retired (owned the Ropers Apartment Building; lived in Apartment 101).

Favorite TV Show: Name That Tune (Helen claims it happened "ever since he guessed the National Anthem in seven notes").

Favorite Bedtime Drink: Hot cocoa.

Favorite Pastime: Entering contests. On *Three's Company*, it was peeping (through binoculars) at "the gorgeous blonde in Apartment 107" through the front window.

Favorite Sunday Paper Comic Strip: Andy Capp.

First Love: A voluptuous girl named Gloria Mealy (Gloria LeRoy).

Car: A 1958 Chevrolet.

Collection: Girlie magazines (like *Playhouse*) that he first hides in his toolbox and, later, "in the bathroom." As Stanley claims, he reads them only "for the men's fashion styles."

Character: Not the most romantic of men and avoids physical contact with Helen (although he has an eye for younger women) with flimsy excuses. He claims that if he saw Helen come to bed in the nude, he would be the first one to complain.

Trait: A weird sense of humor that appears to result from someone else's misfortune (Helen claims his sense of humor is a birth defect). She also says that Stanley snores, uses foul language when he gets angry, and takes a nap every afternoon.

Relatives: Niece, Karen (Christina Hart).

HELEN ROPER
Mother: Unnamed (Lucille Benson).

Sisters: Ethel Armbrewster (Dena Dietrich), Hilda (Dulcie Pullman). Rod Colbin plays Ethel's husband, Hubert Armbrewster.

Occupation: Housewife. She worked as a USO (United Serviceman's Organization) entertainer during World War II (where she met Stanley, a soldier, during a show).

Pets: Muffin (a dog); Stanley (a parakeet).

Wardrobe: Not the most appealing of outfits (usually in loose-fitting clothing, which could partially account for Stanley's lack of affection).

Character: Helen accepts Stanley's nonsense because she loves him. Her objective is to break down the barriers that prevent him from becoming romantic. If Helen were to write an autobiography, she would title it "Not Tonight Helen" (as Stanley always says).

Relatives: Aunt, Martha (Irene Tedrow).

OTHER CHARACTERS

Jeffrey Brookes III, his wife Anne, and their impressionable son David live at 44 Peacock Drive. Jeffrey is the owner of the Brookes Real Estate Company and detests the Ropers, as he feels they are far beneath his social standing and will bring down property values. He is president of the Royal Dale Home Owners Association and fails to understand how Anne and David could not only accept Helen and Stanley but also become their friends. A day without seeing Stanley is a day of pure delight for him.

Note: Based on the British series *George and Mildred* (which was a spin-off from *Man about the House*, the basis for *Three's Company*).

The Sandy Duncan Show
(CBS, 1971–1972)

Cast: Sandy Duncan (Sandy Stockton), Nita Talbot (Maggie Prescott), Tom Bosley (Bert Quinn).

Basis: A small-town girl (Sandy) struggles to make a new life for herself in California as a schoolteacher. Information on the original concept, *Funny Face*, is also contained here.

SANDRA "SANDY" STOCKTON

Place of Birth: Taylorville, Illinois (population, before Sandy left, 10,425).

Education: Taylorville Grammar School; Taylorville High School.

Career Ambition: To become a schoolteacher.

The Move: After graduating from high school, Sandy felt the time was right and relocated to Los Angeles to become a student at the University of California, Los Angeles (UCLA) (where her major is education).

First Address: 130 North Weatherly Boulevard (Apartment 12) of the Royal Weatherly Hotel.

Telephone Number: 555-3444.

Best Friend: Alice McRaven (Valorie Armstrong), her neighbor.

Occupation: Part-time model with the Prescott Advertising Agency (*Funny Face* episodes).

Employer: Margaret "Maggie" Prescott, a former fashion model.

Agency Address: 11 West Pico Street.

Agency Telephone Number: 555-3174.

TV Modeling Jobs: Spokesgirl for John E. Apple Seed Used Cars ("In the heart of the San Fernando Valley") and the Yummy Peanut Butter Girl (commercials).

TV Series Role: A nonspeaking part on *Mission: Impossible* (she was discovered by agent Manny Pitler [Avery Schreiber] and played a girl who is killed when a music box explodes in her face).

Second Address: A new apartment (2A) but at an unidentified location.

Second Occupation: Student teacher at UCLA and part-time secretary to Bert Quinn, owner of the Quinn and Cohen Advertising Agency.

Agency Address: 5099 Lincoln Boulevard in Los Angeles.

Friends: Hilary (Pamela Zarit), the agency's scatterbrained secretary; Kay Fox (Marian Mercer), her levelheaded neighbor; and Alex Lembeck (M. Emmet Walsh), a motorcycle cop who yearned to write a book about his police work experiences.

Note: Production on *Funny Face* was halted when Sandy Duncan required emergency eye surgery. For reasons that are not clear, *Funny Face* (which was a top-performing show for CBS) was altered and retitled *The Sandy Duncan Show.*

Sanford and Son
(NBC, 1972–1977)

Cast: Redd Foxx (Fred G. Sanford), Demond Wilson (Lamont Sanford), La-Wanda Page (Esther Anderson), Whitman Mayo (Grady Wilson), Nathaniel Taylor (Rollo Larson).

Basis: A grumpy, 65-year-old African American widower (Fred Sanford) and his son, Lamont, attempt to make a decent living running a decrepit junkyard in Los Angeles.

FRED G. SANFORD

Place of Birth: St. Louis, Missouri. His father was a shoemaker.

Year of Birth: 1908 (also mentioned as 1907).

Sister: Frances Victor (Mary Alice). She is married to Rodney Victor (Allan Drake), a Caucasian entertainer.

Late Wife: Elizabeth Winfield (they married in 1934; Elizabeth passed away in 1959). Elizabeth lived at 3207 Enright in St. Louis when she and Fred dated.

Son: Lamont Sanford.

Business: Sanford and Son Salvage. He considers the junkyard his "empire" and hopes to pass it down to Lamont.

Business/Home Address: 9114 South Central in Los Angeles.

Tax Shelter: The Divine Profit Church (created by Fred to avoid paying taxes).

Background: Fred showed great promise as a singer and dancer and turned that talent into a career by performing in vaudeville (with his partner Juanita). Fred quit vaudeville when he met Elizabeth and in 1945 purchased a 40- by 60-foot lot in Los Angeles. It is here that he built a home and established a junkyard (Sanford Salvage). Fred raised Lamont alone after Elizabeth's passing, and when Lamont turned 18, Fred renamed the business Sanford and Son. Fred never achieved his dream of a "junk empire" but feels comfortable in his surroundings. He also mentions that he lived in Georgia and in 1932 sold apples on the street. To make extra money (1975), he attempted to sell Whopper Choppers, a food-dicing gizmo.

Heritage: The son of a very poor family (they slept five to a room) who had to drop out of school in eighth grade to help provide support.

Education: Dickinson Elementary School. In the final episode, Fred achieves a dream when he earns his high school diploma and becomes class valedictorian.

Favorite Drink: Ripple (his home-brewed alcoholic beverage).

Character: Ornery and cantankerous and set in his ways. Fred is distrustful of people, and when he doesn't get his way, he feigns a heart attack (he places his hand on his heart, looks up to Heaven, and says, "I'm coming Elizabeth, this is it, the big one"; in the first episode, it is mentioned that Fred has already had 15 major heart attacks). When there is heavy work to be done, Fred develops a sudden case of "arth-i-ritis." Fred needs to wear eyeglasses but refuses to see an optometrist (he has a drawer full of discarded glasses and rummages through them to find a suitable pair when he needs to read something).

Catchphrase: "How would you like one across your lips?" (which he says with a fist made when someone irritates him).

Yearly Income: $7,000 ($4,000 from the business; $3,000 from Social Security).

Favorite Vocal Group: The Ink Spots (Fred often sings lines from their various songs). Fred also has a rare collection of singer Blind Mello Jello albums.

Habit: Although Lamont mentions that Fred has been smoking cigarettes "since he was a baby," Fred is seen smoking only once (in the episode "Fred Sanford Has a Baby").

Romantic Interest: Donna Harris (Lynn Hamilton), a nurse who is also much younger than Fred, then Evelyn Lewis (Marguerite Ray), a wealthy woman (lives at 77 Kantwell Drive in Beverly Hills) whose family disapproved of their relationship (due to their social standing differences). Percy Rodriques played Evelyn's snooty brother Winston; Suzanne Stone was Evelyn's daughter Cissy Lewis.

Best Friend: Grady Wilson. Grady is not the brightest man Fred knows, and they appear to have been friends since Fred established his empire. Grady was mentioned as being born in Chicago and was known as the "Sheik of Drexell Avenue" for his ability to charm the ladies. While the character was essential to the series (as Grady provided someone Fred's own age to play off), he was written out for a spin-off called *Grady* (NBC, 1975–1976). Here, Grady moves to Santa Monica (at 636 Carlisle Street) to live with his married daughter Ellie Marshall (Carol Cole) and her husband Hal (Haywood Nelson). His catchphrase was "Good googledy moo."

Neighbor: Julio Fuentes (Gregory Sierra). Although Julio liked Fred, Fred was uncomfortable living next door to a Puerto Rican (he was also annoyed that Julio's pet goat, Chico, would constantly come into his home). When Julio moved, Fred purchased his home and turned it into the Sanford Arms Rooming House. Alma Beltran played Julio's sister Maria Fuentes.

Personal Nightmare: Esther Anderson, called "Aunt Esther." Esther is Fred's sister-in-law (Elizabeth's older sister) and a constant source of irritation for Fred, as he simply cannot stand her (they constantly argue and insult each other). Esther is a deeply religious Baptist (attends the Central Avenue Baptist Church) and calls Fred "a heathen" (and often tells him, "Watch it sucka"). Esther is married to Woody (DeForest Covan, then Raymond Allen), the owner of Woody's Hardware Store (who appears content living with her as long as he is drunk). When the series first began, Aunt Ethel (Beah Richards), Esther's sister, and Fred clashed.

Fred's Biggest Turnoff: "Ugly white women" (as he says).

Relatives: Elizabeth's sisters, Minnie (Esther Sutherland), Flossie (Dorothy Meyer), and Hazel (not seen); uncle, Edgar (Bobby Johanson).

LAMONT SANFORD

Birthday: Questionable: first February 1942, then September 27, 1940. He is said to be 34 when the series begins and 31 in 1974 episodes.

Parents: Fred and Elizabeth Sanford.

Place of Birth: St. Louis.

Middle Name: Grady. Later, Fred tells him that Lamont is his middle name and that he actually has no first name, as he and Elizabeth "never got around to it."

Nickname for Fred: "Pop." Fred calls him "Dummy" (sometimes "You Big Dummy"). Due to Fred's actions, Lamont often calls him "Old Fool."

Truck: A beat-up faded red Ford pickup truck; license plate 43648E.

Education: South Central High School (he was never able to attend college because Fred never put money aside).

Occupation: Junk dealer (while Fred claims he is a junk dealer, Lamont prefers to be called a "collector"). Lamont also held a second job as a salesman at an unnamed men's clothing store.

Hobby: Collecting glass and porcelain figurines.

Favorite Dinner: Steak, French fries, onion rings, and string beans.

Name Change: "Kalunde" (when Lamont felt he should embrace his African heritage).

Best Friend: Rollo Larson, a rather sleazy guy (known for pulling scams). With Rollo's help, Lamont established an all-girl rock group called the Three Degrees.

Character: Lamont is dissatisfied in his current position and looks to better himself but believes Fred is holding him back: "I'll never get married. I'll wind up an old broken down junk dealer like you." He often threatens to quit—"I'm sick of doing all the work around here. One of these days I'm gonna split. I can't stand being poor like this."

The Split: In 1977, Lamont took a stand and left Fred for a job on the Alaska Pipeline.

The New Partner: Alone and needing help, Fred fast-talks Cal Pettie (Dennis Burkley), a not-too-bright friend of Lamont's, into investing $2,000 in the business. Cal (white) becomes Fred's new partner, and the spin-off *Sanford* was born (NBC, 1980–1981). Cal, an overweight southerner, calls Fred "Mr. Sanford." Although the house and junkyard are the same, the address was now given as 4707 South Central in Watts.

The program is based on the British series *Steptoe and Son* (about a team of "rag and bone men" [junk dealers]). In 1965, NBC produced an unaired American pilot called *Steptoe and Son* with Lee Tracy as Albert and Aldo Ray as his son Harold. Prior to the pilot that sold *Sanford and Son*, Norman Lear produced an unaired version with Barnard Hughes as the father and Paul Sorvino as his son.

Note: Prior to the *Sanford* spin-off, NBC aired *Sanford Arms* in 1977. Here, Fred sells his empire to Phil Wheeler (Theodore Wilson), a widower and retired army man with two children, Angie (Tina Andrews) and Nat (John Earl), who turns the junkyard into the Sanford Arms Rooming House.

The Six Million Dollar Man
(ABC, 1973–1978)

Cast: Lee Majors (Steve Austin), Richard Anderson (Oscar Goldman).

Basis: Astronaut Steve Austin, endowed with special abilities after a bionic operation saves his life, performs assignments for Oscar Goldman, head of the OSI (Office of Scientific Intelligence; also called the Office of Scientific Information).

STEVEN "STEVE" AUSTIN

Place of Birth: Ojai, California (the "Home of American Astronaut Steve Austin").

Parents: Helen Elgin (Martha Scott) and her second husband, Jim Elgin (Ford Rainey); Steve's birth father is not mentioned.

Rank: U.S. Air Force colonel (made three voyages to the moon).

Address: The former Marsden Ranch on Decatur Road. When Steve is at OSI headquarters in Washington, D.C., he lives at 219 Potomac Way.

Education: Ojai High School (where he met and dated Jaime Sommers, the girl who becomes the Bionic Woman; see *The Bionic Woman* for information).

Car License Plate: 299 KKL.

The Accident: While testing an experimental NASA aircraft, the M2-F2 (also called an M-3F5), a blowout occurs, and Steve, unable to control the craft, crash-lands. In the ensuing explosion, Steve suffers severe injuries (legs broken beyond repair, a crushed right arm, and a damaged left eye, among other complications).

The Operation: At a cost of $6 million, Steve's damaged limbs are replaced with atomic-powered artificial limbs that endow him with superhuman abilities (incredible strength, heightened vision, and the ability to run up to 60 miles per hour). Believing that he owes a debt to the government, Steve agrees to perform sensitive (and highly dangerous) missions for Oscar Goldman. Dr. Rudy Wells (Alan Oppenheimer, then Martin E. Brooks) is the bionic surgeon; a Level 6 clearance is needed to access the bionic labs. Due to editing of the pilot film (to encompass the regular series theme song and visuals), it is actually Darren McGavin as Oliver Spencer (of the OSS) who authorized the bionic operation, not Oscar Goldman.

STEVE'S BIONICS

Eye: Bionic Visual Cortex Terminal. Catalog number 075 HFB.

Arm: Bionic Neuro Link Forearm/Upper Arm Assembly (Right). Catalog number 2021/PJ-1.

Legs: Bionic Neuro Link Bi-Pedal Assembly. Catalog number 914 PAH.

Power Source: Neuro Feedback Terminated. Power Supply: Atomic Type, AED-4. Catalog number 2021 AED-4. 1,500-Watt Continuous Duty.

Note: Farrah Fawcett, Lee Majors's wife at the time, appeared in several episodes: Air Force Major Kelly Wood; Victoria Webster, a reporter for KNUZ-TV; and Trish Hollander, a clever art thief.

UPDATES

The Return of the Six Million Dollar Man and the Bionic Woman (NBC, 1987) finds Steve, retired and the owner of the Summer Babe charter boat service, and

The Six Million Dollar Man. *ABC/Photofest. ©ABC*

Jaime, the head of a rehabilitation center, being recruited by Oscar to defeat an evil organization (Fortress) with the help of Michael Austin (Tom Schanley), Steve's estranged son (after being injured in a plane crash, Michael, an air force pilot, was given a bionic operation to save his life, replacing both legs, his right arm, 10 ribs, and his right eye).

The Bionic Showdown (NBC, 1979) finds Kate Mason (Sandra Bullock) becoming an OSI agent after she is given a bionic operation to cure her degenerative muscle disease.

Bionic Ever After (CBS, 1994) reunites Steve and Jaime as special operatives working for Oscar Goldman of the OSI.

Starsky and Hutch
(ABC, 1975–1979)

Cast: Paul Michel Glaser (Dave Starsky), David Soul (Ken Hutchinson), Antonio Fargas (Huggy Bear), Bernie Hamilton (Harold Dobey).

Basis: Starsky and Hutch, plainclothes detectives with the Metropolitan Division of the Bay City Police Department, battle crime in their own unique way—and not always within the limits of the law.

DAVID "DAVE" STARSKY

Place of Birth: New York City (moved to California in 1958).

Brother: Nick (John Herzfield). Their father was a cop, their mother a homemaker.

Religion: Jewish.

Birth Year: Through dialogue, it is placed between 1943 and 1945.

Military Service: The army; he enrolled in the Police Academy after his discharge.

Gun: A Colt .45 (a Baretta 9-mm automatic pistol in the pilot).

Address: 2000 Ridgeway Avenue.

Car: Candy apple red with a white stripe; license plate 537 ONW.

Police Car Code: Zebra 3.

Vice: Junk food.

Favorite Movies: Laurel and Hardy comedies.

Fear: Heights and dogs.

Trait: Rather impetuous.

Favorite Holiday: Christmas.

Childhood Memory: Imagined his backyard as Doodletown, a magical playland.

Trademark: A cardigan sweater.

KENNETH HUTCHINSON

Nicknames: "Ken" and "Hutch."

Place of Birth: California.

Address: A Venice Apartments beach house at 1027½ Ocean in Sea Point.

The Partnership: Ken met Dave at the Police Academy in 1969. They became patrol officers in 1970 (worked out of Metro Division) and undercover cops in 1974.

Car: A scratched, dented, gas-guzzling, muffler-smoking gray car, license plate 552 LQD. It has a bumper sticker that reads "Cops Need Love Too."

Police Car Code: Zebra 3.

Trait: Prefers health foods; vitamin E and wheat germ are most important.

Musical Ability: Plays the guitar and sings.

Gun: A .357 Magnum. In the pilot, Ken used a Smith & Wesson .38.

Rule: Since Dave and Ken share each other's cars for assignments, Ken refuses to allow Dave to drive his car when he is eating—"You're dangerous."

Holiday Spirit: Ken does not enjoy the holidays and tries not to let specific holidays, like Christmas, affect him.

Habit: Slamming their captain's office door and aggravating him. "I'm working on it," he says when Captain Dobey complains.

Childhood Memory: Ken bought toys from Uncle Elmo's Toy Shop. It is now Uncle Elmo's Adult Toy Shop.

Education: Xavier High School (where he was friends with a rich kid and called the "Pauper"; he was also class valedictorian and voted "Most Likely to Succeed").

Dream: To quit the police force and live life as a ship's captain.

HUGGY BEAR

Occupation: Snitch (Ken and Dave's information man).

Character: Fancies himself as a magician ("Huggy, the Houdini with Soul") but is actually a man of many talents (most of which border on the illegal). In one episode, he is given the last name of Brown. He owns a nightclub called Huggy Bear's (also called Huggy's and Huggy's Restaurant). Later, he is seen as the owner of a bar called the Pits.

Favorite Hangout: The Jungle Club (a girlie bar).

License Plates Seen on Huggy's Office Wall: IE 2174, 504 EB5, 237 308, 182 174.

HAROLD DOBEY

Occupation: Captain of detectives.

Complaints: Starsky and Hutch's unorthodox methods of investigating and disregarding his instructions; Hutch handing in their daily reports on a weekly basis; Dave's habit of forgetting (on purpose) to fill in report dates; their continual bickering; and playing practical jokes.

Mobile Phone Extension: 2268 (later 3056). 900-21 is the mobile phone number for Starsky and Hutch to reach him. Richard Ward played Captain Dobey in the pilot.

Taxi

(ABC, 1978–1982; NBC, 1982–1983)

Cast: Judd Hirsch (Alex Reiger), Danny DeVito (Louie DePalma), Marilu Henner (Elaine Nardo), Tony Danza (Tony Banta), Jeff Conaway (Bobby Wheeler), Christopher Lloyd (Jim Ignatowski), Andy Kaufman (Latka Gravas), Carol Kane (Simka Gravas).

Basis: Incidents in the lives of drivers for the Manhattan-based Sunshine Cab Company.

OVERALL SERIES INFORMATION

Cab Rates: 75 cents for the first mile; 15 cents each additional mile (later 90 cents and $1.00 each additional mile).

Company Phone Number: 555-6328.

Most Popular Cab: 804 (driven by almost every cabbie and holds the record at half a million miles).

Worst Cab: 413 (known as the "Widow Maker").

Most Pleasing Cab: 704 (known as the "Memory Cab").

Most Famous Driver: Actor James Caan—"But he'll be back," says Louie.

Hangout: Mario's, a bar/restaurant.

Cab Cleaning: Washed at Cars-a-Poppin (at 23rd Street between Fifth and Sixth avenues).

Posted Notice: "Dayline Drivers Must Report or Phone in by 6 a.m. Nightline Drivers Must Report or Phone in by 3 p.m."

Vending Machine: Dispenses coffee, soup, or hot chocolate for 25 cents.

Opening Theme: Tony Banta is seen driving across the Queensboro Bridge (the sequence is looped, so the same scene appears several times).

Closing Theme: Cab 804 is seen; however, when it changes to show the cab at a different angle, it is cab 734, then cab 239. The license plate is 9207T1.

ALEXANDER "ALEX" REIGER

Father: Joseph "Joe" Reiger (Jack Gilford).

Sister: Charlotte (Joan Hackett). Joe deserted the family when they were children.

Marital Status: Divorced from Phyllis Reiger (Louise Lasser).

Daughter: Cathy Reiger (Talia Balsam); she lives with her mother.

Occupation: Cab driver. He also worked as night watchman and waiter at Mario's bar.

Home: Apartment 2A (address not given).

Character: The oldest and wisest of the cabbies (acts like a father figure to his coworkers as he listens to their problems and tries to solve them). He is also not very ambitious and just accepts where he is in life ("I'm a cab driver, and I don't mind").

Pet Dog: Buddy.

Thoughts about Louie: "If God had a reason for creating snakes, lice, and vermin, he had a reason for creating Louie."

LOUIS "LOUIE" DEPALMA

Occupation: Dispatcher. He became a cabbie in 1963 and claims his first fare was actor Errol Flynn. He also held a temporary job as a Wall Street stockbroker.

Taxi. ABC/Photofest. ©ABC

Office: "The Cage" (which he calls "my window on the world"—as he spies on the cabbies from it).

Belief: All his drivers are losers, "people who never amount to anything."

No-No Word: "Never, never, but never say the word *accident*."

Character: Overall just plain nasty. He is lecherous, believes he is a ladies' man, and loves money. As people say, "The difference between Louie and other people is two million years of evolution" and "When one sees repulsive things floating around in water, one should think of Louie. He'd like that." When cabbies retire, Louie presents them with a map of U.S. highways. If he needs a favor, he says simply, "Who wants a good cab today." If Louie takes a phone message for a cabbie, he charges $1.

Marital Status: Single.

Romance: Louie had a brief affair with Zina Sherman (Rhea Perlman), the candy machine vending girl.

Favorite TV Program: The Phil Donahue Show (then popular talk show).

Relatives: Brother, Nick DePalma (Richard Foronjy); mother, Gabriella De Palma (Julia DeVito).

ELAINE NARDO

Occupation: Cab driver (also works as an art appraiser at the Hazelton Galleries).

Maiden Name: Elaine O'Connor.

Marital Status: Divorced.

Children: Jennifer (Melanie Gaffin) and Jason (David Mendenhall).

Home: Apartment 6A (address not given).

Telephone Number: 555-4276.

Education: Eastside High School (where she was voted "Most Likely to Succeed"; her children attend P.S. 33 in Manhattan).

Measurements: 37-26-26.

Dislike: Louie's constant unwanted attention. He calls her breasts "headlights" (although his line "Nardo's got knobs" was also said); unknown to Elaine, Louie has made a peephole in the ladies' room so he can watch her undress.

ANTHONY "TONY" BANTA

Father: Angie Banta (Donnelly Rhodes).

Sister: Monica Douglas (Julie Kavner).

Occupation: Cab driver (also held a temporary job as a money collector for a bookie).

Marital Status: Single.

Aspiration: To become a world-class boxer.

Current Status: Middleweight (loses most of his matches).

Military Service: Army private during the Vietnam War.

Pet Goldfish: George and Wanda.

ROBERT "BOBBY" WHEELER

Occupation: Cab driver (worked temporarily as a children's party entertainer).

Place of Birth: The Bronx (he moved to Manhattan to pursue his acting career).

Idol: Sir Laurence Olivier.

Marital Status: Single.

TV Debut: "Skip" on the soap opera *For Better, for Worse*. His appearance on the TV soap opera *Boise* enabled him to move to Hollywood to achieve his dream.

One-Man Play: Charles Darwin Tonight.

Trait: Believes he is talented and sexy but often can't translate that to roles (as he is often told by producers that he "is not sexy enough").

JAMES "JIM" IGNATOWSKI

Father: James Caldwell Sr. (Victor Buono).

Siblings: Sister, Lila Caldwell (Barbara Deitch); brother, Tom Caldwell (Walter Olkewicz).

Occupation: Cab driver. He also held a job as a door-to-door salesman selling the Magic Carpet Wizard Vacuum Cleaner (although he thought he was selling encyclopedias).

Problem: Spaced out from years of drug use; still believes it is the 1960s.

Nickname: "Iggie."

Real Name: James Caldwell.

Education: Harvard University (where the studious Jim first encountered drug-laced "funny brownies").

Name Change: It was the 1960s, and one night while high on drugs, Jim changed his last name to Ignatowski, believing it was "Star Child" spelled backwards.

Drug Side Effects: Jim is now an expert on marijuana—he can tell you the day, week, and year a particular weed was grown. He screams in his sleep, doesn't realize he is doing something (like humming), plays concert piano (as he says, "I must-a had lessons"), and makes bank guards nervous (place their hands on their guns) when he walks into a bank.

Home: A condemned building in Brooklyn. When the building was torn down, he moved in with Louie (and burned down the apartment when he left a bean bag on the oven).

Heroes: St. Thomas Aquinas, Alan Alda, and Louie DePalma.

Favorite Movies: Star Wars and *E.T.*

Favorite TV Show: Star Trek (although he also mentions *The Bob Newhart Show*, as he had an obsession for the character of Carol [Marcia Wallace]).

Arrest Record: Theft (stealing decorations at the 1968 Democratic Convention).

Racehorse: Gary (which he purchased for $10,000).

Business: When Jim inherited his late father's money ($3.5 million), he bought the hangout, Mario's, and renamed it Jim's Mario's.

Marital Status: Single.

Religion: Jim is an ordained minister in the Church of the Peaceful (he is some-times called "Reverend Jim").

LATKA GRAVAS

Mother: Greta Gravas (Susan Kellerman).

Occupation: Car mechanic. He held a temporary job as a busboy at Mario's.

Place of Birth: A strange, unidentified Eastern European country whose language sounds like gibberish. In one episode, he pinpoints his homeland as being in the Caspian Sea.

Religion: Orthodox.

Country Belief: "Mindless superstitions and pointless rituals are the only things that separate people in my country from the animals."

Childhood: Hails from a very poor family. For the first eight years of his life, he lived outdoors with a chair and a wooden bucket. When his father received a raise in pay, they moved indoors. His mother was mean, as she forced him to spend summers with his Uncle Bobka, who tried to make a man of him.

Lottery "Riches": Figuring the only way to improve himself was to play his coun-try's lottery. He picked the winning numbers and received the top prize—a flyswatter.

Character: Shy and sensitive and afraid of women. To become familiar with Ameri-can women, Latka studied *Playboy* magazine and altered his life to become the confident ladies' man Vic Ferrari (who spoke with perfect unaccented English). A second personality also arose due to his studies—Arlo the cowboy.

Business: Grandma Gravas's Old Fashioned Oatmeal Cookies (an old family recipe that used drugs as the main ingredient).

Girlfriend, Then Wife: Simka Dablitz. They married in their traditional custom: the male wears the bridal dress, the female the tuxedo. A dance called the Plumitz follows the ceremony.

Simka: Born in the same country as Latka but from a different tribe (Simka's people were respectful of others; Latka's people made cruel joke's about Simka's tribe). Simka is romantic and moody but feared by men when she becomes angry (although Latka finds her temper romantic).

Relatives: Simka's cousin, Zifka (Mark Blankfield).

Three's Company
(ABC, 1977–1984)

Cast: John Ritter (Jack Tripper), Suzanne Somers (Chrissy Snow), Joyce De-Witt (Janet Wood), Jenilee Harrison (Cindy Snow), Priscilla Barnes (Teri

Alden), Norman Fell (Stanley Roper), Audra Lindley (Helen Roper), Don
Knotts (Ralph Furley), Richard Kline (Larry Dallas).

Basis: Two single women (Chrissy and Janet) and a bachelor (Jack) attempt to
share an apartment—and maintain a platonic relationship.

OVERALL SERIES INFORMATION

The Ropers Apartment Building in Santa Monica, California, provides the basic
setting. It was originally owned by Stanley Roper and his wife Helen; later, it was
owned by Bart Furley but managed by his brother Ralph Furley.

Chrissy Snow and Janet Wood originally shared the apartment with Eleanor
Garvey. When Eleanor (Marianne Black) leaves to marry (a man named Teddy,
whom she later divorces), Janet and Chrissy throw a farewell party. A party
crasher (Jack) becomes their new roommate when they find him, having had
too much to drink, asleep in their bathtub. Jack had been living at the YMCA.

Chrissy, Janet, and Jack share Apartment 201. Cindy Snow, Chrissy's
cousin, replaces her, and Cindy, in turn, is replaced by Teri Alden. Rent is $300
a month, and the roommates enjoy drinks at the Regal Beagle, a British-styled
pub. In the original opening theme, Suzanne Somers (in a wig) is seen as the
brunette walking on the beach. In the sixth-season opening theme, a toddler is
seen with Joyce DeWitt feeding a goat; the toddler is Jason Ritter, John's son
(revealed on the DVD release of the series).

In the original pilot, based on the British series *Man about the House*, Norman Fell and Audra Lindley played the landlords as George and Mildred (the
names in the British version). It was set in North Hollywood, California, at the
Hacienda Palms apartment complex. Jenny (Valerie Curtin), Samantha (Suzanne Zenor), and David (John Ritter) were the roommates. A second pilot re-
tained Norman Fell and Audra Lindley (now as Stanley and Helen Roper) with
John Ritter as Jack Tripper, Joyce DeWitt as Janet, and Suze Lanier-Bramlett as
Chrissy. Suzanne Somers replaced Suze in a third pilot, which became the first
episode of the series.

JACK TRIPPER

Father: Jack Tripper Sr. (Dick Shawn); mother, unnamed (Georgann Johnson).

Brothers: Lee Tripper (John Getts); Tex Tripper (John Ritter).

Occupation: Chef (eggs Madeira was the first meal he prepared for Chrissy and
Janet). He worked as a fast-food store cook, personal chef, chef at Marconi's
Diner, and finally head chef at Angelino's Italian Restaurant before opening
his own French eatery, Jack's Bistro, at 834 Ocean Vista in Los Angeles.

Place of Birth: San Diego, California (he later says Arizona).

Childhood: Had a pet dog named Coco and was a fan of the 1954 *Davy Crockett*
TV series. His parents met at a church picnic, and his father calls him "Junior."

Education: San Diego High School (won a trophy as a member of the track team); the L.A. Technical School (majoring in French cuisine).

Meal Specialty: Poached salmon aspic.

Hope: "To become the Galloping Gourmet of the 1980s" (reference to the Graham Kerr TV series *The Galloping Gourmet* of the 1970s).

Military Service: The U.S. Navy (where he got a tattoo on his behind that reads "The Love Butt"). Because of his asthma, he was put to work in the galley.

The Cover-Up: For Jack to live with two girls, he must pretend to be gay to please his landlords, who would not permit the living arrangements if Jack were straight.

Jack's Girlfriend: Victoria "Vicky" Bradford (Mary Cadorette), a flight attendant for Trans Allied Airlines. They met in the last episode when Jack attended a chef's convention in San Francisco. Their relationship was continued in the 1984 spin-off series *Three's a Crowd* (also known as *Three's Company, Too*), wherein Jack and Vicky marry and take up residence above Jack's Bistro (which is now said to be in Ocean Vista, California). The "crowd" is James (Robert Mandan), Vicky's intrusive father and Jack's landlord.

Prior Girlfriends: Jack dated many girls (except his roommates) before meeting Vicky; he was most eager to date the sexy Greedy Gretchen (Teresa Ganzel).

Relatives: Grandpa Tripper (Edward Andrews); uncle, Fremont (Don Porter).

CHRISTMAS "CHRISSY" SNOW

Father: Rev. Luther Snow (Peter Mark Richman); mother, unnamed (Priscilla Morrill).

Occupation: Secretary to J.C. Braddock (Emmaline Henry) of J.C. Braddock and Company. She also sold Easy Time Cosmetics door-to-door.

Place of Birth: San Francisco.

Birthday: December 25. Chrissy first says she was named by her father "because I was the best present he ever got" on Christmas Day; she later says her father was a fan of Bing Crosby and named her after his hit song "White Christmas."

Childhood: The daughter of a Methodist minister who grew up feeling that she had to be the best at everything, especially in Bible school. She tried but could not always live up to his expectations. It left a deep-seated fear in her and now causes her to sleepwalk.

Character: Blonde, beautiful, and a bit naive (she can, for example, turn men on without realizing she is doing it). She is sweet and trusting and cries when she gets upset. She is a member of Harvey's Health Spa and can come up

Three's Company. *ABC/Photofest. ©ABC*

with a plan for something on the spot—but she isn't sure what the plan is until after she realizes what the situation is. Chrissy always tries to answer the telephone with her left ear "because if I don't, I'll be listening with the wrong ear." Despite all the dumb things she does, Chrissy claims, "I always make sense. Other people are just not smart enough to understand me."

Bra Size: 36C (she often goes braless, as she was part of an era called "Jiggle TV," presumably begun by Marlo Thomas on *That Girl* and followed by such actresses as Trisha Noble [*Strike Force*] and Farrah Fawcett [*Charlie's Angels*]).

Traits: Leaves lip gloss on half-eaten donuts and the cap off the toothpaste tube and says, "If I have to listen to a dumb idea, I hope I'm not around to hear it." She snorts when she laughs, and if she loses something, she says, "Before it got lost was the last time I saw it."

The Departure: A contract dispute forced Suzanne Somers to leave the series in 1981. She is first seen in cameos (a quick phone call to Jack and Janet telling them that she is in San Francisco caring for her sick mother), then completely written out; her cousin Cindy becomes Jack and Janet's new roommate.

Relatives: Cousin, Daniel Trent (Jay Garfield).

JANET WOOD

Parents: Roland (Macom McCalman) and Paula Wood (Paula Shaw).

Sister: Jennifer "Jenny" Wood (Devon Ericson).

Occupation: Salesgirl (then manager) of the Arcade Flower Shop. After a hard day's work, Janet exclaims, "I could just sit down and take root."

Place of Birth: Massachusetts.

Childhood: At the age of seven, Janet took ballet lessons (she dreamed of becoming a famous dancer); she later took dance lessons and acquired the starring role in the play *Annie Get Your Gun* in Laguna Beach.

Measurements: 34-22-34. (Janet felt having larger [38D] breasts would attract men and contemplated implants. She wore falsies, became uncomfortable, and dropped the idea.)

Hair Color: Brunette (she wore a blonde wig to attract men but found herself changing from nice to mean; she then went back to her natural hair color [actually black]).

Character: Pretty, practical, smart, and witty. Janet talks and nags and usually gets her way ("People just give into me to shut me up"). She likes to find "love, adventure, and romance at the library" and tends to panic when something upsets her.

Boyfriend: Janet stated from the first episode that she was looking to marry and settle down. It happened in the final episode when she married Philip Dawson, an art dealer.

CYNTHIA "CINDY" SNOW

Relationship: Chrissy's cousin (the daughter of a traveling salesman).

Occupation: Student at the University of California, Los Angeles (UCLA) (studying to become a veterinarian); she also hires herself out as a maid to earn extra money. When first introduced, Cindy was seeking to experience life in the big city. She enrolled in UCLA, and Chrissy arranged for her to stay with Jack and Janet (she shares a bedroom with Janet; Jack has his own bedroom). Chrissy also set her up with a job as a secretary to her boss, a Mr. Hadley (not J.C. Braddock), at an unnamed company.

Place of Birth: Mentioned as "a small town in California."

Pet: A basset hound named Wilbur (which she has had since she was 10 years old).

Bra Size: 36C. She has blue eyes and blonde hair.

Character: Very pretty but clumsy and, according to Jack, a walking disaster area (he calls her "a perfect 10 on the Richter scale"). She cannot lie and is a bit naive. (She tends to believe what people tell her. She believes that Jack is the best liar she has ever met.)

The Departure: Cindy left to live in the UCLA dormitory. Jack was always the victim of Cindy's mishaps and missed her "Oops" when something went wrong.

Relatives: Aunt, Becky Madison (Sue Ane Langdon).

THERESA "TERI" ALDEN

Parents: Father (Alan Manson) and mother (Mina Kolb), both unnamed.

Sister: Samantha Alden (Jennifer Walker).

Occupation: Nurse at Wilshire Memorial Hospital in Los Angeles.

Place of Birth: Indiana.

Measurements: 36-23-36. She has blonde hair and blue eyes.

Childhood Dream: Entering the medical profession.

Musical Ability: Believes she can play the violin (but can't).

Character: Independent and doesn't like being told what to do. She hates to be criticized and was the only one of the roommates to fall for Jack (when he wore a fake moustache to impress girls). Teri is very persistent when she has her mind set on something and is a pain (as Jack calls her) until she gets someone to listen to what she has to say.

Favorite Magazine: All Woman.

Favorite Drink: After a day dealing with broken bones, blood transfusions, knife wounds, and other gory things, Teri likes to relax at the Regal Beagle with a Bloody Mary.

Favorite Breakfast: Pizza with anchovies (when working the hospital graveyard shift).

Favorite Salad Dressing: Creamy garlic.

Dating: Teri has a tendency to fall for men who are married or gay.

The Departure: Teri leaves for a job opportunity in Hawaii in the final episode.

STANLEY AND HELEN ROPER

For information, see *The Ropers*, the spin-off series.

RALPH FURLEY

Brother: Barton "Bart" Furley (Hamilton Camp).

Occupation: The apartment building manager for Bart (who purchased the building from Stanley Roper). He occupies Apartment 101. As he says, "I'm the new manager, landlord in residence so to speak. I'll be in total charge."

Background: As a kid, Ralph had a pet cat named Peaches, and during World War II, he worked in a deli (he wanted to serve his country but was classified 4F). He was engaged to a girl named Helga (who left him for a salami salesman).

Character: Ralph considers himself to be a playboy, ladies' man, and all-around swinger. But he confesses, "I failed at everything I tried and amounted to nothing. I'm the laughingstock of my family." Ralph confessed that he always felt inferior to Bart "because my parents told me so." Jack calls him "R.F.," and Ralph claims his apartment is decorated with valuable antiques (actually, tacky items).

Wardrobe: Ralph dresses in outlandish, bright-colored mod clothes. He believes he has a "powerhouse body" and calls himself the "King of Romance" and the "Prince of Passion" (he even tried to reform Jack and make him a "real man" but failed when Jack needed to remain "gay" to live in the apartment).

Relatives: Nephew, Marc Furley (Brian Robbins).

LAWRENCE "LARRY" DALLAS

Real Name: Larry Dalliopoulos (he shortened it to Dallas, as it was easier to spell).

Relationship: Jack's best friend.

Occupation: Used car salesman, although he appears rather dishonest and takes advantage of people. He calls himself "Honest Larry, the used car salesman."

Residence: Apartment 304 at the Ropers.

Character: A ladies' man who, like Jack, lusts for the ideal date, the gorgeous but flaky Greedy Gretchen. Larry is always in need of money (presumably spending everything he makes entertaining girls) and constantly borrows it from Jack. He never mentions his real occupation to girls, hoping to impress them with a better job.

Vega$
(ABC, 1978–1981)

Cast: Robert Urich (Dan Tanna), Judy Landers (Angie Turner), Phyllis Davis (Bea Travis), Tony Curtis (Philip Roth), Greg Morris (Lieutenant Dave Nelson), Bart Braverman (Binzer).

Basis: Dan Tanna, a Las Vegas–based private detective with a penchant for finding and helping beautiful women in trouble, strives to solve crimes directed at the strip's hotels and casinos, specifically the Desert Inn, where he works as its security chief.

DANIEL "DAN" TANNA

Place of Birth: Nevada (Duluth, Minnesota, is mentioned when he talks about his [unnamed] sister).

Business: Tanna Investigations.

Office: The ground floor of the Desert Inn Casino and Hotel.

Address: 2780 Las Vegas Boulevard, Las Vegas, Nevada 81102.

Telephone Number: 555-7764.

Rates: $200 a day plus expenses. He dislikes "call girl cases" (as they involve pimps and the seedy side of society).

Secretaries: Charlene (not seen), then Angie and Bea (see below).

Car: 1957 red Ford Thunderbird.

License Plate: A29 429 (later TANNA).

Gun: A .357 Magnum (sometimes called That Cannon).

Favorite Drink: Milk. Angie suggests that he purchase a cow for all the milk he drinks.

Employer: Philip Roth, the owner of Roth Hotels, Inc. (includes the Desert Inn, the Dunes, and the Sahara casinos and a retirement hotel). Dan calls him "Slick." Philip (Bernie in the pilot) is worth over $400 million, and gray appears to be his favorite color (he has a gray limousine and 27 gray suits). He came to Las Vegas in 1958 and, being a hustler, established the earliest of the casinos. Roth calls Dan "Daniel," and his favorite drink is "Double usual." By dialogue, he appears to like fishing and tiger hunting.

Police Department Contact: Lieutenant David "Dave" Nelson (called "George Nelson" in the pilot). Raymond St. Jacques played Lieutenant Nelson in one episode. Naomi Stevens as Bella Archer was his original contact (Las Vegas Metropolitan Police Department).

Trait: Cool, handsome, and a ladies' man (always surrounding himself with showgirls).

Favorite Sport: Racquetball.

Military Service: Vietnam (where he served with his friend, Sergeant Harlan Two-Leaf [Will Sampson]; now his occasional legman).

Legman: Bobby "Binzer" Borso (a stooge for the mob that Dan reformed). Binzer drives a car (plate ZG 6BE5) and first worked for Dan to find a magician's missing lion.

ANGELA "ANGIE" TURNER

Occupation: Casino showgirl at the Desert Inn and Riviera Hotel's Follies Bergere dance revues. She does four shows a night (starting at 8:00 p.m.) and needs at least one hour before performing "to get psychologically and mentally prepared." She answers Dan's phone calls with "Hi, it's me, Angie" and is hoping to become an exotic dancer (takes classes at Lenora Exotic Body Movements).

Place of Birth: Philadelphia.

Age: 20 (born in June 1958).

Measurements: 36-25-35 (she wears a 36C bra to enhance her figure onstage). She has blonde hair and blue eyes.

Trait: Beautiful but dim-witted (her looks make up for all her mistakes). She is an expert performer but often becomes confused when Dan asks for assistance. She is starstruck and fascinated by the bright lights and glamour of the Las Vegas Strip.

Address: First said to be 9086 Lincoln Way, then 877 Primrose Drive.

Note: Although Judy Landers was dropped after the first season, her image is still visible in the theme (the girl kissing Dan and the chorus girl in pink tights).

BEATRICE "BEA" TRAVIS

Place of Birth: Texas.

Year of Birth: 1954 (24 when the series begins; in real life, Phyllis Davis was born in 1940, making her 38 at the time).

Occupation: Showgirl (dancer with the Desert Inn Follies Bergere Revue) and Dan's office secretary (but not a "dizzy dame"). She answers his phone calls with either "Dan Tanna Investigations" or "Tanna Investigations."
Address: The Lakewood Apartments (Apartment 303).
Telephone Number: 555-1161.
Bra Size: 36C. She has brunette hair.
Car License Plate: E56 488 (later N5Z 780).

Note: The following casinos are seen in the opening theme: Hilton Flamingo, Frontier, Desert Inn, Star Dust, Gold Nugget, M-G-M Grand, and the Dunes.

The Waltons
(CBS, 1972–1981)

Cast: Ralph Waite (John Walton), Michael Learned (Olivia Walton), Richard Thomas, then Robert Wightman (John-Boy Walton), Will Geer (Zeb Walton), Ellen Corby (Esther Walton), Judy Norton-Taylor (Mary Ellen Walton), Mary Elizabeth McDonough (Erin Walton), Kami Cotler (Elizabeth Walton), John Walmsley (Jason Walton), Eric Scott (Ben Walton), David W. Harper (Jim-Bob Walton), Joe Conley (Ike Godsey), Ronnie Claire Edwards (Cora Beth Godsey), Earl Hamner Jr. (narrator).

Basis: The Waltons, a poor family living in Jefferson County, Virginia, struggle to survive the difficult times of the Great Depression through the end of World War II. John and Olivia are the parents; John-Boy, Mary Ellen, Erin, Elizabeth, Jason, Ben, and Jim-Bob are their children; Zeb and Esther are John's parents.

OVERALL SERIES INFORMATION
It is the year 1789 (also given as 1786 and 1765) when a lone pioneer named Rome Walton and his wife (Becky Lee) settled in the Blue Ridge Mountains of Virginia. The area came to be known as Walton's Mountain, and generation after generation of Waltons maintained the land even though they are not the legal owners; "We sort of hold it in trust," Zeb says.

Series Setting: Begins in the spring of 1933 and ends in June 1946.

Pets: Reckless (family dog), Chance (milk cow; her calf was Bullet), Blue (Zeb's mule), Myrtle (goat; her baby was Gingerbread), Calico (Elizabeth's cat), Rover (Jim-Bob's peacock), Porthos (Jim-Bob's guinea pig), Jay-Bez (Pig; raised by Elizabeth for her class 4-H project), Jim-Bob Jr. (Duck; Jim-Bob later set it free in Drucilla's Pond), Lancelot (a fawn Erin found and later set free), Pete (Elizabeth's raccoon), Chirpee (Esther's canary), Harold (Jeffrey's

female cat; a dog, Nick), Pepper (Elizabeth's horse). As a kid, John-Boy
mentions having a dog (terrier) named Benji.

Neighboring Towns: Charlottesville, Hickory Creek, Scottsville, and Waynes-
boro. The White Arrow Bus Line services the area.

Family Tradition: On Christmas Eve in 1931, as the family gathered in front
of the tree, Elizabeth yawned and was about to say goodnight when Mary
Ellen interrupted: "Don't say goodnight yet. Wait until we're all in bed and
the last light is out." Thus began the traditional program ending with each
family member saying goodnight to one another.

JOHN WALTON SR.

Business: Walton's Lumber Mill (begun by Zeb in 1931 "with one saw and one
axe").

Religion: A "heathen" (as called by Olivia's parents). John is not a churchgoing
man and prefers to worship in his own way. Because of his beliefs, he and
Olivia were forced to elope (married by Preacher Hicks), and a church wedding never occurred.

Education: Walton's Mountain School (in Jefferson County), Class of 1917.

Trait: Hardworking and dedicated to providing for his family.

Military Service: The army during World War 1 (at which time he had a problem
with alcohol and his brother, Ben, was killed in action). During World War
II episodes, he heads the local draft board.

Dislike: The family not being together at dinnertime.

Habit: Smoking a pipe.

1934 Dodge Pickup Truck License Plate: 35 179 (also seen as T6 807, T-9 126,
and T-98254).

Relatives: Cousin, Wade Walton (Richard Hatch).

OLIVIA WALTON

Occupation: Housewife. Olivia was also a sales representative for Pinkess Bubble
Beautifier (a bath oil that sells for 25 cents a bottle; Olivia made a nine-
cent commission); seamstress at Miss Stella Lewis, Modeste, a dress shop in
Charlottesville (where she worked for Stella [Abby Dalton] five days a week
and earned $12 per week).

Maiden Name: Olivia Daly.

Nickname: Called "Liv" by John; "Daughter" by Zeb and Esther; "Livie" also
by Zeb.

Religion: Baptist. She and the children attend the First Baptist Church.

Education: The Walton's Mountain School.

Year of Marriage: 1916. This year contradicts John's history. John mentions to
Olivia that he joined the army in 1917 after graduating from high school,

indicating that they did not know each other a year earlier. To make matters worse, Olivia mentions that she and John "knew each other years before we were married."

Trait: Loving mother and, like John, stern when it comes to disciplining her children. She expects each child to help with the chores but, most importantly, to help each other. She tends to lose her temper when she gets angry and often punishes the children by making them read verses from the Bible.

Favorite Pastimes: Reading the Bible; tending to her vegetable garden.

Hobbies: Quilting (she is a member of the local woman's quilting club) and painting (a landscape she painted hangs on the living room wall).

Famous For: Her applesauce cake.

Best Childhood Friend: Betty Blu Webber.

Brown and Tan Station Wagon License Plate Number: 719 727.

Affiliation: Member of the church choir.

Changes: Olivia developed tuberculosis in 1942 and moved to Arizona to recuperate (she learned at this time that she could no longer have children). After recovering, she returned home and taught third grade at the Walton's Mountain School. In 1943, when women in Jefferson County acquired jobs at Pickett Metal and their children needed caring, Olivia began a day care center from her home. In 1944, Olivia joined the Red Cross and a year later had a relapse of tuberculosis. On doctor's orders, she moved to Arizona to recoup. John later joined her, and both characters were written out.

Replacement: Olivia's widowed cousin, Rose Burton (Peggy Rea); her late husband was named Burt. Serena Burton (Melinda Nix) and Jeffrey Burton (Keith Cogan), her grandchildren, also became a part of the family.

Relatives: cousin, Cody Nelson (Eduard Franz).

JOHN-BOY WALTON

Relationship: The oldest of the children (17). His actual name is John Walton Jr., and he was the only child to have his own bedroom.

Education: The Walton's Mountain School (in narration, the school is also called Miss Hunter's School) and Boatwright University (which he began in 1934).

Occupation: Student, then writer. He began working at age 17 (1933) as an apprentice at the Slaughter Machine Shop (earning $12 a week to help support his family). He was next a reporter for the *Jefferson County Times.* When the paper folded, John-Boy established his own publication, *The Blue Ridge Chronicle.* It was printed on a 1912 Champlin-Price printing press, had eight pages, and sold for three cents. Its motto was "To Search for the Truth." John-Boy also owns a parcel of land called John-Boy's Meadow (named by Zeb on the day John-Boy was born). John-Boy left Walton's

Mountain to pursue his writing career in New York City. He became a writer (as a staff sergeant) for *Stars and Stripes* newspaper during World War II (stationed in Paris) and a wire service reporter for the Associated Press. Following the war, John-Boy became an instructor at Boatwright University when it instituted a television media course in late 1945.

First Writing Attempt: An article about his family for *Collier's* magazine.

Books: Short Stories: A Collection by John Walton Jr. (published by Majestic Press, 201 Main Street in Charlottesville, Virginia); *Walton's Mountain* and *G.I. Journal* (both published by Hastings House in New York City). The series ended with John-Boy struggling to write another novel; he later married a magazine editor (Janet) and moved to California to raise a family.

Car License Plate: 63 982 (later 672 489).

Trait: Believes in family and cared very much for his siblings, especially Elizabeth, with whom he felt a special connection. He is also stubborn and stands up for what he believes in, even if it means going against his parents' wishes.

First Infatuation: Marcia Woolery, a high school classmate. She later moved to Richmond, Virginia, where she worked as a stock girl in a department store.

First Love: Jenny Pendleton (Sian Barbara Allen), a runaway whom Olivia and John took in.

Economic Survival Plan: John-Boy reopened the old Guthrie Mining Company to sell its coal in Virginia; workers were paid $35 a week.

ZEB AND ESTHER WALTON

Zeb (Zebulon Tyler Walton), called "Grandpa," was born in 1865 and claims he can predict the weather by his bones—"They feel one way for good weather, another way for bad weather." Esther, called "Grandma" (sometimes "Old Lady" or "Old Woman" by Zeb), played the church organ and helped Olivia raise her grandchildren until 1976, when Ellen Corby suffered a stroke and was forced to temporarily leave the series. Esther's absence was explained as her being hospitalized after suffering a stroke. In 1978, Ellen returned to the series, and her disability (aphasia [speech difficulty]) also became a part of Esther's character. Zeb mentioned that he had a brother named Matt Walton, a drifter who never settled down. Esther often called Zeb "Old Man" or "Old Fool." When Ellen had a relapse and was unable to perform, she was said to be visiting relatives in Buckingham County. Anzula Walton was mentioned as being Zeb's mother. When Will Geer suffered a heart attack after completing the 1977–1978 season, it was mentioned that Zeb passed after a heart attack (in 1941). Zeb's pride and joy was a wood-carved figure of Annabel Lee, the woman from the Edgar Alan Poe poem of the same name, which he won in the First Baptist Church raffle. Morgan Woodward appeared as Zeb's roustabout brother, Boone Walton.

MARY ELLEN WALTON

Relationship: The second-born child.

Education: Walton's Mountain School; Boatwright University.

Trait: A tomboy (when the series begins). She loved sports (was an expert first baseman), fishing, and hiking and cared for both people and animals (she would hug a cow for comfort when she became upset). She is called "the strongest willed of the children." When Mary Ellen wanted to become a blonde (having brown hair), she experimented on Jim-Bob, turning his hair orange.

Hero: Florence Nightingale.

Occupation: Nursing student, then registered nurse. She was also the nurse at Pickett Metal Products during World War II, and in 1944 she enrolled as a premed student at Boatwright University.

Blue Car License Plate: 672 710 (also seen as T2-619).

Husband: As a nursing student, Mary Ellen dated Dr. David Spencer (Robert S. Woods). When she met Curtis Willard (Tom Bower), a doctor in the nearby town of Rockfish, she fell in love and later married him. They had a son (John Curtis), and Mary Ellen is now called "Mary Ellen Willard." They live in a house (street number 301) that doubles as Curtis's medical practice.

Tragedy: At the outbreak of World War II, Curtis joins the Army Medical Corps. He is transferred to Pearl Harbor in Hawaii and is later reported missing in action and presumed dead after the Japanese bombing. Mary Ellen later learns that Curtis survived the bombing and was living in Larksberg, Florida. Curtis, suffering from injuries that made him impotent, tells Mary Ellen that he can no longer be a good husband, and they agree to divorce; Mary Ellen later marries Arlington "Jonesy" Westcott, a veterinarian.

ERIN ESTHER WALTON

Relationship: The middle daughter (Mary Ellen is her best friend).

Education: Walton's Mountain School; Rockfish Business School.

Occupation: Student. She worked as a telephone operator in the town of Rockfish for the Jefferson County Phone Company (run by Flossie Brimmer; address seen as Route 124) and later as the personnel manager (then assistant company manager) at Pickett Metal Products (J.D. Pickett was her boss); secretary to a Mr. Pringle (company not named). She also cared for the two young children of a widower named James R. Dolworth (who lived at 312 Hazel Avenue in Rockfish) while he worked.

Trait: The prettiest of the sisters. She is very independent when she needs to be, and when she has her mind set on something, it is almost impossible for someone to change her way of thinking. She was the first Walton to have a professionally taken photograph.

Pinup Girl: Erin, in a cheesecake-like pose (wearing shorts, showing her legs, and seated on a piano bench), became the "Sweetheart of Camp Lee" for the soldiers stationed at the military base in Rockfish (her photo, taken by Ben for fun, was published in the "Rotogravure" section of the Charlottesville *Register*; it was chosen from a group of outdoor scenes Ben had photographed hoping to get one published).

Movie Star: In 1943, Erin starred in an unnamed Hollywood documentary about women in the workplace.

Loves: Erin's first romance occurred with George "G.W." Haines, whom she lost when he joined the army and was killed during a training exercise (he originally dated Mary Ellen). She later married Paul Northridge (Morgan Stevens), the son of the owner of Northridge Lumber.

ELIZABETH WALTON

Relationship: The youngest of the sisters.

Education: The Walton's Mountain School.

Trait: Has a mind of her own, is carefree, and is anxious to grow up.

Occupation: Student. Her first job was a lemonade stand (Zeb added to the drink the "Recipe" [moonshine], which made it a pure delight for adults). She also works on occasion at the general store run by Ike Godsey. Elizabeth was later a member of the Peace Corps and opened the Home Front Canteen at the Camp Rockfish army base with Ben's wife, Cindy (offered entertainment for soldiers).

Favorite Radio Program: Mr. District Attorney.

Favorite Book: Jessica: Girl Spy (at one point, she would respond to someone only if they called her "Jessica").

Ambition: Hopes to become a lawyer.

Loves: Takes after John-Boy in his love of reading and writing.

Best Friend: Aimee Godsey (the daughter of Ike and Cora Beth Godsey).

Fear: A carnival Ferris wheel that causes her to have sleepwalking issues.

Cooking Ability: Elizabeth can cook, but her hot chocolate is said to taste burnt.

JASON WALTON

Relationship: The second oldest son.

Education: Walton's Mountain School; the Kleinburg Conservatory (where he composed "Appalachian Portrait" as his spring 1942 senior class musical project).

Occupation: Student. He is seeking to become a musician and songwriter (he composed the song "Will You Be Mine"). He had his first professional job playing banjo and singing with Bobby Bigelow and His Hayseed Band (earned $3.50 per gig). He later joined the Rhythm Kings band, played piano at the Dew Drop Inn (which he eventually came to own), sang with the WQSR Radio Gospelites, played organ for Sunday services at the First Baptist Church, and sold cars at the Jarvis Used Car Lot.

Military Service: The National Guard (1940); the army (1942); stationed at Camp Rockfish, first as a private, then corporal, and finally drill sergeant with the 72nd Division, 2nd Platoon, of Company C.

Wife: Toni Hazelton (Lisa Harrison), a Jewish girl he needlessly feared would cause a problem with his Christian family.

BENJAMIN "BEN" WALTON

Relationship: The third-oldest son.

Education: The Walton's Mountain School.

Trait: Enjoys helping his father run the family sawmill (which he eventually takes over). He is a schemer and always seeks a way to make money.

Occupation: Student. He held jobs as a civil defense worker during World War II and crewman at the Murdock Lumber Mill before becoming his father's foreman.

Military Service: The Seabees (he was captured overseas by the Japanese in 1944 and held as a prisoner of war).

Love: Ruby Davis was Ben's first girlfriend; he later married Cindy Brunson (Leslie Winston) in 1943 (they had two children, Virginia [who died] and Charlie). They eloped and were wed in Maryland. Her red convertible license plate reads 277 923.

Ben's White Car License Plate: 86 297.

Poem: Ben wrote "The Chicken Thief," which was published before John-Boy's articles.

JIM-BOB WALTON

Relationship: The youngest of the boys. He had a twin brother, Joseph Zebulon, who died (presumably at birth).

Date of Birth: January 23, 1923.

Full Name: James-Robert Walton.

Education: The Walton's Mountain School.

Trait: A loner and constantly lost in his dreams.

Occupation: Student. He has a fascination with airplanes and hopes to become a pilot (but later found he was unable due to astigmatism [needed to wear eyeglasses]). In one episode, however, he mentions he would like to become a traveling salesman. He is later seen as a motor mechanic and opening his own business (the Foster-Walton Garage) with a friend in Jefferson County across from the Godsey general store.

Military Service: The Air Corps (joined in 1944; stationed at Langley Field).

Girlfriends: Patsy Brimmer, then Ruby Davis.

Hobby: Operating his ham radio (which is in the barn) and talking to people all over the world; building model airplanes out of wood and fixing cars. In 1945, he made his own TV set from spare parts (but suffered a severe electrical shock during the process).

Black Car License Plate Number: 678 695.

Dream Come True: During World War II, Jim-Bob experimented with building his own airplane, and in late 1945, he flew for the first time when it lifted him into the air. He later becomes a crop duster, then a charter flight pilot.

Mealtime: When it is Jim-Bob's turn to say grace, he does so by mentioning the food that has been prepared.

ISAAC "IKE" AND CORA BETH GODSEY

Occupation: Owners (married) of the Jefferson County general store (General Merchandise, Ike Godsey, Prop.).

Adopted Daughter: Aimee Godsey (Rachel Longaker, then DeAnna Robbins). Like her best friend, Elizabeth Walton, she is anxious to grow up and experience life as an adult. Cora Beth feels that Aimee needs to start acting like a woman and requires her to spend one hour per day sewing and one hour per day reading. She attended Miss Oakland's Finishing School for Girls and the Walton's Mountain School.

Place of Birth: Ike and Aimee (Jefferson County); Cora Beth (Doe Hill). Cora Beth was known as John Walton's spinster cousin before she married Ike. Ronnie Claire Edwards also played Cora Beth's sister Orma Lee.

Store Telephone Number: "Three short rings and one long ring." Ike keeps the keys to the store in the coffee grinder.

Typical Store Merchandise: Pickles sell for five cents each, nails are $2.45 a keg, Lambert's Coffee (later seen as Circle Coffee) sells at two pounds for 39 cents, milk is seven cents a quart, hand soap is six cents a bar, and Harrison Baking Flour and Rex Evaporated Milk can be seen in prominently displayed advertising signs.

Additional Service: Ike is also the local postmaster, and his store also contains a pool table, a tearoom, and a dance hall in the back. During World War II set episodes, Ike was the air raid warden for Jefferson County (although Cora Beth calls him the "director of home defense in Jefferson County").

Ike's Motorcycle License Plate: 39 4857 (Cora Beth often rides in its sidecar).

Ike's Car License Plate: 84625.

Cora Beth's Car License Plate: 617-718.

Cora Beth: Secretly a drinker. She often calls Ike "Mr. Godsey" and eventually became a real estate agent (Cora Beth Godsey, Real Estate). She previously attempted careers as a dancer, dramatic actress, beautician (one of her "victims" was Olivia, whose hair makeover resembled a curly-topped Shirley Temple), and schoolteacher (taught for a brief time at the Walton's Mountain School). She is very prissy and bossy and insists that she must have a cup of coffee in the morning in order to avoid a migraine.

Ike's Favorite Orchestra Leader: Guy Lombardo (although he has only one of his records in his collection).

Ike's Biggest Mistake: Buying 50 Arctic Queen electric refrigerators, forgetting that most of his customers do not have electricity.

OTHER CHARACTERS

Mamie Eudella Winfield Baldwin (Helen Kleeb) and Emily Baldwin (Mary Jackson), called "Miss Mamie" and "Miss Emily," are spinster sisters who live in a grand home (left to them by their wealthy father, a judge, whom they refer to as "Papa"). They are known for the "Recipe," (also called "Papa's Recipe"), an alcoholic brew (moonshine) especially liked by Zeb Walton. The sisters call their still the "Recipe Machine" and also own a cottage at Virginia Beach. Miss Emily had a dog named Dickie; their car license plate reads 79 982 (later 982-869), and they attended Miss Sophie Bell's Finishing School.

Miss Emily often lamented about Ashley Longworth, her long-lost love. She was president of the Rockfish Historical Society and enjoyed Jason's piano playing. Miss Mamie, the vice president of the Historical Society, was a bit more logical than her sister. She and her sister enjoyed passing out "Papa's Recipe" (which they believed was a home-brewed medicine, not actually moonshine). Both were also avid bird-watchers.

Mary Wickes played their cousin Octavia, Denver Pyle their cousin Homer Lee Baldwin, and Jean Marsh their niece Hillary.

Yancy Butler (Robert Donner) was a Walton family friend who seemed to be down on his luck. He was engaged to Cissy Tucker (Cissy Wellman) and had a pet dog named Tiger. He preferred to sleep with animals and would often steal chickens to help feed the poorer people of Walton's Mountain.

Marmaduke Ephraim "Ep" Bridges (John Crawford) is the county sheriff (his car license plate reads 29 561; later 720394). John Ritter played Matthew Fordwick, the local preacher, with Mariclaire Costello as his wife, Rosemary. His character was later written out when Matthew joined the army during World War II.

Note: In the 1971 pilot episode "The Homecoming," Patricia Neal was Olivia Walton; Andrew Duggan, John Walton; Edgar Bergen, Zeb Walton; Woodrow Parfrey, Ike Godsey; and David Huddleston, Sheriff Ep Bridges. Three 1982 NBC TV movies were also produced: *A Wedding on Walton's Mountain* (depicts Erin's marriage to Paul Northridge), *Mother's Day on Walton's Mountain* (finds

Olivia returning to help her children: Mary Ellen when she learns she can no longer have children after a car accident; Elizabeth, who is fighting to grow up; and Ben, whose marriage is failing), and *A Day for Thanks on Walton's Mountain* (depicts Elizabeth's efforts to reunite her family for Thanksgiving Day in 1947).

Welcome Back, Kotter
(ABC, 1975–1979)

Cast: Gabe Kaplan (Gabe Kotter), Marcia Strassman (Julie Kotter). *The Sweathogs:* John Travolta (Vinnie Barbarino), Robert Hegyes (Juan Epstein), Ron Palillo (Arnold Horshack), Lawrence Hilton-Jacobs (Frederick Washington), Debralee Scott (Rosalie Totsi), Vernee Watson (Vernajean Williams), Susan Lanier (Bambi Foster).

Basis: A former high school student (Gabe Kotter) returns to his alma mater 10 years later to teach a group of misfit students called the Sweathogs.

GABRIEL "GABE" KOTTER
Place of Birth: Brooklyn, New York.

Religion: Jewish.

Occupation: Special guidance remedial academics teacher. He is hoping to turn his students' lives around by establishing a meaningful relationship with them (as normal teaching methods do not work on the Sweathogs). He held a temporary job as the greeter (as Captain Chicken) for Mr. Chicken Northern Fried Chicken.

School: James Buchanan High School in Bensonhurst, Brooklyn, New York. He also serves as the faculty adviser for the school newspaper, the *Buchanan Bugle*.

Classroom: Room 11 (he is also the Sweathogs' homeroom teacher). He believes that the antics of Vinnie, Juan, Freddie, and Arnold "are like those of the Marx Brothers Gummo, Groucho, Harpo, and Chico [movie comics of the 1930s]. Only I have four of my own, Wacko, Stupo, Jerko, and Dumbo."

Address: 711 East Ocean Parkway, Apartment 3C; later, Apartment 409 at 1962 Lincoln Boulevard.

Wife: Julie. She and Gabe later become the parents of twins Robin and Rachel.

Background: In 1965, Gabe lived in a tough Brooklyn neighborhood where "gangs didn't carry guns—they pushed the bullets in manually." He was a radical student at Buchanan High and created the name "Sweathogs" to describe students in special education classes. He was branded as the student who started the cafeteria riots, was a star player on the school's basketball team, and was picked on by the neighborhood bully, Tommy Shaughnessy, when he was nine years old. Gabe has a pressed flower in his high school yearbook that he bought for his senior prom date, "but she never showed up."

Dream: To see his students sitting in homeroom before the bell sounds.

Classroom Traditions: Gabe has established a "late fund" (if students are late for class, they must put a quarter in a rubber fish [a halibut]); Freddie is the late fund treasurer. On test days, Gabe comes to school with a green bucket and detergent to wash the answers off Vinnie's and Juan's arms. Arnold is the "official test distributor."

Relatives: While not seen, Gabe mentions he has a brother named Melvyn. He also jokes about numerous relatives in opening and closing segments.

JULIE KOTTER

Mother: Unnamed (Alice Backus).

Sister: Jenny (Susie Pratt).

Maiden Name: Julie Hansen.

Place of Birth: Nebraska.

Occupation: Housewife. She volunteers at the Free Clinic and earns $5 for every 1,000 envelopes she stuffs with polyester fabric samples (company not named).

Most Famous For: Her tuna casserole (which Gabe hates and says, "It will deter dinner guests from returning").

Quirk: When Julie doesn't have enough money for Gabe's birthday present, she gives him a card saying, "I owe you one giant favor."

Tradition: Appearing at school to bring Gabe his lunch, which he often forgets. (Julie is sometimes seen only in the opening and closing segments wherein Gabe tells her a joke about one of his relatives. The "lunch thing" allows Julie to appear more often.)

Note: Before acquiring roles (at the same time) on *Charlie's Angels*, Kate Jackson and Farrah Fawcett auditioned for the role of Julie.

VINCENT "VINNIE" BARBARINO

Place of Birth: Brooklyn, New York.

Heritage: Italian.

Religion: Catholic.

Position: Leader of the Sweathogs. "Room 11 is my place and these [the Sweathogs] are my people." He calls himself the "Sweathog Heartthrob" and believes he can have any girl he desires ("I have a stupefying effect on female girls of the opposite sex").

Homework: "When it comes to homework, Barbarino don't do no reports for no one." He once tried reading a book and studied for 15 minutes, "but nothing happened." He often plays on Gabe's sympathies ("It will hurt my sainted mother if she hears bad things about me") and claims that bad news causes his mother to throw her rosary beads at him.

Catchphrase: "Up your nose with a rubber hose."

Dance: Vinnie created a dance called the Barbarino ("Bar-bar-Barbarino . . .").

Student Politics: Vinnie ran for student body president under the campaign "Vote for Vinnie and Nobody Gets Hurt" (Juan was his "Secretary of Fear"); he lost, receiving only 47 votes.

Quirk: When asked a question, Vinnie responds with "What?" When the question is repeated, he responds with "Where?"

Hope: To be discovered in a drugstore and become an actor (like his hero, Marlon Brando). In the meantime, he works as an orderly at the local (unnamed) hospital.

JUAN EPSTEIN

Sister: Carmen Epstein (Lisa Mordente). He has a large family, but names are not given.

Full Name: Juan Luis Pedro Felipo DeHuevos Epstein.

Heritage: Puerto Rican Jew (as he calls himself).

Place of Birth: Brooklyn.

Reputation: The toughest kid in school and voted The One Most Likely to Take a Life.

Dream: To become a "typhoon" (tycoon) and open Puerto Rican–Jewish restaurants (based on his experience at school—"Don't eat the tuna casserole in the cafeteria").

Pets: Truman Capote (a turtle); Wally, Eddie Haskell, Lumpy, and Jerry Mathers as the Beaver (lizards; based on names from the TV series *Leave It to Beaver*); Jimmy, Cubby, Darlene, and Annette (white mice [names from the TV series *The Mickey Mouse Club*], which he calls his Mouseketeers); Florence, Harpo, and John-Boy (hamsters); and an unnamed chicken ("who escaped from a butcher shop and crossed Bay Parkway").

Trait: When it comes to taking tests or handing in his homework, Juan presents Gabe with one of his famous excuse notes from his mother that is always signed by Juan as "Epstein's Mother." In one episode, Juan was actually sick (stomach virus), missed school, and presented a legit note (signed "Mrs. Epstein"). For his book reports, Juan hopes a movie has been made and copies the descriptions used in *TV Guide*.

Distinction: The only Sweathog who the school's principal, John Lazarus (voice of James Komack), likes (treats him like his own son).

Habit: Has been smoking cigarettes (on and off) since he was 12 years old.

Artistic Ability: Painted a nude mural of Julie Kotter on a school wall.

Relatives: Uncle, Moe Epstein (Herb Edelman).

ARNOLD HORSHACK

Father: Manny (Dean Solomon), a cab driver; mother, unnamed (Ellen Travolta).

Sisters: Doris (Andrea McArdle) and Judy Horshack (Elyssa Davalos).

Place of Birth: Brooklyn.

Middle Name: Dingfelder (his mother's maiden name).

Last-Name Translation: According to Arnold, it means "The Cattle Are Dying." He also says he is the last of the Horshacks ("after they made me, they broke the mold").

Occupation: Student. He originally spoke only when Vinnie gave his permission; he works for his Uncle Harry (James Komack) at Orshacks of Fifth Avenue, a costume shop (Harry dropped the "H" to make it sound better).

Girlfriend: Mary (Irene Arranga), whom he married in the episode "Ooh, Ooh, I Do." He was also the first Sweathog to improve his grades and be placed with regular students. He returned to his Sweathog status when he missed his former life.

Catchphrase: "Ooh, Ooh, Ooh"; he greets people with "Hello, how are you?"

As a Kid: Had a wooden rocking horse named Pepper.

FREDERICK "FREDDIE" WASHINGTON

Nickname: "Boom Boom" ("Because I like boom boom").

Ambition: To become an architect and design the world's tallest building: Boom Boom Towers.

Place of Birth: Brooklyn.

Musical Ability: Plays the bass.

School Athletics: A member of the basketball team (wears jersey 1).

Girlfriend: Vernajean Williams.

Catchphrase: "Hi there." He calls Gabe "Mr. Kot-ter."

Occupation: Student. He also hosted the radio program *Hi There* on station WBAD.

Pet: As a kid, Freddie had an invisible duck named Ralph (who would always sit on his shoulder).

OTHER CHARACTERS

Rosalie "Hotsie" Totsie is a very pretty and sexy girl who hates her nickname ("Because it gives me the image of being easy, and I'm not. I'm a lady"). She was born in Brooklyn and has eyes for Vinnie.

Bambi Foster is a very pretty blonde who was born in Texas and later lived in California. When Gabe asked her what part of California, Bambi responded with "The beach." She calls Mr. Kotter "Gabie." When Gabe objected and requested that she call him something else, she chose "Captain Cosmic." "On second thought,"

Gabe said, "call me Gabie." Bambi mentions that her parents are divorced (she lives with her father) and attended 11 different schools in 11 different states.

Michael Woodman (John Sylvester White) is the vice principal and the authority figure that is actually seen (the principal, John Lazarus, is only heard). Michael is sarcastic and was a nurse's aide during World War II. He is ill-tempered and previously taught history at Buchanan ("Because a good war cheers me up"). Woodman claims, "I have no sense of humor," and calls Gabe's teaching methods "nutty cuckoo." His teaching philosophy: "I teach. They listen." He hates Captain Kangaroo (from the TV series of the same name) as much as he does the Sweathogs and wishes for only one thing: a transfer to Scarsdale (where he believes there are no Sweathogs).

WKRP in Cincinnati
(CBS, 1978–1982)

Cast: Gordon Jump (Arthur Carlson), Loni Anderson (Jennifer Marlowe), Howard Hesseman (Dr. Johnny Fever), Frank Bonner (Herb Tarlek), Jan Smithers (Bailey Quarters), Richard Sanders (Les Nessman), Tim Reid (Venus Flytrap), Gary Sandy (Andy Travis).

Basis: A behind-the-scenes look at the operations of a 5,000-watt AM radio station, WKRP (1590 on the dial), in Cincinnati, Ohio.

OVERALL SERIES INFORMATION
WKRP, originally mentioned as being a 50,000-watt station, is located in suite 1412 of the nine-story Osgood R. Flemm Building. A fish (carp) is the station's mascot; 555-WKRP is its phone number, and WPIG is its main competition. A bandage worn by Les in each episode (but in different places) is a reminder of an injury Richard Sanders sustained on the first day of shooting; for episodes, it is said to be an injury acquired from his vicious, never-seen dog. The bulletin boards seen in the common-space office contain bumper stickers from radio stations across the United States (sent in by deejay fans of the show). The most famous episode is its Thanksgiving program wherein Arthur concocts a promotion to give away free turkeys, dropped from a helicopter to shoppers at a mall. Unaware that turkeys could not fly, the birds fell like bombs on the mall grounds.

ARTHUR CARLSON
Mother: Lillian "Mama" Carlson (Sylvia Sidney, then Carol Bruce).
Wife: Carmen (Allyn Ann McLerie); married for 27 years (later said to be 25 years).
Child: Arthur Jr. (Sparky Marcus); attends the Prussian Military Academy.
Occupation: General manager of WKRP. His father, Hank Carlson, founded the
    station on December 7, 1941, and he became its manager in 1955 (taking

WKRP in Cincinnati. *CBS/Photofest. ©CBS*

over the chore from his stern mother). Mama Carlson reveals in the final episode that she allowed her incompetent son to run the station, as she always intended for WKRP to lose money and be a tax write-off. It is also seen that as powerful and demanding as Mama Carlson was, only her elderly butler, Hirsch (Ian Wolfe), could get the best of her.

Nickname: "Big Guy" (his son is called "Little Big Guy").

Military Career: The Marines during World War II (served in the Pacific Theater).

Trait: Wimpy (fears his mother). He dislikes rock-and-roll music and rarely listens to the station; ignores staff problems and has stopped trying to make WKRP a top station.

Character: Arthur has little interest in the station but shows great interest in fishing, golfing, and playing with toys to pass the time of day. In his youth, Arthur was a baseball player called "Moose."

Favorite Magazine: Ohio Fisherman.

Note: In the 1992 update *The New WKRP in Cincinnati*, Arthur still manages the station; Carmen has opened a business called Carmen's Crystal Corner in the Pinedale Mall.

JENNIFER ELIZABETH MARLOWE

Occupation: Secretary (the highest-paid employee at the station).

Salary: $24,000 a year.

Place of Birth: Rock Throw, West Virginia.

Address: The Fairview Towers, Apartment 330. She later lives in a Victorian home (for which she paid $125,000) in the town of Landerville.

Apartment Doorbell Song: "Fly Me to the Moon."

Bra Size: 36C. She has blonde hair and blue eyes.

Marital Status: Single.

Wardrobe: Tight skirts and blouses. Jennifer knows, "I am a very sexy and desirable woman, but other women see me as a threat to their husbands." Other women describe her as "the best-looking woman I have ever seen."

Dating: Always seen in the company of older men because she feels safe and secure with them. Although she will never do favors for men or loan them money, they buy her things—"cars, acoustical ceilings, microwaves, and appliances." She also receives tickets for box seats at all Cincinnati Reds ball games but never uses them.

Membership: The International Sisterhood of Blonde Receptionists.

Philosophy: "Do your job, but don't do too much of it."

Note: Jennifer is a wealthy widow and engaged to Reynaldo Roberto Ricky Ricardo Goulegant (Robert Goulet), the prince of a European country called Rosario Roberto in the 1991 update *The New WKRP in Cincinnati*.

HERBERT R. TARLEK II

Father: Herbert Tarlek Sr. (Bert Parks).

Wife: Lucille (Edie McClurg).

Children: Bunny (Stacey Heather Tolkin) and Herbert Jr. (N.P. Schoch).

Occupation: Sales manager.

Place of Birth: Arkansas.

Nickname: "Herb." The "R" in his name stands for "Ruggles."

Education: University of Arkansas (where he majored in business).

Fears: Losing his job (as selling time to advertisers on WKRP is difficult and he must devise ingenious ways to get their business). Office meetings terrorize Herb, as he always wonders, "Am I in trouble?" He also will not sign any petitions—"Herbert R. Tarlek doesn't sign anything."

Character: Rather obnoxious. He dresses in loud and tacky clothing and has an unrelenting crush on Jennifer. He and Lucille have a comfortable relationship, but Lucille believes sex is a reward and will give it only when Herb does something to earn it (like "Mow the lawn Herb, or no num num tonight").

Catchphrase: "Okay. Fine."

Coffee Mug: A close look reveals that it is labeled with a University of Arkansas Razorbacks logo (as Frank Bonner was born in Arkansas).

Note: In the 1991 update *The New WKRP in Cincinnati*, Herb still works as the station's salesman, is still married to Lucille, and still has a roving eye for beautiful women.

DR. JOHNNY FEVER

Occupation: Disc jockey.

Salary: $17,000 a year.

Place of Birth: Los Angeles, California.

Address: An apartment at the Gone with the Wind Estates.

Real Name: Johnny Caravella. Johnny has also worked under the names Johnny Cool, Johnny Midnight, Johnny Duke, Johnny Style, Johnny Sunshine, and Professor Sunshine (the names can be seen in close-ups when Johnny picks up his coffee mug). Johnny was fired from his job in Los Angeles for using the word "booger" on the air. He then drifted around the country and found his way to WKRP when it changed formats from beautiful music to rock; he hosts the morning shift (and repeated that previously taboo word).

Nickname for WKRP: Johnny calls the station the "Mighty KRP."

Favorite Charity: The Vine Street Mission (for the free food he can get).

Ex-Wife: Paula (Ruth Silveria). Johnny is currently single.

Daughter: Lori Caravelli (Pattie Allen).

Character: Spaced out (from drug and alcohol use over the years). He has a bad habit of listening to conversations behind closed doors (his way of knowing whether to join in) and keeps a bottle of some unknown alcoholic brew in his desk that Jennifer, after sampling it, claimed, "I think Johnny gets it in a hardware store." Johnny resurfaced during the second season (1992–1993) of the update *The New WKRP in Cincinnati* as his old self but hosting the midnight-to-6:00 a.m. slot. It is learned that he left WKRP in 1982 and moved to New York's Greenwich Village. He worked at various deejay jobs while attempting to write a book about rock music. When that failed, he returned to WKRP, the only station he really called home.

LESTER "LES" NESSMAN

Occupation: News director (the self-proclaimed News Beacon of the Ohio Valley).

Place of Birth: Dayton, Ohio.

Education: Xavier University.

Programs: As the newscaster, Les signs on at 8:00 a.m. and ends the day with the 6:00 p.m. newscast. He also does the sports, "Eyewitness Weather," and an interview program called "Show Beat." He uses his motor scooter as the WKRP Mobile News Unit.

Awards: Won the Silver Sow Award for his hog reports (which he believes are the most important part of his newscasts; he keeps up to date by reading *Pig American* magazine). He also won the Buckeye News Hawk Award for his newscasts.

Office: Les works in an open-office atmosphere but has imaginary walls and a door (marked with tape on the floor) that his coworkers respect, although Herb finds it a bit ridiculous having to knock on an invisible door.

Pet Dog: Phil.

Record Collection: Only one record, *Chances Are*, by Johnny Mathis.

Hobby: Exploring dark basements and attics (hoping to find a ghost or some unearthly being).

Musical Ability: Plays the violin.

Childhood Ambition: To become a handyman (until he tried to make a footstool and blew out the back of the garage), then a great baseball player (but was bad at catching).

Club: Member of the Ho Down Square Dancing Club.

Les's Newscast Opening: "London! Madrid! Bangkok! Moscow! Cincinnati! From the four corners of the world, from the news capitals at home and abroad, the day's headlines brought into focus. The issues and events that shape our times! WKRP, the information bureau of the Ohio Valley, presents Les Nessman and the News" (spoken by William Woodson).

Les's Program Closing: "This is Les Nessman saying this is Les Nessman" or "This is Les Nessman saying good day, and may the good news be yours."

Note: In the 1991 update *The New WKRP in Cincinnati*, Les is still the newsman, still wears a bandage, and still has the invisible walls. He now has a pet bird named Hilda.

VENUS FLYTRAP

Occupation: Disc jockey (hosts the overnight program of romantic music). He was also said to be a schoolteacher in New Orleans (and the city's number one radio disc jockey); rock band leader and minor league baseball player.

Real Name: Gordon Simms (he uses the alias Venus Flytrap to avoid capture by the military). Gordon was an army private during the Vietnam War who, after serving 10 months and 29 days, realized he made a big mistake by enlisting and went AWOL (absent without leave). He is now wanted as a military fugitive but feels safe being a nondescript disc jockey at a low-rated and insignificant radio station. He tries to remain inconspicuous in all situations that involve his duties away from the safety of WKRP. He fears any attention being thrust on him and rarely voices his objections to station policy. While he does fear getting caught, he never associates a woman as being with the military (he believes it's a military "guy" out to get him).

Car: A yellow 1970s Chevrolet Vega (exact year not mentioned).

Character: Venus plays a mix of romantic and rock music. He is a ladies' man, and to set the mood, he usually burns scented candles in the broadcast booth. He also romances his lady friends while spinning records and has a glass or two of wine during the show.

BAILEY QUARTERS

Occupation: Traffic manager (schedules commercials); she is later an on-the-air personality, doing two of the 10 daily "WKRP News Roundups" (sponsored by Golden Bean Coffee). She also produced *Cincinnati Beat*, a public affairs program of local citizen interviews hosted by Johnny.

Place of Birth: Cincinnati.

Education: Ohio University (where she acquired a degree in journalism).

Measurements: 34-25-35. She stands 5 feet, 7 inches tall and has blonde hair.

Character: Bailey, the only other female seen as a WKRP employee, stands up for what she believes in, especially equal rights for women. She was originally depicted as a plain Jane (glasses, nonflattering clothes, and pulled-back hair). As the series progressed, Bailey became more glamorous but did not lose her independent and liberal outlook.

ANDREW "ANDY" TRAVIS

Sister: Carol Travis (Allison Argo).

Occupation: Program director. He previously worked in Santa Fe, New Mexico, and was hired by Mama Carlson to try and improve its standing at number 14 in a 26-station radio market (WKRP was, at one point, number 10). Andy can stand up to Mama Carlson and believes that "I'm an easygoing young guy with a natural ability to lead. Except no one listens." The theme song reflects Andy's decision to settle down in Cincinnati ("Baby, if you've

wondered, wondered whatever became of me, I'm livin' on the air in Cincinnati, Cincinnati, WKRP. . .").
Dog: Pecos Bill (which he found on Mount Baldy).
Girlfriend: Linda Taylor (Barrie Youngfellow).

Wonder Woman
(ABC, 1975–1976; CBS, 1977–1979)

ABC Cast: Lynda Carter (Diana Prince/Wonder Woman), Lyle Waggoner (Steve Trevor), Debra Winger (Drusilla/Wonder Girl), Cloris Leachman, then Carolyn Jones (Queen Mother).
CBS Cast: Lynda Carter (Diana Prince/Wonder Woman), Lyle Waggoner (Steve Trevor Jr.), Beatrice Straight (Queen Mother), Norman Burton (Joe Atkinson), Saundra Sharpe (Eve).
ABC Basis: Diana Prince, alias Wonder Woman, uses her super abilities to help the United States battle the Nazis during World War II.
CBS Basis: Set in modern times, Diana Prince, now a government agent, secretly battles evil as the mysterious Wonder Woman.

PRINCESS DIANA
Mother: Hippolyta, called the "Queen Mother."
Heritage: Amazon.
Age: Diana, an immortal, is centuries old but appears to be in her mid-twenties.
Home: Paradise Island (named by Hippolyta, as its women live "in peace and sisterhood," and it is "free of men and their barbaric ways"). It is located in the Bermuda Triangle (protected by the refraction light) and remains invisible to the outside world.
Creation: In 200 B.C., when the rival gods Aphrodite and Mars battled for the conquest of the Earth, Aphrodite created a race of superwomen called Amazons to defeat him but failed when her queen, Hippolyta, was seduced by Mars. Realizing that she had been unfaithful to Aphrodite, Hippolyta fashioned a small statue out of clay and offered it to Aphrodite in forgiveness. Aphrodite forgave her and brought the statue to life as the baby Diana, a child whom Hippolyta chose to raise and groom to become a future ruler.
Name Origin: Diana received the name of Wonder Woman from Hippolyta ("In the words of ordinary men, you are a Wonder Woman").

WONDER WOMAN
Abilities: Incredible strength, speed, and agility and the ability (speed and coordination) to deflect bullets with her gold bracelets (made from Feminun, a metal that can be found only on Paradise Island).

Costume: On Paradise Island, Diana normally wears short white dresses. As Wonder Woman, Diana wears a revealing red, white, and blue strapless one-piece–like bathing suit (to signify her allegiance to the American flag). It has a blue bottom with white stars and a red with gold top (around her bustline).

Accessories: A gold belt (called Aphrodite's Girdle, to maintain her abilities away from Paradise Island), a Magic Lariat (also called the Lasso of Truth, which compels people to tell the truth), and a gold tiara with a red ruby in the center.

Weakness: While it is not known how to kill Wonder Woman, her enemies have discovered that she can be subdued with chloroform.

First Commandment: Keep Paradise Island secret.

Cover: To conceal her true identity in the outside world, Diana adopts the alias Diana Prince. To become Wonder Woman, Diana does a twirling strip-tease. As she twirls, a slow-motion film mix shows Diana shedding her street clothes for her Wonder Woman outfit (later Diana, in her street clothes, does a balletlike spin and transforms into Wonder Woman in a flash of bright light followed by a burst of thunder). Most transformations show Diana checking her gold belt and tiara after the occurrence.

ABC EPISODES

Time: 1942 at the height of World War II.

The Incident: U.S. fighter pilot Steve Leonard Trevor is on a mission to intercept a Nazi plane (en route to bomb the Brooklyn shipyards) when his plane is hit by enemy gunfire. The plane crash-lands on Paradise Island, and Steve is rescued by Princess Diana. As Steve recovers, Diana learns about Nazis and their plan to take over the world.

The Mission: After a Tournament of Athletic Games is held and Diana proves her abilities, Hippolyta gives her permission to leave the island to help battle the Nazis. Steve is given a special drug from the Hybernium Tree, which erases his memory of his time on Paradise Island. Diana flies Steve to Washington, D.C., in her invisible plane (takes him to the Armed Services Hospital) and sets out on a quest to defeat the Nazis.

The Disguise: To conceal her true identity as Wonder Woman and learn of Nazi activities, Diana enlists in the navy and becomes Yeoman Diana Prince.

Position: Secretary to U.S. Air Force Major Steve Trevor at the War Department.

Wardrobe: Diana dresses in rather drab outfits and is often seen in her blue military uniform with large glasses and pulled-back hair. She did appear "out of character" (wig and sexy clothes) when Diana entered the Miss G.I. Dream Girl of 1942 beauty pageant (as Diana Paradise) to uncover a plot to destroy a radar scanner.

Address: Apartment 308 (address not given).

Phone Number: Capitol 7-362.

Regret: Diana cannot return home until she completes her mission ("If I do, there may not be a Paradise Island—it will suffer with the rest of the free world if the Nazis win"). The Nazis consider Wonder Woman an American secret weapon. Although the Japanese were also the enemy, they are not incorporated into any stories.

Diana's Sister: Drusilla, called "Dru," had originally been dispatched by the Queen Mother to find Diana and bring her home to assume her royal duties. Dru, however, becomes fascinated by life in America and convinces Diana to let her stay and help. She assists by becoming Wonder Girl (possesses the same abilities as Diana but wears a much less revealing costume). She loves ice cream and hot dogs and conceals her true identity by posing as a typical teenage girl who has come to spend time with her older sister.

STEVEN LEONARD TREVOR

Address: An apartment on D Street.

Distinguishing Marks: A battle injury scar (right shoulder) shaped liked the letter "J."

Occupation: Intelligence agent with the U.S. Air Corps.

Rank: Major. He retired with the rank of major general.

Base of Operation: The Military Building, Air Corps Intelligence Division (also called the War Department).

Office Safe Combination: 24-36-33.

Quirk: When done with a top-secret report, Steve tosses it into his wastebasket and brings it to an incinerator himself. He also uses a 20-mm shell casing as a paperweight.

OTHER CHARACTERS (ABC)

General Philip Blankenship (Richard Erdman) is Steve's superior. Yeoman Etta Candy (Beatrice Colen) is Steve's secretary.

CBS EPISODES

Setting: Washington, D.C., 1977.

The Transition: Although the ABC version ended with the war still in progress, it is assumed that Wonder Woman accomplished her goal and returned to Paradise Island. It is 1977, and Steve Trevor Jr., the son of the major Diana previously assisted, is an agent for I.A.D.C. (Inter Agency Defense Command). He is aboard a plane (ID N027C) to attend a secret meeting in Latin America to deal with terrorist threats when the plane is sabotaged (a gas released) and the crew and passengers are disabled. The plane enters the Bermuda Triangle and comes under the control of the Scientific Council of Paradise Island (which enables its safe landing). When Diana learns, through a drug given to Steve, that the world is threatened by terrorism, she convinces her mother to let her again become Wonder Woman to help stop a threat that could destroy their home. The crew and passengers are returned to the plane and released from a hypnotic-like state as Diana uses her invisible plane to guide it to Latin America (where Steve, under a hypnotic trance, is to accept Diana Prince as his new associate).

WONDER WOMAN

Disguise: Diana Prince.

Occupation: Agent for the I.A.D.C., a computerized government organization dedicated to battling the enemies of the world.

Address: 2890 West 20th Street, Washington, D.C.

Measurements: 37-25-35. She wears a size 4 dress; stands 5 feet, 9 inches tall; and has hazel eyes and brown hair. Her wardrobe is much more becoming and typical of women in the workplace.

Costume: The same basic Wonder Woman attire, although the bustier is cut lower to reveal more of Lynda Carter's cleavage; her "satin tights" are cut higher in the thighs, and her bracelets changed from silver-gray to bright gold. The tiara ruby is now a communications link to Paradise Island (it can also transform into a boomerang); her lasso can also make people forget things. The revised spin technique from the ABC episodes is also used for the Diana–to–Wonder Woman transformation.

STEVEN LEONARD TREVOR JR.

Birthday: April 13, 1935.

Height: 6 feet, 4 inches tall.

Address: 27 Lincoln Boulevard, Washington, D.C.

Telephone Number: 555-5455.

Official ID Card: Issued in 1976; lists him as the I.A.D.C. deputy director with the security clearance number HQ 69412.

THE AGENCY

Assisting Steve and Diana is IRAC (Informative Retrieval Associative Computer; IRA for short. It deduced that Diana and Wonder Woman are the same person). Rover is the mobile robot that performs menial duties (like fetching coffee and sorting mail).

Because Diana does not officially exist as an I.A.D.C. agent, she programmed the following information into IRA: *Identity:* Diana Prince. *Sex:* Female. *Age:* 25. *Past Employment:* Inter Agency Defense Command, Overseas Division, Past 3 Years. *Prior:* Student at the University of California, Berkeley.

Records damaged; confirmation by interview. *Current Grade:* GS-16. Diana is recognized as an agency employee but apparently is not paid; she acquires money by cashing rare drachmas her mother gave her (worth $25,000 each).

OTHER CHARACTERS (CBS)

Joe Atkinson was originally Steve and Diana's superior; he was later dropped, and Steve became the new agency head. Eve was added as Steve's secretary, and Eve Plumb played Joe's daughter, Elena. Also known as *The New, Original Wonder Woman* (ABC) and *The New Adventures of Wonder Woman* (CBS).

Note: The episode "The Man Who Could Not Be Killed" established a revised format wherein Diana, transferred to the Los Angeles branch of the I.A.D.C., would now be working with Dale Hawthorn (John Durren), her superior, and Bryce Crandall (Bob Seagren), a genetically enhanced man who could not be killed (hence the episode title). CBS chose not to continue the series after the episode was filmed.

PRIOR VERSIONS

In 1968, the first known *Wonder Woman* pilot was produced with Ellie Wood Walker as Diana Prince/Wonder Woman. Here, in a comical version, Diana lives with her domineering mother (Maudie Prickett) in a modern-day apartment. Diana (not as busty as Lynda Carter's Diana) is quite accident prone and very vain (enjoys looking at herself in a mirror). She has a secret room in the apartment for her transformation from Diana to Wonder Woman. The six-minute test film ends with Diana embarking on a mission (as she says, "Away, away, you vision of enchantment, you've got a job to do").

On March 12, 1974, ABC aired the pilot *Wonder Woman* with Cathy Lee Crosby as Diana Prince/Wonder Woman and Charlene Holt as the Queen Mother. Here, Diana was secretary to government agent Steve Trevor (Kaz Garas) and found herself battling Ahnjayla (Anitra Ford), a renegade Amazon who joined forces with the evil Abner Smith (Ricardo Montalban) to steal top-secret information.

REBOOT

In 2011, NBC produced an updated (but unaired) version titled *Wonder Woman* with Adrienne Palicki as Diana/Wonder Woman. Diana now lives in Los Angeles and has three identities: Diana Prince, a lonely girl who lives in a small apartment with her cat, Sylvester; Diana Therymscira, the founder and president of Therymscira Industries; and Wonder Woman, a vicious vigilante crime fighter.

How Diana became Wonder Woman, her past on Paradise Island, or how she established Therymscira Industries (or why she chose that name and exactly what the multi-million-dollar company does) is not explained. It is revealed that the world is aware of the fact that Diana Therymscira is Wonder Woman and that she uses her company to "fund her crime-fighting activities." The Justice Department has become aware of Wonder Woman's activities and has assigned its top lawyer, Steve Trevor (Justin Bruening), to monitor her activities.

The pilot establishes Wonder Woman as a gorgeous champion for justice—and in a bosom-revealing red and gold top and tight blue pants. Etta (Tracie Thoms) is Diana Therymscira's personal assistant; Henry (Cary Evans) is her company chief executive officer.

Index

About the Author

Vincent Terrace has worked as a researcher for ABC and is currently the TV historian for BPOLIN Productions, LLC (for which he created and wrote the pilot episode for a projected TV series called *April's Dream*). The author of 37 books on television and radio history, Terrace has teamed with James Robert Parish for the *Actors' Television Credits* series of books for Scarecrow Press. He has also written such books as *Television Series of the 1950s: Essential Facts and Quirky Details* (Rowman & Littlefield, 2016), *Television Series of the 1960s: Essential Facts and Quirky Details* (Rowman & Littlefield, 2016), *Television Introductions: Narrated TV Program Openings since 1949* (Scarecrow, 2013), *The Encyclopedia of Television Pilots, 1937–2012* (2013), *Television Specials, 1936–2012* (2013), *The Encyclopedia of Television Subjects, Themes, and Settings* (2011), and *The Encyclopedia of Television Programs, 1925–2010, Second Edition* (2011).